CW00918964

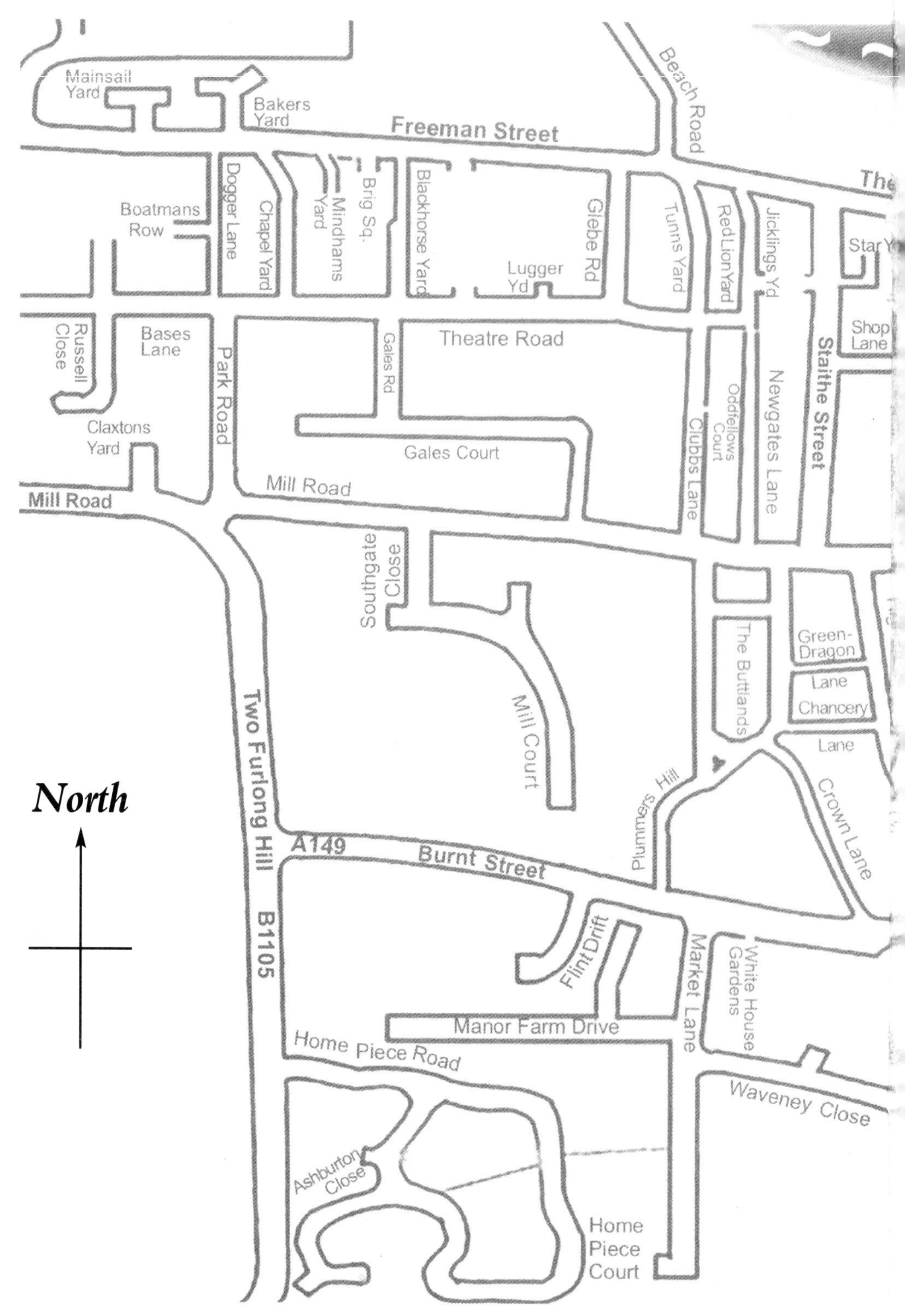
Mainsail Yard
Bakers Yard
Freeman Street
Beach Road
The
Boatmans Row
Dogger Lane
Chapel Yard
Mindhams Yard
Brig Sq.
Blackhorse Yard
Lugger Yd
Glebe Rd
Tunns Yard
Red Lion Yard
Jicklings Yd
Star Y
Russell Close
Bases Lane
Park Road
Gales Rd
Theatre Road
Shop Lane
Staithe Street
Oddfellows Court
Newgates Lane
Clubbs Lane
Claxtons Yard
Gales Court
Mill Road
Mill Road
Southgate Close
Mill Court
The Buttlands
Green-Dragon
Lane
Chancery
Lane
Plummers Hill
Crown Lane
North
Two Furlong Hill
B1105
A149
Burnt Street
Flint Drift
Market Lane
White House Gardens
Manor Farm Drive
Home Piece Road
Waveney Close
Ashburton Close
Home Piece Court

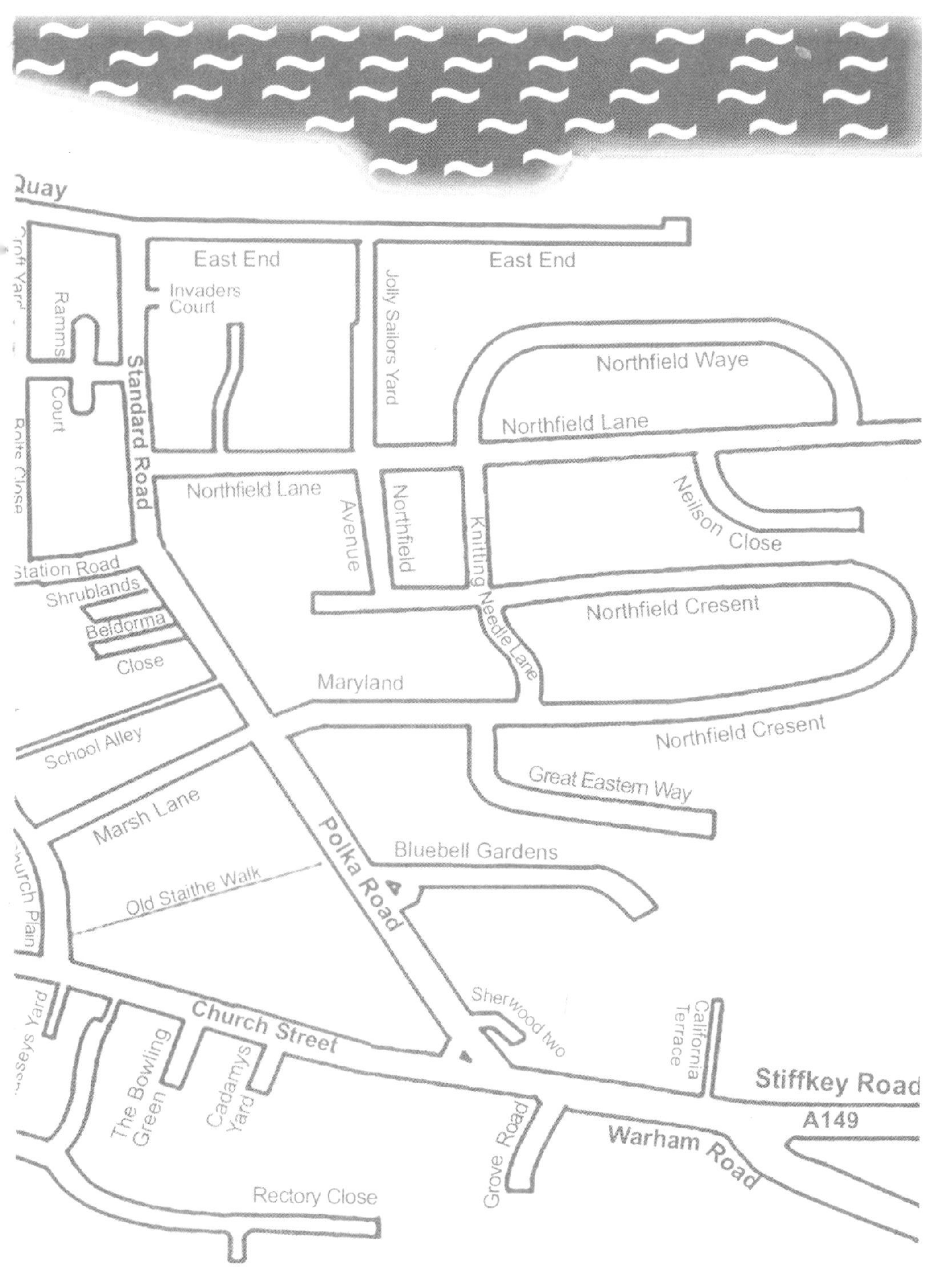

Wells next the Sea

With thanks to Wells Local History Group
for initiating my interest in the history of the town;
to so many people in the town, some of whose names
appear later in the book; to the memory of Alun Howkins,
social historian and friend, and to Geoff Perkins whose
pictorial representations of a huge number of Wells folk have
kept the memory of so many locals alive.

Finally, with apologies, to my wife for having taken so
much time out of our marriage, hopefully to some purpose.

Wells-next-the-Sea

The Long Last Century 1859-1999

Roger Arguile

ISBN 978-0-9568515-1-2

Published by Jubilee Publications, 10, Marsh Lane,
Wells-next-the-Sea, Norfolk NR23 1EG

Picture credits
Pictures other than those cited below are from John Tuck's huge collection of photographs for whose help the author is extremely grateful.
Author: 35, 37, 54, 245, 247, 252, 253
Author's collection: 33 (upper), 45, 72, 80, 128, 195, 198 (both pictures), 232 (lower)
Campbell McCallum collection: 16 (lower), 28, 33 (lower), 43, 76, 81, 82, 85, 88 (lower), 156 (lower)
ECF: 188
EDP: 146
Holkham Estate: 25
John Tuck collection: see above
Percy Phillips: 190
Peter Lynn: 110
Richard Shackle (WLHG archive): 194 (upper), 230 (both pictures), 231 (both pictures), 232, (upper), 234, 235, 236
Robin Golding: 166 (lower)
Mike Welland collection: cover, 34, 64, 117, 192 (upper)
Bob Curtis: 216
Betty Tipler: 160, 187, 215
Fakenham Community Archive: 202 (lower)
Wensum Trust: 219
Linda Gower: 237, 249, 250, 251

Cover painting by Walter Frederick Osborne, 1859-1903
Wells Town Council map at the front of the book by Jim Parkinson

Many of the pictures have been copied so many times without attribution that it has proved impossible to identify sources. The author apologises for any pictures which have been reproduced without the necessary permission.

Design by Sara Phillips
Printed and bound in Wales by Gomer Press, Llandysul,
Ceredigion SA4 4JL

Contents

Preface

When I wrote an earlier book about Wells people were nice about it but some of them complained that it did not tell the stories of the Wells they knew. It was mostly about people long ago. I had done this deliberately. To tell stories about people known to some of the readership might be to mention matters which some would rather were forgotten. People tend to have partial memories of those they loved (and also to remember the bad things about those whom they disliked.) It seemed as if I could please nobody and had better forget about the project and just enjoy sailing.

But finding out about time past has proved to be an addiction. I was also frustrated by how little I knew about the town. So I have become an asker of questions, a seeker after information, some of it only in people's heads. I have become, so far as some people are concerned, irritatingly nosey. Like any outsider my interpretation of events will never match the intimacy of those who were there or who were told stories by their elders. It is also true that when telling the stories of the living or recently dead, there are stories that cannot be told. On the other hand, I have tried to stitch stories together into a larger whole and to set Wells in a wider context of national and international events. I have also I hope preserved some information that would otherwise be lost. It is amazing how forgetful some institutions can be, how easily an organisation can lose touch with its roots and, as a result I believe, lose something of its proper sense of future direction. I am also aware that there are areas of life which I have scarcely touched on: football clubs are one; dramatic societies another. I have written little about youth organisations. I have clearly left plenty of stories for others to tell.

In putting together these stories I have had in mind two different readerships: those whose families have lived in and around Wells, some for generations, and who want to see something of their story preserved and those who know little about the town other than perhaps having visited it and even moved here. Some of the background explanations are intended to make the stories more intelligible to the second group. Likewise the naming of names will mean much to some and nothing to others. Inevitably the cast of thousands has been reduced to several dozen. I apologise to those whose names have been omitted. So many more stories could be told.

I have made a wider use of photographs than previously, something which is only possible when sticking to the period after photography was invented. That has been an excuse also for extending the period under consideration before the turn of the twentieth century: hence the title of the book. Wells as a modern town has its origins around the mid-nineteenth century when the both harbour and town were the subject of comprehensive legislation, when the beach bank was built and the railways came.

I have relied upon many sources to put the work together. Written source material has included the records of the Wells Improvement Commissioners, which unfortunately have not all survived – the minute books from 1875 to 1893 are missing – as well as the minutes of its successor, the Urban District Council which was abolished in 1974. They are held by the Norfolk Records Office to whose staff I offer my hearty thanks. I have also read the Log Books of Wells Schools from 1860 to 1995. The National Archives in London have provided some material and many books about aspects of Wells life have been plundered. I have spoken to many local people, sometimes by arrangement and sometimes in snatches. I am aware not only of the occasional unreliability of memory but also of the need to be sensitive about the recent past. I have to thank in particular, for their assistance in adding to the narrative Christine Abel, Marion Abramowitz, Madge and Brian Barker, Bob Brownjohn, Alan Bushell, Mel Catton, Davina Catton, Eddie and Judy Cast, Rodney Crafer, Helen Dunn, Philip Eaglen, Charles Ebrill, John Edwards, Ted Everitt, Mick Frary, Marcus French, Paul Hart, Richard Harvey, Jonathan Hazell, David Hewitt, Christine Hiskey, David Hudson, Keith Leesmith, Pete Lynn, Diana McCallum, Daniel Money, Terry Norton, Alastair Ogle, Sue Page, Percy Phillips, Peter Rainsford, Richard Seeley, Anne Sibley, Ray Smith, Robert Smith, Rachel Stroulgar, Stephen Temple, John Tuck, Diana Walker, Simon Walsingham, Desmond Wright and Mike Welland. Mike made detailed and invaluable comments on the text. A certain amount of what I have written appears in the earlier book but is here much expanded and corrected.

History writing is an attempt to recover and to make sense of the past. It is not the same as having lived then, whenever that was, and gathering from past events some kind of order. No doubt some will dispute the accuracy of what I have written; wherever possible I have cited sources so that people can check whether I was correct though in many cases particularly in the case of the recent past my sources were conversations with living people. Overall my hope is that I have provided a series of pictures of vanished worlds whose traces have nevertheless left us with the place as it is. It is an inheritance not just of bricks, mud and water, but of lives lived in a place which so many people love, but which is constantly changing. I felt that some of the memories are too valuable to be lost.

Roger Arguile
July 2022

Introduction – the town of Wells

Wells calls itself a town, which may seem rather grand to some people, given its winter population of fewer than 2,000 souls. The word town was actually once much less discriminatingly used than it is now; it was not a matter of mere population. It is also true that there have been times in Wells' history when the town has been of considerable importance.

It was important first of all because it was a port. In the days before good roads, only a matter of two hundred years ago, seaports were much more accessible than inland communities. Secondly, Wells was a port lying on the edge of the richest part of the country, close to the continent of Europe, within easy reach of London by sea, and provided with relatively fertile soils. To these factors may be added something indefinable. Human character is not simply a product of external factors, but while it is hard to put a finger on what it was that made and sometimes unmade the town, character traits cannot be left out. It may have been what drove men to sea in bad weather when mariners in other places would not venture out; what made them sometimes resent outsiders; what caused them to resist control; what made good land out of poor ground. Someone once said 'there is an enterprise in the people of Wells which is not to be found generally'. 'It is', he said 'the eye of Norfolk'.

Whether that captures the spirit of the town, or whether it is mere fancy, what follows makes the simple point that this was never just a

Map by Willem Blaue 1630 showing Lynn, Wells and Yarmouth in Norfolk

fishing village. The map of Europe produced by Dutch cartographer Willem Blaue in 1630 shows three ports on the Norfolk coast, Lynn, Yarmouth and Wells; and only one other, Colchester, in East Anglia. Just over a hundred years later Wells is recorded as supplying a third of the country's exports of malt to the continent, nearly 16,000 tonnes. Only Yarmouth sent more. As for fishing, for several hundred years locals once routinely sailed as far as Iceland for cod, relying on little more than a compass, their sailing skills and their wits. I have written about the earlier history elsewhere and the story is one of rise and fall of importance as wider forces dictated. It is probably enough to say that because of its small size Wells was often under the control of magnates from other places: monarchs in one generation; great landowners in another. And that those local people who became influential in the town had to go elsewhere to make their fortunes.

For the benefit of those who know little of the town, it stands on the most northerly point of the Norfolk coast. The creek system, of which the harbour is the southern focus, runs through a wide strip of salt marshes, the result of millennia of siltation, the deposition of solid matter carried in by a succession of tides. The salt marshes have been colonised and stabilised by a variety of plants capable of coping with regular or occasional inundation by the sea. The marshes are now a haven for wildlife and as such enjoy some protection; once upon a time they were grazed by sheep; even tilled.

As for the harbour, there is no river to scour the channel out to sea, a lack which human ingenuity has sought to meet by dredging and digging over many centuries. This has kept the harbour open to shipping.

Lying between land and sea, the land rising gently behind is underlain by chalk covered with a light sandy soil which has proved very suitable for growing barley. The use of sheep to keep this light land in good heart has gone on for over a thousand years, 'tathing' it, as the word has it, with their dung after harvest. Barley makes the best beer and so, for several hundred years, the town has turned its barley into malt and sent its malt up and down the coast and across the sea. Local maltsters would later come to send it by rail and by road. In return, for more than five hundred years the town received coal by sea to feed its ancillary industries and keep itself warm.

The many yards which run down to the quay were once a mixture of wretched cottages and malthouses, granaries and coalhouses, intermingled with a few cow houses and pigsties. Among them were and are a number of grander houses, mostly invisible to the casual eye, standing behind, rather than fronting, the many streets. They were once occupied by merchants. At the east end of the quay where fishing boats have long been moored there were, in the nineteenth century, two shipyards in which sailing vessels were built, routinely of over a hundred tons but occasionally much larger. The Shipwrights, on the marsh edge and formerly a pub, is the sole reminder of those days. The church, once another focus of the community, lies on the south side of the ridge which parallels the harbour at the southern end. Running down to it is a once lively shopping street, now a street of cottages largely owned by second-home owners. Running east and west past the church is the old coast road where there were a number of farms. Blacksmiths once supplied their needs as well as those of the town. The rise of the town's fortunes in the later Georgian times produced, around a green called the Buttlands, more merchants' houses. The town was prosperous in the nineteenth century and its population grew to over 3,000 in consequence.

It was a time, however, of great contrasts between rich and poor. Visitors may notice, in different parts of the town, a number of what were once council houses. Wells was once said to have the greatest proportion of such houses in Europe. This was a response to the existence of those cramped, poor and insanitary cottages in the yards running down to the harbour whose conditions were only slowly recognised as being unacceptable for human habitation. Like most things in Wells, as perhaps elsewhere, developments such as those were achieved as a result of vision on the part of some and despite local opposition. There is an irony in the fact that those cottages which remain have come to be regarded as charming, desirable holiday homes albeit following the expenditure of large sums to achieve their renovation.

Wells entered the nineteenth century as a community much harmed by the Napoleonic wars, in a country whose population had grown fast as a result of agricultural change, whose resources were stretched and whose infrastructure was inadequate. The mid-century civil engineering works intended to improve both the harbour and the town made a big difference. Road improvements and the coming of the railway threatened the port's viability; issues of health and hygiene were recognised as in need of attention; educational provision was patchy and largely inadequate. Tourism had not visibly changed the character of the town. The town's industries were apparently thriving but change would come fast and furiously. The sheer unpredictability of the future, as always, presented a challenge to the people who had to deal with change while often making futile attempts to hold it back. Those who saw themselves as beneficiaries of change might urge it onwards; those whose condition was founded on vested interests might oppose it.

Enough of generalisations; what follow are some stories.

Part 1: Towards a new century (1857 to 1914)

1. The many faces of the town – 1911

The half century leading to the First World War saw immense change in the town. The coming of the railway in 1857 was only one element of this but it was symptomatic of those changes. The mechanisation of manufacturing, of transport and of agriculture and the opening up of the world through communications was to have massive economic consequences. Nevertheless, to some people this was not yet apparent.

To take one year, 1911, towards the end of this first period, we can see how far change had happened and how far things remained the same. At the end of the nineteenth century there were over a million men working in agriculture in England. Norfolk was overwhelmingly an agricultural county and Wells was still as much an agricultural community as it was a commercial port and an industrial town. In 1911[1] there were over 170 agricultural labourers living in Wells and Holkham, more than twice the number of fishermen. To that number may be added blacksmiths, dairymen and casual labourers, all adjuncts of the business of agriculture. The harvest controlled the school even after education became compulsory in 1881. Before that the attempts to get children into school were always going to be defeated at certain times of the year. Children simply disappeared when the fields needed attention, whether it was ploughing, planting, stone picking, bird scaring, hoeing or harvesting.

The passage of the seasons was the controlling feature in the life of the town: from 'cleaning' the fields, as it was called – removing couch

Harvesting with scythes was labour intensive

[1] This chapter derives much of its information from the 1911 Census

grass and weeds – to stone picking; to 'singling' rows of beet. These were all done by hand, by many hands in fact. Bird scaring was the work of small children. Labourers were wanted from April to September, after which many would have to find other work or seek parish relief. It was a horse culture. Ploughing, harrowing, drilling, and reaping all required skilled men. Men prided themselves on how straight a furrow they could plough, how they could drill a field; keeping horses in good condition so as to avoid using the vet were all skills common to those unlettered men,[2] though when several teams were required to plough a field a boy of ten might lead a team of horses. George Edwards, sometime MP for South Norfolk, who was born in 1850, did just that. The haysel - the hay harvest - and then the corn harvest took whole families to the fields. Reaper binders had come in, though some still used a scythe to cut the corn. Scythes were needed in any case to clear the headlands so that a machine could get onto the field and to harvest wind or rain-laid crops.

And there were sheep upon the marshes as well as inland, as there had been for hundreds of years, each flock requiring a solitary shepherd assisted by his dog. His was a highly skilled job, required to treat the injured and diseased – a tar pot to treat foot rot and prevent the dreaded fly-strike – maggots that burrowed under the skin – and lead them safely inland at high tides and in winter. In June, at a busy time of the farming year, when the haysel was in progress, the sheep had to be sheared. A single shepherd could not manage a large flock, sheared still by hand. So another group of men, whose occupations do not appear in the census, and whose other occupations might include fishing, would be deployed to shear the sheep, a hundred a day each, moving from flock to flock during the month.[3]

There were cattle, some brought in from Ireland and fattened during the summer. Dairy cattle provided for local needs and were driven twice a day to and from the fields to a milking parlour in the farmyard. Those who tended them could have no days off. There was dung to be shifted and spread on the fields. There was hedging and ditching to be done to keep animals within the fields and to prevent flooding from heavy rains.

Wells farms lay on the fringes of the town; three exceeded three hundred acres: Manor Farm on Burnt Street, Mill Farm off Mill Road and New Farm off Warham Road. The latter had been taken on by the Coe family in 1881, whose three sons, Thomas, Robert and William, gradually increased their acreage. Ernest Flint took over Manor Farm in 1911 which he likewise proceeded to enlarge. Isaac Wright did the same at Mill Farm which he took on in 1899. He and his sons, Frederick and George, were more sheep dealers than farmers; like Arthur Ramm who had grazing in the town, he had several butchers' shops. In 1912 there were seven butchers in the town and every village had one. There were still small farms, of fifty

---

[2] GE Evans *Where Beards Wag All* (Faber 1970) Ch 6
[3] GE Evans *Ask the fellows who cut the hay* (Faber 1956,2018) p.42ff,

acres and less. In 1871 there were eight farmers of one sort or another. William Hall's Orchard Farm on Burnt Street had a dairy; it would become an orchard (and much later a caravan park). All were tenancies from Holkham.

Farming was as much part of the town as the harbour. Not only were animals driven through the streets but some were kept within its dwellings. There was a foundry in the town which specialised in making and repairing agricultural machinery. There were a number of blacksmiths, one of them on Burnt Street. Horses were the means of motive power. They were the means of transport for goods and people alike. Grooms and ostlers attended to horses which carried the gentry in their carriages. Horses were used to pull railway trucks along the quay. Harnesses and bridles were made and sold in the town. The grisly equivalent of a scrap yard in those days was the premises of the horse slaughterer. Pigs and cows were also kept in the town itself. This was to become the object of controversy – it was not sensible for animals to be kept adjacent to cooking or washing facilities or near the wells which supplied water for the townspeople; but it happened. The farms did not just provide barley for the maltings; they provided wheat for bread; they provided butchers' meat; they provided milk: there were several farm dairies in the town which delivered twice a day, the milk being measured out from a churn into jugs. Even so, in summer the milk often had to be boiled if it were not to go sour. Butter and cheese were made locally.

Ploughing by traction engine at Branthill 1913

There were some signs of the changes to come in farming practice but they were few. Steam traction engines were beginning to be seen, mostly on large farms able to raise the capital for these giants. They were used to haul waggons and to drive threshing machines. Their use in ploughing was confined to hauling a plough from one side of a field to another on long cables, with a traction engine at each side, and where the field was rectangular, not by any means always the case.

As there had always been good harvests and bad, now increasingly the price of what grew in the fields was influenced by international factors. The great agricultural depression lasted from 1873 to 1896; its cause was the collapse in the price of corn caused by cheap Canadian imports which, despite shipping costs, severely undercut the domestic product. The effects were felt by small and great farmers alike;

tenants let go of their land and moved away; estates were sold up. Fields were no longer properly fenced. Hedges grew unkempt so that 'they used to grow each side of the road until they met'. So it was said. The worsening conditions caused men to join the union. Farm workers' wages were a third of those of men working in Norwich factories. They wanted better wages and lower prices; farmers wanted low wages and high prices. Men would be let go if they were known to be union members. It was a recipe for previously unseen conflict in which Wells was to be a locus. The strikes of 1891-2 resulted in permanent estrangement even between members of the same Methodist chapel.[4] Strange as it may seem to us as we look at the empty fields, Norfolk became one of the centres of agricultural trades unionism; two of its MPs at different times, Joseph Arch in the 1870s and George Edwards in the 1920s, were both trade unionists. The national headquarters of the union was in Fakenham. The changed mood affected the town's industries too. Wells was only intermittently a focus of union activity but in 1897 the maltsters struck too.

The position of women had much changed. Women and children were no longer available for land work in the way that they had been. Gang labour by which women and children were casually employed for weeding and stone picking had gone. The Gangs Act of 1867, restricting the use of children on the land, saw to that. The census records the number of women employed as shop assistants, mostly within families but a few in larger shops; a great number, over fifty, were employed in some form of domestic service. Thirty-two are described simply as servants. Wells had clearly developed a substantial middle-class whose larger houses required servicing, cooks, laundresses, housemaids, housekeepers and charwomen; some, of course, would work at Holkham. There were fewer engaged in the more specialist trades; no hatters or glovers any longer; more items were bought in rather than made in the town. But most clothes worn by working people, and even by the better-off, were made either at home or in the homes of local dressmakers. Thirty-three women described themselves as dressmakers. Many women identified themselves as doing housework whereas in earlier days they were described as having no occupation. Perceptions as well as jobs were changing.

Wells Post office staff in 1905, including six women

Children were at school in some numbers. Schooling had been made compulsory in 1881. Attendance was required until the age of 13. Some few, probably those not readily employable, remained thereafter, a total of nearly 600. Doubtless these figures, taken from the

[4] Howkins (1985) p. 173

Men waiting for work at Standard Barn on the quay

census, are reasonably accurate. That they do not accord with the number on the register of the school may tell us something about either the turnover of scholars, the level of attendance or the existence of private schools. Families were large. Population was growing nationally though at a slower rate than earlier in the century. Families of eight were not unusual, much greater than replacement numbers.

Some industries were in decline. Ship building had ceased back in 1869 (though it never directly employed a great number). The *Roseola* was the last commercial sailing ship to be built in the town in that year. Nearly two hundred sailing ships had been built, their varied sail plans barely known to the modern age: barques, brigs, brigantines, luggers, schooners, snows and so on, up to 334 tons, but mostly between 50 and 150 tons. Most had two masts – brigs, brigantines and snows; schooners had two masts but their sails were fore-and-aft instead of square sails.[5] Such vessels continued to bring in coal and take out grain but also all manner of commodities for the town: cloth, furniture, fancy clothes and decorative items. Astonishingly, though the names of half a dozen naval pensioners are recorded, there was but one mariner. Twenty years before there were twenty-five and seventy years before there were over 140. Others may have been at sea or unrecorded but the evidence is pretty conclusive: Wells was no longer an effective trading port.

In the town industry, and malting in particular, seemed to be thriving. The building of the huge granary overlooking the quay in 1904 was a testament to that. The advent of mechanical power was improving the rate of production and changing its character. The intensification of the malting industry meant that in the census forty-five men identified themselves as maltsters of one sort or another, whereas very few had done so hitherto. The flour mill employed far fewer, a

[5] Michael Stammers *Shipbuilding in Wells in the 18th and 19th Centuries* (WLHG 2011)

dozen or so. Whereas for generations windmills had silhouetted the skyline, now the tall chimney of Dewing and Kersley's new steam-driven mill, built in 1893 down the road by the railway station, was visible all over the town. Dewing had acquired Brown's windmill fifty years earlier. The new site enabled the transhipment of flour from the mill directly to the waggons. A railway siding was extended for the purpose. The engine provided the interior of the mill with electric light, the first building in the town to be so equipped. The windmill was taken down in 1905.

Some local manufactories adapted. The blacksmiths made ship's anchors and whelk pots as well as practising their horse-related trades, and there were also a few lorries and cars, the former being driven by steam.

There were new jobs, some of them such as the workers' grandparents would not have understood. The census records that over forty men worked on the railway. The town needed a couple of telegraph messengers and half a dozen postmen. There were still carpenters and builders and, of course, fishermen, some sixty of them. Many of the fishermen and their families lived in the East End; others, their rivals, lived around Freeman Street. Ever opportunistic, they would bring in whatever could be caught; it was mostly shellfish, cockles and whelks. Cockling on the sands at low tide was a major industry; whelking was in its infancy. The oyster fishery had died. Out to sea, long-lining brought in cod and skate; herring and bass could be netted. They would be displayed on the quay for sale or hawked around the streets and surrounding villages as well as sold in the shops of Freeman Street.

There was also an appreciable number of men who described themselves as being of private means and those less prosperous might be described as 'retired', no longer as paupers. The creation of a pension scheme for those over 70 in 1908 meant that the numbers of

Polka Road at the turn of the century

High Street early twentieth century

such folk had to be recorded even if the amount of five shillings a week they received was ungenerous. As the national life expectancy was 47, it might have been assumed to apply to only a few, but the town boasted 141 folk of 70 years and more; a couple over ninety; 10% of its population was over 60 years of age. On the other hand job security was lacking, as it had been since the casualisation of agricultural labour a century before, and fishing depended on the weather. Men did not in any case go to sea in winter. So if there was no work either in the fields, the various maltings or the quay, men stood around idle. It was this state of affairs which Sam Peel, Quaker and soon-to-be politician, was to recognise and seek to address when he came to Wells only a year or two later.

As for origins, scarcely anyone had been born across the channel; over half were born in the town itself; the rest within ten miles, other than one or two Scots, a dozen Irish, fifty or so Londoners, two or three from the other side of the Atlantic and a smaller number, including the vicar, the Revd George Ingle, who had been born in India.

Some people were leaving. The population of the town fell dramatically from 3,675 according to the 1851 Census to 2,633 in 1911. Some evidently sought employment elsewhere in the country, notably in the brewing industry whose maltings drew on local experience here. Others went elsewhere entirely, even abroad. Advertisements for a new life in the colonies appeared in local newspapers as the colonial administrations sought to attract potential settlers to their new worlds. Many people left the town in response, departing for Australia, South Africa and Canada in particular. One advertisement for South Australia asked for 'Artisans, Agricultural and other Labourers, Miners and Gardeners, single domestic servants and widows (without children under 12) not exceeding 40 years old'. The state of Queensland was offering 40 acres per adult for those who wanted to go. It was not only working people but well-to-do folk like Frank Mann of the ironmongering dynasty who left for a new life in the colonies. In addition mill owners and manufacturers had their agents visit the town and recruit inhabitants of Wells to work for their businesses in northern England.[6] That there were also many incomers indicates fluidity in the composition of the population, which goes against the perception that its people were mostly native to the area.

Of course, for some the town seemed prosperous and commodious. Kelly's Directory for 1912 records the various shops and businesses whose goods were brought now over land, increasingly by rail, though some came by sea: 'London goods' as they were called. Much was still made locally. In the early years of the century the three major streets of the town, Freeman Street, Staithe Street and High Street were full of shops. High Street would be almost unrecognisable now, apart from its only hotel, the Edinburgh, rebuilt in 1887; it had seventeen shops and three more pubs: the Vine – now Angus House, the Dukes Head, uphill of Green Dragon Lane and the Eight Ringers, the last being almost opposite the church. The rather grand Milton House, at

Staithe Street in 1912 leading down to the quay

the top of the street, was the onetime home of William Edwards, master mariner and skipper of the harbour tug *Marie*. Two pork butchers and two hairdressers lay close by two drapers and a tailor. Arthur Ramm's butcher's shop stood two houses up from School Alley. Ramm also owned Church Marsh, keeping hay in a barn, still standing, on Marsh Lane, next to his pig sheds and slaughterhouse. A printer, several confectioners and Rose's ironmongers and another butcher lay on the west side of the street. There was the odd carpenter and bricklayer carrying on their businesses. There were several grocers'

[6] Advertisements 1870s lent by Mike Welland (WLHG Archive)

and bakeries; James Thurgur's glass and china warehouse was on the corner of Church Plain – it survived until the 1960s. Further down opposite was Mary Leggett's lodging house, said to be of ill-repute.[7] Whether this had anything to do with the building of the police station in 1891 is unlikely. Finally Frederick Rushmore, local assistant schoolmaster, had his house opposite the church.

Staithe Street, by comparison, had just two public houses: apart from the Fleece on the quay, at the opposite end on the corner lay the Prince of Wales, now a café. On the eastern side lay Mayshiel, the home of maltster George Frederick Smith with its extensive gardens occupying a third of the street behind a forbidding wall. There were three butchers and two bakers and the rather grand premises of grocer Thomas Leggett with its Doric columns at the top of the street opposite the Prince of Wales. Leggett was to retire and sell out to the

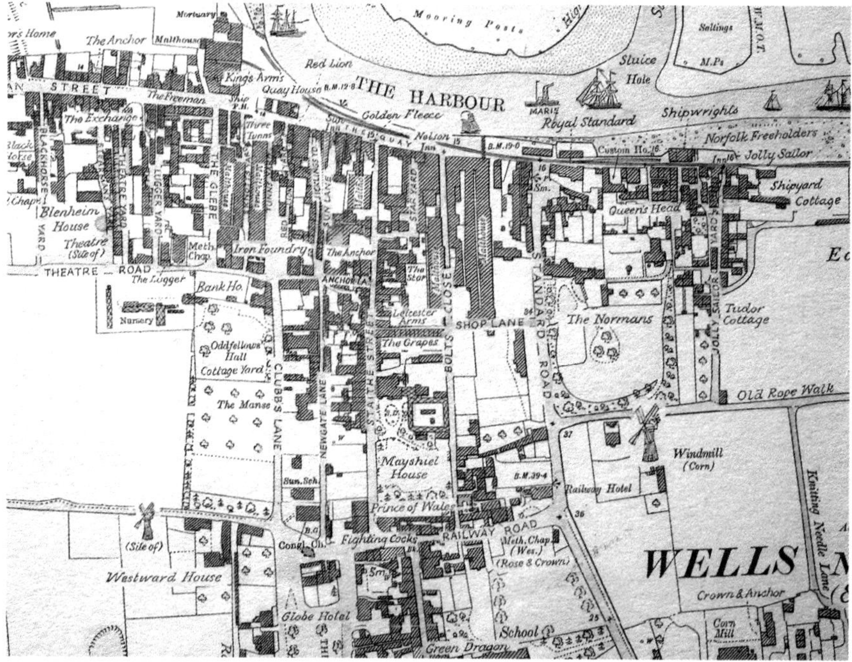

Map of Wells, 1906 by Reg Gerken

International Tea Stores in 1913. Down the street on the opposite side Arthur Ralling ran his family grocery business supplying teas, wines and spirits and was an agent for Allsopp's and Whitbread's Burton ales. By repute there had been a grocer there since 1777. Various trades were carried on in the street: harness makers, carpenters and bootmakers and for many years, until it moved to its present site in 1905, the town post office. The harbourmaster, William Temple, lived on the street at one time, as did the postmaster, Francis Southgate. Many retailers delivered to the houses, a practice that would continue long into the age of the motor van. Coal, bread, meat, groceries and

[7] Kelly's Directories 1900/1912

shellfish and white fish came to the door.

In 1911 Freeman Street boasted just three public houses, the Queen Adelaide, The Ship and the shortly-to-be-closed Kings Arms.[8] Its twenty modest shops supplied the west end of the town with provisions; it also boasted four fish shops.

The water cart, 1900

The number of inns, taverns and beer houses had steadily been reducing over the previous decades as regulations were tightened and as commercial breweries such as Bullards, Morgans, and Steward & Patteson bought into the town, consolidating their holdings by closing the least successful outlets. From 1902 applicants had to submit plans of their premises twenty-one days before the annual licensing meetings. Those factors coupled with the decline in the town's population led to there being only twelve outlets by the early twentieth century.[9]

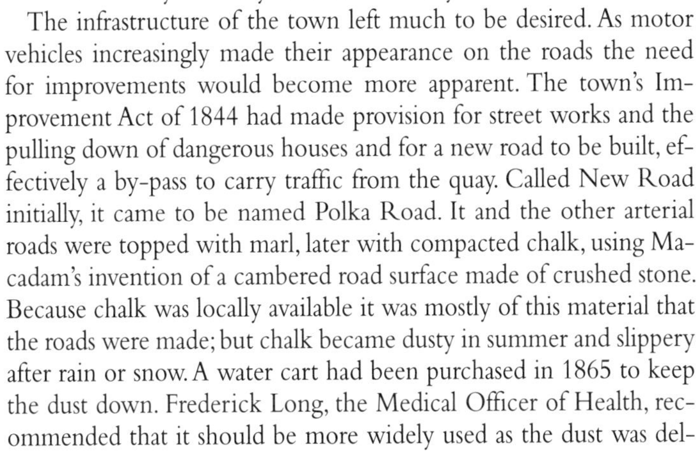

The infrastructure of the town left much to be desired. As motor vehicles increasingly made their appearance on the roads the need for improvements would become more apparent. The town's Improvement Act of 1844 had made provision for street works and the pulling down of dangerous houses and for a new road to be built, effectively a by-pass to carry traffic from the quay. Called New Road initially, it came to be named Polka Road. It and the other arterial roads were topped with marl, later with compacted chalk, using Macadam's invention of a cambered road surface made of crushed stone. Because chalk was locally available it was mostly of this material that the roads were made; but chalk became dusty in summer and slippery after rain or snow. A water cart had been purchased in 1865 to keep the dust down. Frederick Long, the Medical Officer of Health, recommended that it should be more widely used as the dust was deleterious to health. Salt water was used, pumped from the quay at Standard Yard – but not, Long insisted, at low tide when sewage effluent from the various outfalls might be pumped onto the cart! Frequent mention of the water cart indicates how much

The New Road, still lacking pavements

[8] Welland Mike, *The History of the Inns and Public Houses of Wells* (WLHG 2012)
[9] Welland (2012) pp. xivff.

it was needed, particularly when strong winds whipped up the dust into a minor storm. Finally, in 1904, the council decided that the chalk should be replaced by granite which was brought by sea from Antwerp. It was deployed in the first instance for the major town roads, Burnt Street, Church Street and Two Furlong Hill, but subsequently on all the main thoroughfares in the town. Its use required the hiring of a steam roller to level the roads. Over the next few years hundreds of tons of granite would be brought, first by sea and then later overland by train from Leicestershire. Eventually the surfaces would be sprayed with tar to create a much smoother surface. The first curbed footpaths were put in place on Polka Road to improve pedestrian access to the railway station and later on Freeman Street, Staithe Street and Mill Lane. Asphalt, subsequently used to metal the roads, was contracted for the pathways.

The town would continue to struggle to accommodate wheeled traffic, but gradually the jumble of buildings of a hundred and more years past was cleared to allow comparatively free movement. Even after the building of Polka Road, High Street required some attention, particularly at its junctions. At its northern end it was too narrow to turn, left or right. The bottleneck at the bottom of Staithe Street prevented access to the quay. It was proposed to take down and rebuild the gable end of The Fleece at the bottom of Staithe Street in order to widen the corner. The owner of The Fleece Inn, James Alexander Davidson, was at first in agreement but subsequently changed his mind and the proposal was never implemented. When the new Post Office was built in 1905 on Station Road, replacing a bakery and several cottages, the building line was moved back to enable the road to be widened.[10] The railings of the Methodist chapel were moved back towards the building with the same object. But the many yards running north to the quay were not paved at all; they were muddy tracks full of potholes between which grass grew. They would be like that for many years to come.

Yards were mostly grassy in summer and muddy in winter

Outside the town, the lanes were only gradually being metaled; otherwise they were not much better than bridle ways; only the old toll roads to Fakenham were of a standard to enable the passage of reasonably fast horse-drawn traffic, even still at no more than twelve miles an hour. London, now easily accessible by train, could only be reached by road after a long day, some fifteen hours; Norwich was half a day away.

The town's streets were lit by gas, also provided for in the 1844 legislation. The

[10] *UDC Minutes* NRO DC18/4/3 p558

gas works were completed in 1846. The installation of gas lights, to be lit each night and extinguished at 11pm, took time. By 1867, there were 78 lights, provided free of charge by the council, lit 'from 1 September to 30 April from one hour after sunset until 11 o'clock (except upon six nights at each full moon)'. Parsimony qualified safety: it took no account of cloudy nights. The income, of course, came from those who burnt gas in their homes. How quickly lamps were installed is unknown but as late as 1907 Lugger Yard, Blackhorse Yard and Stearman's Yard were only just being provided with street lights. Theatre Road received an addition to its lights the following year.

The town was, in its geographical extent, tiny by comparison with what it would become but its population was greater than it would be in the twenty-first century; many of its people lived in what can only be described as intolerably cramped conditions. Before a single

Rackhams Yard: the Busby and Gee families

council house had been built; when the future Northfield estate was but a rope walk, a field and an allotment; when there lacked a single dwelling to the south of Mill Road as far down the hill as Burnt Street's cottages and farm buildings; before the building of the little estates of neat bungalows at the east and south of the town; when therefore the bulk of the population lived in the yards running up from Freeman Street, the quay and the East End: in that year of 1911 the town's population was still greater than it would be a century later. The difference lay in their conditions of life. 294 people – men, women and children – lived in the East End alone. The many yards which ran down to Freeman Street, including Freeman Street itself, contained over 700 family members. Some of the houses were no more than thirty feet square, paved with flagstones. They had no running water, their cooking facilities consisted at best of a coal-fuelled range and a brick bread oven. A pump outside provided water for several families and an earth closet outside provided for personal hygiene, shared between several houses. A tin bath, hung up on a wall when not in use, provided bathing facilities. A communal wash-house lay beside the closets. Poor drainage and proximity of cesspools was often made worse by the presence of rats which shared the living space.

The contrast between their lives and those of the inhabitants of the substantial houses around the Buttlands or in even grander dwellings, like Mayshiel or Marsh House, secluded as they were in their considerable grounds by high walls, could not have been greater.

As to what they thought and believed, evidence is scant; the only records of church attendance were in 1851, when the huge majority appear to have conformed. On Sundays, more than half the population was in the several churches of the town. The Census had shown that there were as many worshippers at non-conformist places of worship as there were at the established church.

In particular, and notably in Norfolk, the Primitive Methodist movement, since its inception in 1807, had mushroomed. In short order virtually every village in Norfolk would have its Primitive Methodist chapel. Ejected by its parent body the 'Prims', as they were known, intended to return to its founder's ideals. They spread through the country, Norfolk in particular, like a stubble fire. Very much a working man's religion, its members were heavily involved with the agricultural trade union movement. Joseph Arch, the founder of agricultural trade unionism nationally was a Primitive Methodist lay preacher; he came to Norfolk and was to become one of its MPs. The relationship between the Prims and trade unionism would become uneasy, but as late as the 1905 election, the final examinations for its trainee ministers were put off so that they could campaign for the Liberals in the general election. By then its days of holding open air camp meetings were long past; in Wells it had opened a chapel in 1836 in what would be called Ranters Yard. Originally a coach house belonging to one of the large houses in the town, Blenheim House, it measured only 54 feet by 27 feet, too small for its burgeoning congregation which by 1851 allegedly numbered nearly 500 at its two services. In 1890 the new superintendent minister Revd H Bennett proposed the purchase of land to put up a new building. Land on Theatre Road was obtained and the first service in the new building took place in September 1891. The older established Wesleyan Methodist Chapel on Station Road had been built in 1808.

A select group of Quakers met at the Meeting House on Church Street. They had been a presence in the town since the seventeenth century. Burials in their ground date from 1680 and they enlarged their premises by taking on the site of the old workhouse; but by the 1890s, following a decline in their numbers, the Meeting House was no longer used. It would take the arrival of Sam Peel in 1909 and the evangelical meetings he held for it to come back into use. He was instrumental in its extension back and front in 1913 with a basement, and a moveable partition to provide two meeting rooms. [11]

---

[11] M. Welland *The Quay* May 2010 p.23

The Congregational church was one of the oldest dissenting bodies. It was established following the ejection in 1660 of ministers who would not use the state-approved forms of worship. In Wells it took substantial form when, in 1816, a large room was rented for weekly lectures by neighbouring independent ministers. Whose initiative it was is not known. This room gave way to a larger barn, and when this proved to be inadequate, to a newly erected chapel building. A site was purchased under a 99 year lease and the foundation stone was laid on 8 May 1817 and the chapel was licensed for public worship on 20 September 1817, actually opening on 24 September. The total cost of building was £750. In 1825/6, additional gallery seating was erected. On 11 February 1839, the chapel was licensed for the solemnisation of marriages. By 1874 its Sunday school membership alone numbered 151 pupils and its minister, George Stallworthy, decided to build a new manse and Sunday school combined. This was what is now Scarborough House. The project was over-ambitious and never came to fruition. Unfortunately costs outran the resources of the church and it was sold, first to Joseph Haycock and then to local surgeon Dr Alfred Whitlock who gave it its current name. Stallworthy moved away in 1883. His several successors lived on the Buttlands. None stayed long.[12]

Wells church after the fire 1879

Support for the parish church was strongest among the more prosperous members of Wells society. It was demonstrated spectacularly when the church was struck by lightning on the night of 4 August 1879 and burnt almost to the ground. Only the tower remained intact. The lack of a proper fire service was well demonstrated by the unrestrained conflagration; a contemporary engraving shows men climbing a ladder with a bucket to cast upon the flames. The vicar,

[12] Article by Mike Welland (unpublished)

Robert Leeder, died within a fortnight, but JR Pilling, the young curate, lost no time in securing the building of an 'iron church' probably on the land opposite the building which was completed by November that year. Its iron frame was clad with corrugated iron and internally with wooden panels. Able to accommodate 350 worshippers, it was said to provide for every need; in other words baptisms, weddings and funerals as well as the round of Sunday worship were resumed. Meanwhile, nearly £3,500 had been raised within a month of the fire, £1,000 from the Earl of Leicester. Pilling's father, who had bought the right to appoint a vicar,[13] assumed office in the new year but it was the son who ensured the rebuilding of the church. When no longer needed, on the completion of the rebuilt stone church, the temporary replacement was sold for £250 in 1892.

The rebuilding of the church was completed by 1883, on the same ground plan as its predecessor, following a design produced by the diocesan architect Herbert Green. The cost of rebuilding was on a different scale from that of its Methodist rival, some £10,000. Its style was largely similar to the old building – pointed arches, narrow fluted pillars, and a two-stage roof with upper clerestory windows – though the east window was of a different style, so-called Perpendicular. The influence of non-conformity was evident in the style of its contents. The stained glass windows were replaced by plain glass and when Hugh Rump, local physician, left £2,000 for the replacement of the contents his executors tried to insist that the congregation should sit on plain benches rather than ornate carved pews topped with traditional poppy-heads. Rump died in 1885, his rector the following year, so there was a high degree of uncertainty over what were to be major decisions as to the character of the interior. Eventually the new rector, John Player, and his vestry won the day, and carved oak pews were installed together with a fine organ to support the singing. In those days the church had a large robed choir, a relatively recent introduction emanating from the high church lobby which was almost everywhere influencing opinion. Choirs were there to sing but were placed not in a gallery at the back of the church as hitherto but instead in the chancel where colleges of clergy of old had said their daily prayers for all to see and thus had to be robed.[14]

The Sunday ministry of the church still supported by large numbers was, in this new spirit, enough, but George Ingle, who was vicar from 1893 until 1929, recognised the absence from worship of fisherman and labourers. He proposed to set up a daughter church and Sunday school on Freeman Street where they lived. He was not simply interested in recruiting church members. He proposed the appointment of a qualified nurse to take some care of the physical needs of the people. Whether he lacked the means, the will or the support required it does not appear to have come to anything.

There was, as yet, no Catholic church in the town. Catholics had

[13] Called an advowson this was a property right not long abolished.
[14] Roger Arguile *History of the Church* 2021

only been relieved of their many civic disabilities in 1829 and the first Catholic bishops were appointed in 1850. Norfolk was part of the diocese of Northampton and there were, in the early days, only six Catholic churches in the whole county; there were none anywhere along the coast from King's Lynn to Yarmouth. It was the building of the railways bringing visitors to the seaside that generated the idea of creating summer missions along the coast, beginning at Hunstanton in 1902 and Cromer in 1903.[15] In 1904 a Miss Charlotte Boyd, a Catholic convert, bought the old slipper chapel at Walsingham, then a barn, and offered it to the diocese; the existence of the railway line to Wells seemed to offer a golden opportunity for another church. Land had to be found and paid for but it would be another twenty and more years before the Catholics of the town had their own church.

By and large the fishing community were not adherents. No one went to sea on a Sunday but they did not go to church. There is no record of blessing of fishing nets such as took place in King's Lynn. Superstitions however abounded, including the belief that it was bad luck to have a parson on board. All manner of events could be bad luck, carrying money out to sea, whistling, or leaving a broom on deck. There was so much uncertainty at sea that any source of good luck might be sought.

It remains to describe the emergency services in the town. The church fire raised the issue of the need for a fire engine and a place to put it. Only a year after the blaze the first Wells Fire Brigade was formed. It took as its model the Dereham brigade and its first appliance was a horse drawn affair with a water tank and a hand pump. It lasted fifteen years during which time no record exists as to its use. Its replacement in 1895 was partly paid for by the Norwich Union Insurance Company. It cost £16 10s but by 1901 a Fire Engine Committee was appointed to deal with the fact that there was now no fire appliance in the town. Initially it made little progress. It took another fire, in 1908 at the premises of Herbert Standford, grocer and outfitter of Staithe Street, for a new engine to be purchased. At the time of the fire, a telegram was sent to Fakenham asking that their appliance be sent. The reply came back asking who would pay for its use. The fire was dealt with by men from the nearby maltings. The new machine, similar to the earlier model, was stored in the now no longer used lifeboat station which had been bought by the council in 1897 and let out at one time as a sports changing room and at another as a tea room and known as the Jubilee house.[16] Volunteer firemen were sought.

Then there was the matter of policing. Wells had long had a reputation for being a lawless town, resistant to authority, apt to riotous assemblies and a resort of smugglers. Many of its inhabitants lived on the fringes of society. Highway robbery, burglary and smuggling were

[15] Francis Young ed., *Catholic East Anglia* (Gracewing 2016) p. 168
[16] *UDC Minutes* June 1908. NRO DC18/4/3

rife. Those with land, such as the Cokes, had their own gamekeepers, while merchants deployed various forms of protection; the poor had nothing.[17] Wells' first paid policeman, Robert Parker, was appointed in 1840 under the County Police Act 1839. There was, until 1891, no police station and no cells other than the bridewell in Walsingham. Those arrested were chained up at some convenient spot, a not very satisfactory arrangement which was frequently criticised. The new police were appointed from outside their own communities in order to prevent their being susceptible to bribery or influenced by local loyalty; Wells was no exception. Henry Haylett was the first officer at the police station on Church Plain, which consisted of a magistrate's room and accommodation for a sergeant and a constable.[18] Officers served under the local justices until 1888 when responsibility was transferred to the County Council, which may account for the building of the police station.

Having attempted to describe how the town looked and how it worked, it seems a good idea to tell how it got to be so in more detail.

[17] Steve Adcock *Early Policing in Wells* (WLHG Newsletter No 69 Autumn 2019)
[18] *UDC Minutes*: NRO DC18/4/5 1916

2. The harbour

From time immemorial Wells had looked out to sea to where its primary communications lay. If it was remote then its remoteness was from the towns and cities to the west. The harbour was its link with the world and its condition was vital to the life of the town. The story has been told elsewhere, but of all the changes the biggest occurred at the beginning of our story. Back in 1859 the harbour had been transformed by the building of a bank, running north from the old lifeboat station which stood at the west end of the quay and is now the harbour office, to the dunes a mile to the north. Hitherto a number of creeks, fleets as some of them were called, ran into the main channel from the east and west and out to sea, constrained only by the marshes. The West Fleet drained the land from Holkham where a little harbour had once existed, running out to the channel just south of the east end of Holkham Meals. Previous works had been undertaken to embank and enclose the west marshes, the most recent being that of 1719 when a wide strip of land north of the

The various marshes and banks circa 1782

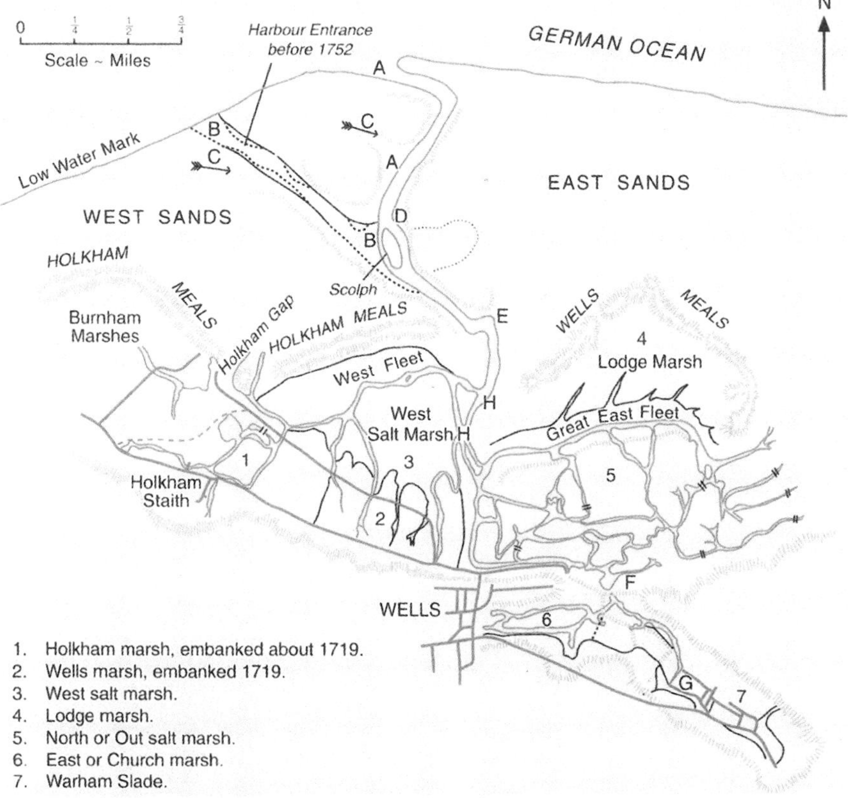

coast road had been enclosed and made into farmland, the bank running roughly east-west and turning south within the town. It was the joint enterprise of the Cokes and Sir John Turner who between them owned much of the land in Wells. Turner built another bank to the east, the so-called North Point Bank, that is now part of the Norfolk coast path to Morston and Stiffkey.

The building of the new bank completed the enclosure of the land to the west of the harbour, providing the Holkham estate with an additional 550 acres of farmland making marsh into arable. The process was a matter of controversy; it had been opposed by no less than the national Harbours Commission which deliberated in Wells as elsewhere over the state of the many harbours on which the nation relied not only for its fish, but also its trade and its protection from invasion. The plans had been produced by a London surveyor, James Rendel, on behalf of the second Earl of Leicester who had taken over from his late father in 1842. Its stated intention was that of protecting vessels coming in from the sea and providing greater flow of water on the ebb tide, thus scouring the channel and preventing it from silting up. The idea was promoted that the east side of the Wells channel should be embanked as well but was never proceeded with.

Whatever the intention, Rendel's solution did not answer the problem. As vessels became bigger and bigger, up to several hundred tons, keeping the harbour open demanded more intervention. Water flows inwards with the flood tide in a matter of three hours; it flows outwards on the ebb at a much more leisurely rate. The consequence is that silt is deposited at high tide when the water is temporarily still but is not carried away as the tide falls. The problem was found to have become acute later in the century.

At the same time, receipts from harbour dues, which peaked in 1869, had fallen significantly and by 1894 were at a quarter of their highest levels. In 1844 there were twelve pilots for incoming and outgoing vessels. By 1890 there were only three. The fall in income meant that there was little money to spend on the harbour which had now silted up badly and had become tortuous between the quay and the pool. By 1876, the blocked exits from the east marsh had eroded or been swept away entirely.

Various solutions were sought, one of which, never proceeded with, was the building of a railway extension 'across the marshes to the deep water harbour about a mile distant'[19] The report gives no details of a possible route but it is clear that it was not meant to follow the beach bank because there is also mention of extending the quay tramway along the bank for the benefit of beach users. How the main channel at the quay, Stonemeals Creek, was to be bridged was not made clear. It never happened.

More practical and much less expensive – though clearly beyond the means of the commissioners – the services of Sir John Coode,

---

[19] *Eastern Daily Press* July 14th 1882

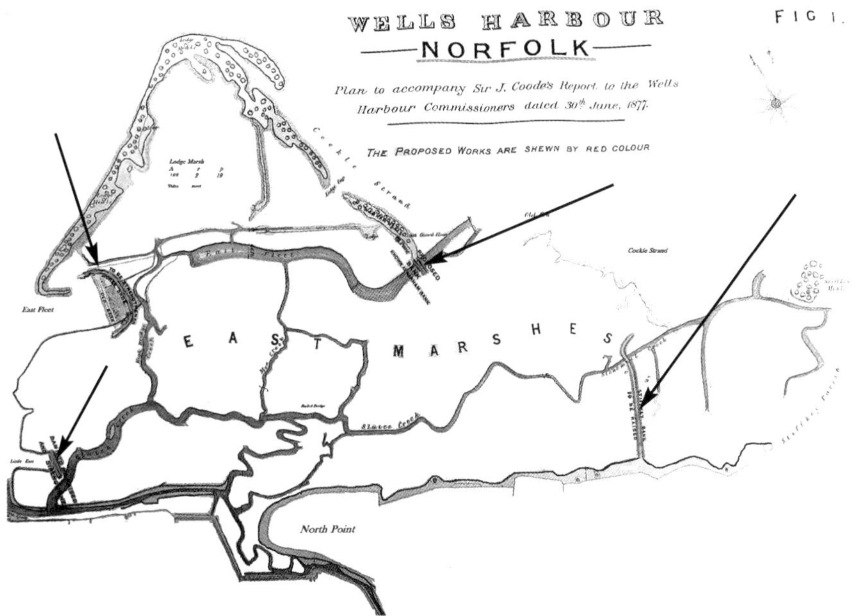

Coode's map of 1877 showing (by arrows) the proposed strengthened banks

the distinguished London engineer, were obtained, apparently without charge. Coode had done work on Portland harbour and the east London docks. He recommended a range of work, including the reinstatement of the four banks (see picture above) on the east marsh and the straightening of the Wells channel. The banks, which had decayed, lay east and west of the marshes and were intended to divert the ebb down via the quay thus achieving the much wanted flushing effect. Required expenditure was £1,165 for just essential works and a further £5,000 if a training wall were built. Bondholders were initially unwilling to fund the work; an acrimonious correspondence ran over six years which included a threat to have them made bankrupt for non-payment of fees. Finally in 1884 they were persuaded by the issue of new bonds and the threat that if nothing were done they would lose their investment entirely. They followed Coode's advice, digging out a bank of hard clay in the main channel, thus straightening it and speeding the flow. The banks at the eastern and western ends of the East Fleet were built up, Stiffkey bank was renewed and a bank built up at Little East fleet. It was enough. The inner channel was straightened and the outer route lay across sands to the north-west, an alignment which was owed to the forces of nature; the former was owed to Coode. It was reported that 'a vessel lying in the quay, as soon as it can float, can now proceed to sea'.[20]

Nevertheless, marine traffic continued to decline as traders made use of inland means of transport. Harbour dues, averaged over ten years to 1869, were £780; by 1879 they had fallen to £469; by 1904

[20] *Wells Harbour Office: records of Harbour Commissioners; finance records and printed reports* in Barney p. 31-2

Marie towing a sailing vessel out to sea – after 1912

to £240 and by 1914 to £140.[21] In 1893 fifteen vessels came from foreign ports, mostly from Denmark; by 1895 this number had fallen to five, three from Riga, while there were 39 coasters bringing mostly coal to the harbour. By 1903 the number had risen to 44; foreign vessels were in penny numbers. Mostly they brought in coal and oil-cake and took away barley. The odd vessel from Antwerp brought in road stone. The number of incoming vessels was not to rise above forty-five until the war when traffic all but ceased. [22]

Sailing boats still dominated the harbour trade into the new century. A series of tugs were used to assist them into and out of the harbour. The first of these, *Economy*, was bought by local merchants in 1840. She was replaced by the much larger *Olive Branch* and in turn by the even bigger sixty-seven ton *Promise*[23] in 1877. She it was who took part in the events leading to the loss of the Wells lifeboat *Eliza Adams* in 1880: she towed the lifeboat out to the *Ocean Queen* which had foundered on East Sands.

The last tug was *Marie*, owned jointly by two maltsters, Smiths and Marriotts. As steamers gradually replaced sailing ships they considered selling her but instead, having had her reboilered, her two funnels replaced by one in 1912, they then sold her in 1917, only for her to be requisitioned by the navy and sunk by a mine.

One reason for the slowness in going over to steam was expense. Wind was free. It was also a matter of capacity. Bunkering coal took up a lot of space which would otherwise be made available for cargo or passengers. A sailing vessel could travel any distance provided the crew could be fed and watered; the distance a steamer could manage was heavily restricted and trips on the high seas were out of the

---

[21] Barney p.32
[22] NRO DC 18/4/3-5
[23] Called *Provider* by Mike Stammers in *Victorian North Norfolk Sailing Ships* pp. 21,44,47

Albion, Violet, Sharon's Rose, and Louise after the 1880 storm

question. The steam engine itself was bulky. When it came to large boats, this problem could be overcome because the ratio of power needed to the weight of the vessel was much reduced, but it was not economical or practical to power cargo vessels by steam until the advance of the screw propeller.

On the other hand, the cost in vessels, cargoes and human lives when sailing vessels foundered in adverse weather continued to be suffered by merchants, by ship-owners and by families. The 1880 storm which took the lives of all but one of the crew of the *Eliza Adams* was not an isolated incident. The loss of life, marked by the memorial near the harbour office, was in the service of three stricken vessels that night. Several more were lost in the same storm, which no one reached. CJ Cornish, who chronicled the lives of the early wildfowlers, records walking the beach east of Wells at low tide and seeing dozens of sailing vessels in various states of decay, settling into the sand.[24] More than a hundred years later anchors and other fragments of sailing vessels were still being picked up by local whelk fishermen. The fact was that the narrow outer channel had moved eastwards so that the coastal tide running across it to the east with the rising tide could easily carry a vessel onto the sands beyond East Hills. Ships were largely square rigged, and could not sail close to the wind as modern yachts can. These factors conspired together to make losses almost inevitable in bad weather.

The 1880s saw no let up in the demands made on lifeboat crew who were often helpless before the sight of vessels driven ashore and lost. The *Anne Persunna* carrying pitch pine in October 1881 bound for Grimsby was lost with all her crew of twenty-one who could not be reached. The new lifeboat, the first *Baltic,* was unable to get up the channel two years later to the *Duke of Cornwall* whose crew gratefully

[24] CJ Cornish *Nights with an Old Gunner* (London 1897) p.7

walked ashore after the tide had gone out.[25] When the *Hickman* was sunk in the mouth of Wells harbour a day or so after that, the lifeboat crew were so exhausted by their efforts to get to her that their boat was beached at Holkham. Some of the crew then took to a salvage boat, the *Friends*, to row out to three men who had been hanging on to the rigging and who were saved. A fourth, a young man who had been lashed onto the taffrail, had died. William Crawford, who had volunteered to take the second boat, expressed the common view saying 'It's now or never'. The *Marie* was put to service with the

Baltic No 2
naming ceremony
1895

lifeboat in 1900 when it went out to the *Hopewell* which had anchored in Holkham bay when its anchor warp parted. The crew of three jumped into the lifeboat just as the foremast fell and the vessel became a total wreck.[26]

The advance of steam would make boats safer. It was achieved through greater efficiency by the introduction of the screw propeller. Even so *Heathfield*, sailing past Wells from Blyth in Northumberland on 12 October 1910 in a force 12 storm, hit one of the many sand shoals off the coast and was lost. On the morning of 14 October her masts and funnels and rigging were seen above the water and there were bodies lashed to the rigging. The dead were brought ashore to Wells and ten of them were buried in Wells cemetery after a service in church attended by hundreds, not including many who had lined the route of the cortege from the old lifeboat station.[27] Considering that neither the ship nor its crew owed anything to Wells it was an extraordinary exhibition of the solidarity of seamen.

---

[25] Graham Walker *The Memoirs of William John Harman 1854-1944* (Walker 1995) passim
[26] Walker | (1995) . p. 39-40
[27] *The Journal* Feb. 21st. 1964

The lifeboats would continue to be powered by sails and oars until 1936. The building of the new lifeboat station and slipway at the end of the beach bank in 1895 was a definite improvement. At high tide a lifeboat could be on the water in minutes; at low tide a carriage drawn by horses would take it out to the water's edge. The old lifeboat station by the quay was sold to the council in 1897 which christened it the Golden Jubilee house and intended it for use as a reading room and shelter for sailors. It was subsequently rented out as a tearoom and is now the harbour office.

The new lifeboat station housed the second *Baltic*, newly purchased that year. The first boat of that name, bought in 1888, was so called after the Baltic Lifeboat Fund which had raised the money for her; as did its members for the second boat of that name. She was replaced in 1913 by the *James Stevens* which saw out the war.

Those who risked their lives in the service of others were not limited to the RNLI volunteers. The coastguard service, which long predated that of the lifeboats, established a shore station in Wells in 1841. The service had two main functions, one related to the prevention of smuggling, the other to rescue at sea. For both of these purposes the coastguard had its own fleet of cutters. In 1881 the inspecting officer, Lieutenant Bellett, had 49 men under his command, including 23 boatmen and a carpenter. This service suffered the loss of one of its boats in 1898. When going to meet a naval vessel, the *Alarm*, to take off stores in heavy weather the cutter capsized with the loss of her crew of five; a boat from the *Alarm* was also subsequently lost. The *Baltic* was able to prevent further loss of life by going out to the *Alarm* herself.

The earliest records of Wells as a fishing port go back to 1337 when thirteen fishing boats were reported to government as operating from the harbour. The more recent story of the fishery has been told

James Jarvis outside his whelk house on Tug Boat Yard

elsewhere but it needs updating. Just before the turn of the century, a number of families from Sheringham came to the town – Shannocks as they were known. Fishermen have been notoriously nomadic, seeking fishing where it can be found. The Coxes came first, followed by the Grimes, the Coopers, the Peggs and the Littles. George Cox married a local girl; the Grimes and Coopers brought their several families with them. The Jarvises came from Stiffkey at the same time. Initially, they came for a few days fishing, sailing home for the weekend but eventually they rented houses in the town. The Peggs likewise settled here. As outsiders they initially met with hostility from locals. George Cox recorded that he was stoned when he first arrived. Fights among fishermen and with local people were routine, fuelled by alcohol. Though many of the shoreline public houses were being closed about that time, the Sun, the Fleece and the Shipwrights provided adequate sustenance. The Fleece, suitably gentrified, survives and the fishermen are much more moderate in their habits these days. The fishermen's children on the East Quay, dozens of them, emulated their parents by fighting the children from the west side of town, the sons of shopkeepers and agricultural workers. 'We all'us won!' said George's son, known as 'Loady', years later.[28] These were the children that headmaster Frederick Raven coerced into school by means of the school attendance officer and tried to teach. Spelling was hard to teach 'on account of their provincial pronunciation.'

With the decline of the oyster fishery, the local fishermen had relied on mussels, cockles and long-line fishing. The newcomers brought with them the skills of fishing for whelks, which was to become the mainstay of the Wells fishery for many years. Their boats, light and shallow drafted, intended to be hauled over the shingle beaches to the east, were double-ended, and powered by oars or a single lug sail. It was much later, from the 1920s onwards, that the idea came of fitting them with marinised petrol engines but they retained their sails for many years. Hauling pots in shanks of twenty-five was done by hand, a cruel job as the tarred rope tore even into their mitten-clad hands. Using bigger boats, known locally as hovellers, they could go further out to sea than the long-liners.[29] Sometimes they practised drift netting for mackerel and herring to provide themselves with bait.

Once upon a time whelks themselves had been chiefly used as bait for long-lining along the coast. The old cod smacks had lines stretching for miles with baited hooks every yard or so. It was a method which went back hundreds of years; the only difference now being the length of the line. Long-lining continued and was in war-time one of the most important kinds of fishing carried on hereabouts. When it came to fishing for whelks for food, they were caught in hexagonal pots, roped together into shanks, to be hauled aboard and emptied onto the deck, sorted, sieved and bagged. The hermit crabs among

[28] Charles 'Loady' Cox in Sally Festing *Fishermen* 1974 p.59
[29] 'Loady' Cox in Festing p.71

them were thrown overboard while the starfish, great destroyers of whelk beds, would be left to dry out and die. When the boats came in sight, with their red lug sails, someone on shore would be deputed to cycle off to the whelk sheds to light the fires for the boilers. Once ashore they would be boiled in big coppers in the sheds at the East End and sent to London by rail. They might sell their catch afar – to Yorkshire and beyond.

In bad weather, the pots set on heavy iron frames would be made and repaired, tied up with layers of rope to contain the catch, with only a hole in the top to allow entry. The iron frames were made by the local foundry and the tar to preserve the rope came from the gas works. Soon the whole frame would be made of iron, produced by the foundry at Walsingham.

The character of life in Wells in those days, dependant as it was on external factors against which there was no financial cushion, is illustrated by the life of William Harman, one of a very few people who recorded his life in the town. Harman's pedigree as a local goes back at least to the eighteenth century though like many men his father had travelled around the country in search of work. Born in 1854, his father drowned when William was four years old. Early on he learned the importance of contributing to the family income. As a schoolboy he helped his widowed mother in their shop on Freeman Street; he worked as a paper boy; later he assisted salvagers, 'wreckers' as they were called, recovering timber from ships sunk in the creeks; eventually he went on to tending his grandfather's mussel lays, one of many which in those days ran from the Sluice Creek, along the quay, and down the channel all the way out to the lifeboat station. He acquired several more lays when they became available. In summer he would take visitors out to East Hills in his boat; in winter he practised longshore netting which, in those days brought in salmon, sea trout and bass. The practice, almost extinct now, entailed paying out a weighted net from a boat rowed out from shore leaving a man on shore holding one end, and describing a semi-circle to enclose whatever fish were close to the beach, after which the net would be hauled in by the two men trapping the fish within it. In winter he harvested his mussel lays. He was also a lifeboatman, continuing to assist into his sixties. He recorded the loss of dozens of ships, most of them colliers, off the coast at or near Wells over the years and the loss of their crews before and after the *Eliza Adams* disaster. He died in 1944 at the age of 90, having witnessed the coming of the first motor-driven lifeboat from his house on the Glebe where, even when he was too old to go to sea, he could be found mending his nets.[30]

---

[30] Walker (1995) p. 9ff.

3. The marshes

Sheep on Wells marsh, circa 1900

If Wells was on the cusp of change, some aspects of its life appeared to be changeless. The marshes still seemed to be an untouched wilderness. It was of course an illusion. Though permanent occupation proved to be beyond human powers, yet Wells marsh had been farmed for nigh on a thousand years and had been intermittently peopled for at least as long. Its very inaccessibility was a blessing and an opportunity: the marsh had been a protection for the harbour from wind and wave; it was a hiding place for miscreants and smugglers over centuries; it was sought after by those who wished to increase their holding of arable land by draining and embanking; and it was a source of food for local fisherman and gentlemen wildfowlers (and has become latterly a refuge for wildlife, some of it very rare). The farming required the digging of banks not only to direct the incoming and outgoing tides but also to create grazing land. One long bank stretched from east to west, north of East Fleet to which sheep were driven above high tide. Attempts were made at various times to grow crops, such as asparagus. Apart from the banks, drainage channels were dug at different times, whose intention was to take water away from grazing pasture. They can still be seen clearly from the air. They were also the resort and the breeding grounds for birds - waders, ducks and geese.

As far back as 1740 duck had been entrapped with decoys at Holkham. It was a common activity wherever duck were known to congregate. Decoys were ponds of open water from which were led tapering net-covered ditches down which ducks were first enticed

Netting geese was an effective alternative to shooting

and then driven and trapped.[31] These were the practices of great estates. After the embanking of the west marsh in 1859, the lands from Wells to Blakeney continued to be a source of income. In the years up to 1914 shepherds and wildfowlers were to be found there, the latter feeding themselves and their families, using nets and guns. After the Napoleonic wars, men had come back with guns of various kinds, all of them muzzle-loaded and requiring time and skill to load and reload. One instrument of choice for those earning their living by wildfowling was the punt gun loaded with shot, powder, wads and caps all rammed home and fixed to the bow of a punt. This was then paddled through the creeks and pointed in the expected direction of low flying geese. The intention was that when fired, it would bring down a large number of geese. Goose nets, hung on stakes, were a very effective alternative. Geese were taken as they flew on dark nights or when swimming with the tide.

Sheep farming was recorded as early as Domesday, and was still practiced in the early years of the twentieth century. Often managed by a single shepherd and his dog, the sheep grazed the vegetation by

Fred and Percy Barrett – wildfowlers

[31] Christine Hiskey *Holkham* (2016) p. 444

day during the summer and were led across the many gated bridges over the creeks each night.[32] Sheep and geese were a symbiotic combination. The resultant extents of *Zostera*, eel grass, cropped short by the sheep, were favoured by the huge flocks of ducks and geese – Brent and pink foot – widgeon, teal and mallard which came to feed at night and were shot for the pot and for sale. A brace of Brent geese for the pot would fetch five shillings in Leadenhall Market in London in the 1800s, a child's wage for a week.[33]

The muzzle-loaders continued in use into the twentieth century. Though much less accurate than a breach loader, the cost of a cartridge far exceeded the cost of some black powder, shot and newspaper used as wadding. Fishermen and fowlers might meet as the former, having beached their boats when the wind dropped, trudged home over the sheep bridges to recover their vessels and the catch in the morning.[34]

The development of the breach-loaded cartridge, fired from a twin-barrelled shot gun, carried over the arm, opened up new opportunities. Local publican and coal merchant James Alexander Davidson took advantage of the new development and set up a small factory for their manufacture on the Buttlands. Another profitable enterprise derived from fowling was the market in stuffed birds. Taxidermy, now virtually a lost art, was practised by the likes of Thomas Gunn of Norwich, to whom rare birds could be sold for handsome sums.[35] A second source of employment was that of guiding the gentlemen wildfowlers from London and elsewhere who began to appear, eager to take home a goose they had shot. Some of these were happiest staying in Wells hotels; the hardier of them would stay overnight in the various houseboats moored out in the creeks. Wells wildfowlers like Pat Cringle and Fred and Percy Barrett became much sought-after as guides to the prized quarry. Not only geese, but knots, stints,

North Point Bridge with the club house seen in background

[32] Mike Cringle *The Gamekeeper's Boy* (Larks Press 2001) p. 51
[33] *Wildfowling at Wells* (WLHG 2011) article by Kevin Thatcher p. 1
[34] Cringle p.52
[35] Examples of Gunn's work can be seen in the Victoria Hotel at Holkham.

grey, green and golden plover, curlew, redshanks, apparently in their thousands, could be seen and shot, not to mention rabbits and partridge. [36]

The profusion of birds seemed inexhaustible, and shooting them seemed to have no impact on their numbers. Nevertheless, there were the beginnings of an interest in conservation. The Wells Society for the Preservation of Wild Birds came into existence in the latter years of the nineteenth century, devoted to the protection of the tern colony whose last redoubt in Norfolk was Wells.[37] Cringle himself had, as a very young man, been employed by Holkham during the summer to guard the breeding terns which established themselves on Wells beach, spending nights in a houseboat moored in a creek not far away from the stretch of sand and shingle where the birds nested.[38]

Cringle recorded his life in articles which he wrote for the *Shooting Times*. Frank Southgate recorded his impressions in paint. A local man, his paintings of fowlers and of birds flying over the marshes were to be followed by many others, another impetus to changed attitudes towards the natural order.

A quite different recreational use for the marshes was as a golf course. The much more recent pitch-and-putt course on the reclaimed west marsh was often thought of as the site of the earlier course, but it was not so. The original Wells golf course lay to the east on the edge of the marsh past North Point Bank. It was in fact in Warham parish. It was accessed via one of a number of footbridges over smaller creeks to the south of Stonemeals Creek, the principal of which was known as North Point Bridge and whose remains, at the time of writing, can still be seen. The course itself was horseshoe-shaped between two creeks. The origins of the course are obscure but the club which was to manage it was set up at a meeting on 25 June 1894 at

East Hills with the remains of the North Point Bridge

[36] CJ Cornish (1897) pp. 33-4, 50
[37] Cornish p. 66
[38] Cringle p. 15

the Edinburgh Inn presided over by EB Loynes, solicitor and clerk to the council. One of its joint secretaries was the aforementioned James Alexander Davidson, owner of the establishment. The other was AJ Napier of Holkham who was to become the driving force behind the club's activities. Permission for the use of the land was sought from Major JE Groom who can be presumed to be the owner or manager of the marsh. The land was poor but was evidently thought suitable, for a year later funds and support were sought for a club house which was duly built by Thomas Platten in 1895. Competitions were held and visits to other clubs undertaken; various trophies were donated to be competed for. Ladies were admitted to membership. Access was not easy and a roadway was built to the bridge.[39] Its membership included some of the substantial citizens of the town including GF Smith and several members of the Everitt family, all maltsters. Its income enabled the paying off of the debt of the club-house and making improvements to the course itself.

Records exist of the club continuing until about 1912 and mention is made of the course throughout the 1930s but the neglect consequent upon war and the 1953 floods would have destroyed any evidence of it.

---

[39] Welland *Wells-next-the-Sea Golf Club* (WLHG Archive)

4. Maltings

F&G Smith floor malting at Great Ryburgh, 2009

The wild beauty of the marshes, replete with strutting gulls and carefully stepping waders, is but a yard or so from the industrial town. To the north of the harbour wall lay vessels, large and small, dependent on their ability to survive the sea's wilder moods. Inland by a yard or two lay the many industrial premises that drove the town.

Malting in Wells went back hundreds of years. Vessels carried malt and grain up and down the coast when road transport was poor or non-existent, bringing back coal to feed its drying kilns, to fuel the blacksmiths' forges and to warm folks' houses. In the eighteenth century malting grew from being an occupation of every farming community to being a commercial activity, supplying the Dutch gin distilleries as well as the inland breweries which in turn supplied local public houses. Many public houses continued to have their own brew houses, but by the midcentury, commercial breweries had begun to supplant them.

The maltsters themselves had ceased to be farmers and become merchants employing others to do the actual work. James Everitt was one such. He bought, leased or built maltings in the town which, with the assistance of the new railway, he proceeded to supply malt to breweries as far away as the renowned Burton upon Trent establishments. Randle Brereton, Martha Rust and Stephen Leeds were among others in Wells who built and worked and subsequently leased their maltings in the town. Martha Rust, the daughter of one of the town's shipbuilders, had married into malting. Others, like Robert

Leaman, were from farming stock; he was from Whitwell. Such traders had accumulated properties as individuals suffering the risk of bankruptcy – to which many of them succumbed. Leaman was very much the entrepreneur, concerning himself with the 1844 Improvement Act and subsequently buying up Randle Brereton's malting. He followed that by buying up five pubs, several granaries, brew houses, wharves, coalhouses, a number of malt houses, a brick works and a town house.[40] He left the town in 1868 complaining of the 'hostile spirit' when he suffered a fivefold increase in the rent of the brickworks which he had leased. Alas, he would not be the last to feel ill-treated by the town, believing that he could single-handedly change it.

A new generation took another step. Among farmers turned maltsters were the Smith family, originally of Ryburgh. They differed in one important respect from their predecessors. They began their progress as individuals buying everyone else out but did so latterly as a corporate body with a succession. In 1890 they formed an incorporated company with limited liability. In future they could raise capital not only by borrowing but by the issue of shares.

The brief history is as follows. The brothers Frederick and George, having been farmers in Ryburgh, had diversified into the making of malt. Canadian imports had undermined the market in wheat but the excellent quality of Norfolk barley meant that the market for malt remained buoyant. Their first malting in Dereham, built in 1870, was served from Ryburgh by the new railway. From there, in 1878, they expanded to Wells which was conveniently at the end of the same railway line, leasing Stephen Leeds' malting on Staithe Street. They proceeded to expand further but the weakness of their position was exposed by Frederick's death in 1881 which left his widow, Anne, and her eight children to carry on the business. Her eldest son George was then 19. In 1890, just before Anne's death, the company was incorporated with George, now 28, as chairman.

F&G Smith and Co. Ltd. began to develop and add to their stock of maltings at their three sites, at Ryburgh, Dereham and Wells. Though Wells was to be the registered office, directors' meetings were held at the offices of the accountants HP Gould & Son in Norwich. George moved, on his marriage in 1886, to an eighteenth century town house half way up Staithe Street in Wells, within easy walking distance of the maltings on the quay. It was also close to the station for his trips to Ryburgh and Dereham. He renamed it Mayshiel after a shooting estate in Scotland which he had frequented.

From then onwards Smiths bought, built or extended a number of maltings and granaries, some of which they had previously rented. Their first attempt to buy Everitt's maltings failed. They then bought out James Chapman in 1893. In the same year they ordered the installation of new rollers to replace the old stone mills at Ryburgh. They built two sweating kilns, one at Ryburgh, the other at Wells at

[40] NRO BR 320/1-9

the same time in 1895.[41] In 1902 they spent £2,051 on what must have been a massive extension of what became No 18 Malting between Tunns Yard and Knotts Yard. In 1903 they purchased four more maltings and several public houses belonging to the trustees of Robert Leaman and Stephen Leeds (on which they already had leases).[42] Finally, in April 1904, they entered into a contract with Thompsons of Nottingham for the building of the now iconic Granary, then described as a malt storage warehouse, on the quay at a cost of £3,280. They were on a spending spree.

Supply of some of the equipment for the maltings was put out to tender but they also used local suppliers. Local iron founder John Woods had patented an iron tile for use in malt drying kilns. These appear to have been a success, being widely sold. Jabez Cornish, who bought Woods out in 1885, advertised himself as a supplier of 'Patent Malt Kiln tiles' to the trade as well as the run of agricultural machinery.[43]

They also improved the necessary infrastructure adjunct to their enterprise by buying a length of quay. The harbour commissioners had bought up some properties on the quay, using the powers of the 1844 Act, but they had never completed it as proposed. Smiths took

Marie *in her twin funnel days towing a sailing barque inward, circa 1900*

advantage of the situation and bought the length to the east of the Granary from James Chapman. They then strengthened that section of the quay to accommodate their supply vessels, deepening it at the same time.[44]

Though they had turned to using the railway, taking advantage of

[41] Christine Clark *The British malting industry since 1830* (Hambleton 1998) p.92; F & G Smith Ltd Directors Minute Book Jan.26th. 1895

[42] F&G Smith passim; the Staithe street maltings continued to operate under the name of Richard Dewing & Co. until they closed in 1929.

[43] M. Welland *The Cornish family of Iron Founders* (2016) unpubl. (WLHG Archive)

[44] Betty Wharton *The Smith's of Ryburgh* (Crisp Malting 1990) p. 32

Aerial picture of the town showing the many long malting sheds, 1925

the cheaper tariffs, their trade with Guinness, the Dublin brewers, required the use of sea transport. How longstanding it was is not known but in any case malt exports continued unaffected by the agricultural depression of the 1870s. Having acquired shares in the tug *Promise* in 1877, ten years later they bought *Marie* to service incoming vessels. The Dublin trade, carried on now mostly by Welsh vessels, had the advantage that on the return journey from Ireland, ships could pick up a cargo of anthracite from Swansea, a high carbon smokeless coal with which to fire the kilns used to dry and roast the malted barley. From 1886 onwards until 1904 there were regular deliveries at the rate of two shipments a year, back and forth.[45]

By the end of the century there were probably twelve maltings along the length of the quay. By 1913 Smiths were to be one of the twelve leading sales-maltsters in the country by production capacity.[46] Developments at the other two sites proceeded at a similar pace.

Smiths' conduct of business was not without its troubles. The press reported an attempted strike in February of 1892. The report describes the physical nature of the work: the need to carry heavy sacks from waggons to the various chambers; the hot working conditions of the malting floors; the irregular hours which workers were obliged to work; and the fact that malting could only be done for less than six months of the year (and the best malt produced in four).[47] Men would routinely carry 12 stone (75 kilo) wicker baskets of coal across the quay into the fire-hold.[48] In the event 22 of the 29 men went

[45] Mike Stammers in *Maritime Wales* vol. 20 (1999) p.77
[46] Clark p. 62; the 1903 purchase increased the capacity by 243 quarters: Wharton p.32
[47] Wharton p.34-5
[48] Clark p. 123

back to work without any agreement; their bid for an increase in wages was ignored. And the directors did nothing to meet the grievances. In 1901 Smiths sustained a horrendous loss, a self-inflicted wound, from the collapse of the Greenwich brewery of Lovibond which they had supplied on credit to the sum of nearly £20,000.

George Smith meanwhile lived a life of comparative ease, unconcerned with the conditions of the labour force. The family 'seem to have been primarily concerned with their own comfortable lives and the level of the dividends which are most carefully recorded.'[49] The day-to-day management of the company seems to have been in the hands of their accountant and general managers. Dividends remained high, too high in the view of Harry Gould, the firm's accountant, occasionally as high as 10% and never less than 4%. Ominously the increasingly shaky signature of George Smith indicated a man of failing powers; the meetings became shorter and his contributions fewer. He drank too much. On his death in 1917, he was succeeded by his brother Herbert and on his death in 1921 by George's youngest son, Ladas.

The Smiths had long relied upon those outside the family to keep the company going. 'Teddy' Hill, manager at both Dereham and Wells, effectively took over much of the decision-making. Times were becoming harder. The falling demand for malt is suggested by the decision to send one member of the family, Harry Jacobs-Smith, to seek new orders in the north of England on commission. The property at Overy was sold. *Marie* had gone the same year that George died. Drum malting, which provided much greater control over temperature, humidity and disease, was beginning to replace the traditional floor malting system of countless ages, but the Smiths did not take it up.[50] There was increasing pressure on the industry to accommodate change. It was something for which they were not prepared, having turned their interest towards investments in unrelated government stocks with an expectation of high returns. These were clouds no bigger than a man's hand.

---

[49] Wharton p. 36

[50] Lawrence Briant and Cuthbert Vaux *Drum Malting* Journal of the Federated Institutes of Brewing Vol. 7 Issue 5 p. 404; it was not until the 1950s that Smiths actually bought a drum!

5. The railway age

The railway came to Wells in 1857. By its means, the town began falteringly but deliberately to turn its face southwards. For a thousand years it had been easier to travel by sea than by land, to get to Antwerp

Wells station, late 19th century – note the windmill extreme right

rather than to Birmingham. London and Newcastle were both easily accessible by sea. Roads had improved enormously, particularly since the coming of the turnpikes in the 1820s, but even so travel inland was slow. The internal combustion engine had not yet been invented but now travel was possible to anywhere in the country.

The idea of making Wells a modern port with access to the rest of the country by means of the new transport phenomenon was led by Thomas Coke, the second Earl, at Holkham who, like his father, was an agricultural improver. He began campaigning for a railway as early as 1846, together with a number of local merchants and the occasional adventurer. The process had, in truth, many elements: the port needed to be accessible to larger ships; the town needed to be accessible to goods coming from inland and being taken out; the new railway would enable long distance transport to be speedier than anything that could be contemplated by road. Coke saw the railways primarily as a means of transporting goods, not people. Unlike Cromer and Hunstanton, Wells was not, in his view, to be a holiday resort but a thriving industrial town. He contributed the considerable sum of £10,000; local traders added a further £14,000. Supporters of the railway included other landowners such as Sir Willoughby Jones of Cranmer Hall but also local merchants interested in profitable investments. These included local ship-owner, builder and opportunist, Joseph Southgate, the banker JH Gurney, James Everitt, maltster, and Sir Samuel Morton Peto, a go-getting engineer with a string of enterprises to his name and interests in railways across East Anglia.[51]

The 1840s saw the eruption of so-called railway mania with different interests promoting different schemes, often with more thought of personal gain than public advantage. Peto was one such, offering unrealistic returns to Wells subscribers to encourage them to put their money into the new venture while doing little to advance the actual building of the railway. Parliamentary approval was not secured until 1854 and even when the line was completed by 1856, no agreement could be reached with the Norfolk Railway or its successor the Eastern Counties Railway, as to when trains would actually start running.

The unrealistic financial package, with its promises of high returns, began to unravel. Peto's primary aim was to develop Lowestoft rather than Wells as a major port. At a meeting in Wells in August 1857 to secure the running of trains, Southgate was the only director to turn up. Eventually, the promised high rates of return were replaced by a much more modest package. The building of the line had been expensive and Peto was sure not to make a loss. Because of the steepness of the hill a cutting had to be made at Fakenham in order to reduce the gradient. The river Stiffkey, which ran through a marshy valley, had to be crossed by a viaduct and a short tunnel, both at Barsham. The river crossing was managed by the construction of an American style wooden trestle viaduct, a cheaper option than building an embankment.

Barsham viaduct as originally built

The line finally opened in December of that year, running from Wells to Fakenham and then onwards to Dereham, joining the main line from Norwich at Wymondham. The opening day was declared to be a public holiday with hundreds gathered at the station and

[51] Stanley Jenkins *The Wells-next-the-Sea Branch* (The Oakwood Press 2011) p.17ff.

Horse-drawn waggons on the quay

along the line to witness the arrival of the first train from Fakenham. The streets of the town were decorated with flags; Coke held a celebratory lunch for the directors at Holkham and a crowd descended on the thirteen-coach train to take them to Fakenham, returning after an interval to Wells. A dinner for eighty people was held in The Crown, while labourers who had worked on the line were given dinner at the Tunns Inn.

The harbour branch, a tramway from the station to the quay, suffered its own delays, not opening until 1859. Until its completion, cargoes had to be unloaded from boats onto carts which then proceeded through the town to be transhipped to railway waggons, a laborious and costly practice which was continued after completion as a result of the initial refusal of the railway company to operate it. Another problem was the fact that the tramway impeded the launching of vessels from the two shipyards, for which reason it was opposed by one of the shipbuilders; they threatened to take proceedings against the company.[52] A compromise was achieved by which compensation was paid to the ship-owners. How vessels were launched over the line is not clear. Horses were used to pull the waggons along the quay to the east end where a steam locomotive picked them up and took them through the cutting in the town's chalk bank to the station. In the reverse direction, locomotives were allowed no further than the east end of the quay after which the horses took over. The tramway was laid level with the roadway which may have been the agreed compromise.

In practice railway and port were competitors. Sometimes when ships were stormbound their cargoes were unloaded and transferred to the railway to ensure prompt delivery. Nevertheless, the new railway did not prosper and in 1862 the Wells and Fakenham Railway transferred its assets to the newly formed Great Eastern Railway with

[52] Letter to the directors in Michael Stammers *Shipbuilding in Wells* (WLHG) p. 21

Wells station after the accident of 1879

over half the stock being written off at some cost to local investors.[53]

Wells was to remain a terminus. The line ran to Fakenham and Wymondham (via Dereham); a proposed link with Blakeney was never built. A line from Wells to Heacham was built in 1866 but it was not well patronised and was never a success, partly because the line which it joined, between Hunstanton and Lynn, was inadequate to cope with increased traffic. Its use was never encouraged by the Great Eastern when it took over both lines in 1890. It never ran more than four passenger trains a day and a single freight train. [54]

For some businesses the railway was a godsend. James Everitt, whose maltings had been acquired in the 1850s, began to supply the Bass brewery in Burton upon Trent. He did not merely supply; he acted as agent for the brewery in purchasing barley for its use. Malt could now be dispatched quickly and cheaply to the centres of urban growth.[55] Everitt was from a local farming family and, as a young man in the 1820s, had been involved in the family brewery business with its string of twenty five public houses.[56] Likewise, the 1879 accounts for F&G Smith show their transport costs as being almost entirely for rail freight.[57] One can understand why: in the early days of the railway, malt cost 1s 4d per quarter to transport from Norwich to London against 2s 5d by sea.[58] The malting at Ryburgh was immediately adjacent to the railway line.

The number of passenger trains to Norwich rose during the century from four to six and, though the distance to London was much longer via Norwich than via Heacham, timetabling encouraged the use of

53 Jenkins p.29
54 Jenkins p. 30ff.
55 Clark p. 23
56 Clark p. 53; *Select Committee on the Malt Tax* (1867) pp. 52
57 Wharton (1990) p. 10
58 Clark p. 21

The collapse of the Barsham viaduct after heavy rains in 1912

the former route. By the 1880s it was possible to catch the 8.30am train from Wells and arrive in London, making one change, at 11.14am. A return journey leaving London at 5pm would get a passenger into Wells by 9.15pm, changing at Wymondham. The railway did not, in those days, much benefit the rise of tourism. Day trippers were a more likely prospect than those who would stay overnight, let alone for the season. If people came to stay it was likely that they would be wildfowlers.

The railway was, on the whole, a safe means of transport but on 3 June 1879, the sharp gradient running into the station proved the undoing of the driver who was unable to slow the train down. It hit the buffer stops, broke down the section of platform beyond and smashed the wall of the porters' room and the toilets, where it came to a halt. George Cooke, who had come to meet someone off the train and who had gone into the toilet, was killed.

Perhaps even more dramatic, though without loss of life, was the flooding of the river Stiffkey on 26 August 1912, caused by exceptionally heavy rains which washed away part of the embankment at East Barsham, between Fakenham and Wells, and which carried away the bridge. A freight train had been crossing the bridge at the time, but most of the waggons reached safety before it collapsed. It was quickly repaired.

6. Schools for the poor

The first public school in Wells opened in 1837. Private academies existed in the town, open to the children of the merchant classes. Samuel Bradley ran a boarding school in Blenheim House; a charity school had been set up in 1678 by the will of Christopher Ringer but it was small – 30 boys and 30 girls – as were its resources. The new school was paid for by public subscription. It was opposed by the vicar, the Revd John Hopper, as a derogation of the rights of the established church which had opened a so-called National School using the old workhouse on Church Street in 1834. The National Society for the encouragement of education according to the tenets of the church of England had been established in 1811.

Those who wished for a broader based education set up their own school in opposition to it three years later under the aegis of a non-conformist body, the British and Foreign School Society. This more inclusive option found support from, among others, the Countess of Leicester and the rector of Warham, Thomas Robert Keppel. The great and the good, under the patronage of no less than the Duke of Sussex, presumably solicited by the Earl, thus sponsored fund-raising events for the new school. As the Wells Parochial British School it would be managed by a committee of local businessmen headed by the agent at Holkham, Samuel Shellabear and ship-owner Joseph Springall Southgate (who appeared to have his finger in every pie in the town).

The first head teachers were, in quick succession, Miss Garwood and William Gamble, both of whom had previously run private academies; Gamble had married the daughter of John Fryer, sailing master of *HMS Bounty*, who assisted him. Gamble continued for some years until 1860. The school grew and by 1856 it had 195 pupils from three years of age upwards. With such a small teaching force some of the older scholars were deployed assisting in the teaching of the younger ones, the so-called monitorial system. The head would lecture to the whole cohort of boys after which they would be divided up into sections to be taught by the monitors. It spread the load but it was often the case that little was learnt, acting merely as child care. It could scarcely survive the growing need for literate and numerate children.

Gamble was followed in 1860 by Sidney Uren, the first master to record his doings in a log book. It is to him that we owe the first description of the conditions of teaching in the school. He did not stay long and in 1863 the Society recruited to its headship Samuel Lewton, a registered teacher from Chichester. Lewton was to see the school through some of the major developments in education in the country. He did not like what he saw. The school buildings were in good condition; the standard of teaching was not. Maria Gamble, who had taught the infants' class, left shortly after his arrival, perhaps finding the new regime not to her liking. (She thereafter joined the staff of Ringer's School.)

Lewton's new stricter regime coincided with the production, by the education committee of the Privy Council, of the so-called 'revised code'. This was to be a very simple national curriculum, setting out standards to be achieved at each of six standards of children between the ages of 7 and 13. Central government had only comparatively recently taken any interest in the state of education and the Newcastle Commission, set up by the Privy Council in 1839, was tasked with the examination of the state of elementary education across the country.[59] The resultant code furnished Lewton with what he needed, standards for reading, writing and arithmetic. Various pub-

Samuel Lewton the master, right and Rolf with scholars in 1897

lishing companies supplied him with reading books for each standard. Finally, his job was made secure by the Privy Council's decision to grant four shillings for each scholar's attendance and eight shillings 'subject to examination'. Staff could now be properly paid. Their efficiency would determine their security of tenure.

The next major development was the passing of the Elementary Schools Act of 1870. Its stated purpose, that of its progenitor, the Liberal MP William Forster, was to fill the gaps in national educational provision thus ensuring that every community had a school. They

[59] Derek Gillard *Education in England* (revised edition May 2018) assembles a vast array of source material on the subject: http://www.educationengland.org.uk/history Revised Code of Minutes and Regulations of the Committee of the Privy Council 1862 Gillard Ch. 6.

were to be called board schools. Most village schools were church schools but not all villages had such schools; they were much rarer in towns and cities. The Act provided for the teaching of pupils from five to ten and empowered schools to take pupils up to the age of thirteen regardless of ability to pay. At the annual meeting of subscribers in April 1875, the school managers decided upon the transfer of the school to the local board under the Act. The board consisted of much the same people as the earlier committee: Sam Shellabear the Holkham agent, Hugh Rump, local surgeon, Joseph Southgate, Joshua Gales, proprietor the *Wells Herald* newspaper, the Revd George Stallworthy, Congregational minister, with Edward Bunting Loynes, local solicitor, as secretary. It was now what would later be called a state school. The next development, which came in 1880, was when elementary education was formally made compulsory. In 1891 it was made free, paid for by local and central government.

Under Lewton's direction the school was enlarged in 1876 and again in 1885 to cope with its increased number of pupils who now totalled 420. In 1876 the teaching of boys and girls was made entirely separate. For most of that time Lewton was assisted only by monitors and pupil teachers, the latter being another invention of the Privy Council – older teenagers themselves whose education Lewton had to progress at the beginning or end of the school day. Youngsters, who might be thinking of a career in teaching, were recruited on a five year apprenticeship with a view to attending one of the new teacher training colleges. Better than monitors, they were still immature for the task. Qualified assistant teachers, when they came, were often a disaster. When Mr Kendle, a former pupil teacher from Rudham, left after 16 months in 1877 he left the school 'in great confusion; with 140 children and little help the Master feels overpowered and leaves school disheartened'. Kendle, though, was better than his predecessor Mr Cooke of whom Lewton wrote: 'he leaves school this afternoon without a word to his children or the master. When the key was given up on the following morning it was discovered that nearly all his slates, pens and pencils had been lost or broken.'

Another serious impediment to learning was the spread of disease. Epidemics severely hampered educational progress: in 1888 the school was closed from January to early April because of scarlet fever. Whooping cough closed the school for three weeks in 1899. The head himself was sick in 1881 from February until late May, thus threatening the continuation of the school altogether; he was sick again for several weeks in 1883. School closures were necessary. Bringing over 400 children into contact with each other was a guaranteed means of spreading diseases which were pretty much untreatable at the time.

In 1898 a further proposal was then put that the school be further extended. The proposal, when reported to the district council, was regarded locally as amounting to the provision of a new school.[60]

[60] *UDC Minutes* NRO D18/4/4 p. 558

The school would, on completion, consist of a boys' schoolroom and classroom, a girls' schoolroom and classroom and an infants' schoolroom and classroom and be capable of serving 590 children. The cost would be £7,765.

Lewton continued as head until 1900, assisted by Miss Hermon Taylor who taught mixed infants and Miss Betty Rayfield, who taught the girls. Both proved to be long stayers: Taylor died in office in 1915; Betty Rayfield retired in 1925. After a period of dislocation the new head, appointed in 1903, was Frederick Raven. Raven was to carry the school through 27 years of the century, through a World War and

School staff 1904. Frederick Raven (centre) flanked by Miss Hermon Taylor and Miss Betty Rayfield

the depression which shortly after followed it. He would make his contribution to the life of the town as head teacher but also as a magistrate, as a district councillor, as a harbour commissioner, secretary of the hospital management committee and as treasurer of the town football club.

In 1902 supervision of the school and evaluation of its effectiveness passed to the County Board of Education which would henceforth undertake a regular annual inspection.[61] The school would now be subject to HMI and to the county inspector. It was a big school. Raven reported in 1907 that there were 246 boys, 232 girls and 168 infants, a total of 636. A contemporary photograph shows a staff of fourteen plus three pupil teachers, making for an average class size of 45. How many of these teachers were not qualified is not known; lack of qualified teachers would certainly be a problem later.

The HMI report of 1908 declared that 'This school is one of the most important in the county... [and] to the ability and enthusiasm of the headmaster the school owes a great deal of its reputation'. The

---

[61] NA ED2/327

following year however the report noted that there were too few qualified teachers and that the classes were too large; sub-division for reading was recommended. The transfer from infants' to the boys' and girls' schools was not well managed: 'Teachers of the lower classes should have some knowledge of teaching in an infants' school'. Comment was made and continued to be made about the lack of satisfactory ventilation and lighting in the infants' school. Toilets were a problem. Pails, to be emptied weekly, were proposed instead of the 'pit system' or earth closets. As adverse comment continued to be made about the buildings, positive comments were made about the teachers. 'This is on the whole a very good school. The upper group are intelligent, better informed and more active and take a great interest in their work', the Inspector wrote in 1913.[62] It was to grow and grow.

The bulk of the population had missed the opportunity of education. Few had the advantage of George Edwards who learned to read at his wife's elbow when he was in his twenties. Evening schools were an opportunity to make good the loss. In 1903 a committee of management under chairmanship of the rector, George Ingle, was set up to organise an evening class under Raven's overall headship. Sixteen scholars, of age unknown, attended the first session, paying three shillings each. Apart from basic literacy they were treated to lantern slides. Numbers rose to over 30, though attendance was affected by choir practices and on one occasion by 'moonlit' football. They met three times a week. It was not just a piece of local initiative. One of HM inspectors visited them. He wrote 'This is a new class that has made a good beginning. The subjects under instruction are being soundly taught and those in attendance are making a wise choice of their opportunities'.[63] The opportunities included shorthand as well as arithmetic, history and geography, drawing, woodwork and French. There were now two classes.

Of these classes, there is no record after 1908. In the short term any provision would have to be a matter of private initiative. Sam Peel, who was about to become a significant figure in the life of the town and who was to establish himself as something of a social reformer was, among other things, a believer in education. Soon after arriving in 1910 he set up an adult school at the Friends' Meeting House. The school subsequently moved to Staithe Street. His purpose was twofold: to keep men out of the pubs on a Sunday evening and to give them something of an education. It was, of course, religious conviction that drove him. In the summer meetings were held on the quay where up to a thousand people would gather to hear Sankey's hymns and to listen to various speakers who stood on an empty railway truck.[64]

---

[62] NA. ED70/1887
[63] *Log Book for Evening Schools School No. 45244* September 1903 p.8
[64] John Tuck *Conversations with Alderman Sam Peel OBE* (WLHG Newsletter No 46 2010)

7. Health and housing

Health is partly a matter of prevention and partly of cure. Prevention is achieved by the control of the external conditions: primarily the availability of clean water, adequate waste disposal and decent housing, but also a matter of lifestyle. Means of cure before the advent of modern medicine were primitive. Wells' physicians got an occasional mention in the eighteenth century when people made use of the services of a veterinary rather than a doctor because he would be cheaper. Some diseases were better understood than others and the remarkable story of the use of variolation, an early form of vaccination when a smallpox outbreak occurred in 1758 needs a mention. Who the doctor was at the time is not known. Some 250 people in the town were treated. None of them died. The overall death toll was over a hundred.[65] A later epidemic of the disease in 1769 found the town better prepared: 30 people died out of 500 who caught the infection. Unfortunately as a port the town was vulnerable to disease brought in by visiting vessels. Not all surgeons, as they were then called, had a dismal job. Henry Girdlestone was described in 1793 as a surgeon and man-midwife.

Doctors were to become more and more important not only for their medical expertise but for their contribution to the life of the town. The succession of three generations of the Rump family, from 1789 when the first Hugh Rump came to the town, to 1887 when the last of the line died, would be a story in itself; they were widely admired for their service to the town both medically and because of their charitable works. The second Hugh paid for the church clock and the third, Hugh Robert, contributed a third of the cost of rebuilding the church after the fire of 1879. The second of the line bought The Normans, an eighteenth century town house which would be intermittently occupied by Wells doctors until the retirement of Dr Hicks in 1969. The Rumps remained in the town after their retirement in 1864.

Another of the acts of charity of Hugh Robert had been to donate towards the establishment of the West Norfolk and Lynn hospital in 1848. No one thought of building a hospital in Wells until 1890 when the idea was mooted by a Norwich printer, BE Fletcher; the Earl of Leicester offered £20,000 as an endowment for its continuation but it was only in 1910, at the instigation of local doctor EFW Sturdee, a Scot by birth, that the hospital was built as a memorial to the Earl, who had died in 1909. It was supported by public subscription. The third Earl of Leicester provided the site. Opening in 1911,

[65] Wells Parish Register 1758

it was stated to be 'for the benefit of poor persons suffering from accident or non-infectious disease who cannot be properly attended to in their homes and primarily for those resident in Wells and district'.[66] Long term conditions such as consumption, as tuberculosis was then called, and chronic disease were specifically excluded. The maximum length of stay was to be four weeks. In practice the average length of stay was ten days. It was to have no outpatient department nor were minor casualties to be treated. Patients would pay 2s 6d (12½p) per week in advance 'according to their circumstances'. Thirty-seven subscribers attended the first meeting whose support was obviously voluntary though there were inducements to major donations: those whose subscription exceeded 10s 6d could recommend one patient annually. Two villages, Walsingham and Hindringham, ran schemes which brought in 15s (75p) a week as did the Great Eastern Railway Company. The hospital's staff, consisting of Sturdee, Gordon Calthrop and Alfred Whitlock, all local practitioners, were to provide their services gratuitously, unless treating their own patients. In addition, the hospital had the occasional services of two consultants, FW Burton-Fanning, a nationally renowned physician and Sir Hamilton Ballance, a London surgeon.

Operations were undertaken from an early stage. The first reference to an appendectomy was in April 1912, that of a Walsingham pauper. This drew criticism from the committee. No one should be admitted unless they had paid their 2s 6d. Calthrop, whose experience of poverty and need in the community had already been tested by his day job, was to stand up to his committee over other matters as well as this. The Earl, who took a more than occasional interest in the work of the hospital, was to suggest that the removal of tonsils, which was a widespread practice, could take place in patients' homes to save money. Calthrop's response was that these were the homes of the poorest whose houses were insanitary and not suitable for such procedures.

Sturdee did most of the surgery. He was described as 'a very clever surgeon and by aiding him [Whitlock and Calthrop] had been able to perform a large number of difficult operations such as appendectomies and hernias.' Clearly not all survived. The mortuary was built in 1914.

The Rumps had made a further contribution to the town's medical provision. In 1851 Russell Rump, nephew of Hugh the third, leased and subsequently bought the newly built pharmacy on Staithe Street, describing himself in 1856 as 'Chemist, Druggist, British Wine Dealer and Agent for the East of England Bank'. It was sold to George Poll in 1904.

Being a surgeon was not all about plaudits. In 1860 Hugh the third was called upon to make a judgement on his colleague, Patrick Vincent, who was accused of poisoning, albeit accidentally, one Tolvers

[66] Wells Cottage Hospital Management Committee Minutes Feb. 1st 1911 NRO ACC2008/268

Silvers, a local schoolmaster who had died a painful death after treatment. A post mortem was ordered to be performed by Rump. He concluded that no blame should be attached to Vincent for his treatment of Silvers; but the furore, fanned by rumours around the town, was pretty intense for a short while.[67]

Bread oven and hearth 1873 Holkham

The conditions of life of ordinary Wells people call for some comment. The hearings before the House of Lords in 1844 had heard how narrow and ill-paved the streets were. Wells compared poorly with the Georgian town of Holt with its wide streets, but its houses were at least built of brick, unlike many inland where as late as 1863 a few families still lived in a single room of a wattle and daub thatched dwelling, often in a state of decay.[68] Even so some of the conditions in Wells were not hugely better. For one thing, almost all cottages had one or at most two bedrooms. Having been built with a single upstairs room, many of the cottages on High Street had additional frontages, adding a living room (or sometimes a shop) with a second bedroom upstairs. A family with upwards of five children of both sexes could not be accommodated easily in such conditions. The 1861 Census records up to ten people, sometimes of three generations, in a house. How a couple and their two married and one unmarried son organised their domestic arrangements we don't know.[69] A single hearth provided all the heating for the house. Domestic provision for cooking and washing was often in a separate outhouse with a bread oven, copper and range, all heated by coal. In some yards a single

---

[67] Mike Welland *The Rump family of Wells* (unpub. WLHG Archive)
[68] Report in *Norfolk News* in John Burnett, *A Social History of Housing 1815-1985* (Routledge 1986) p. 129 – accounts of Saxlingham and Corpusty
[69] 1861 Census (WLHG Archive)

communal washhouse might provide for the laundry needs of half a dozen cottages. It is understandable that men sought warmth and sociability in the many public houses in the town.

Stearmans Yard looking to Freeman Street

Sexual abuse was the subject of comment in several reports to government on conditions. One in ten Norfolk children were illegitimate at a time when marriage was pretty much universal. A curtain hung across a room would preserve a degree of modesty; it would not always suffice. '...with the beds lying as thickly as they can be packed, father, mother, young men, lads, grown and growing up girls – two and sometimes three generations – are herded promiscuously; where every operation of the toilette and of nature – dressings, undressing, births and deaths – is performed by each within the sight and hearing of all; where children of both sexes to as high an age as 12 or 14 or even more, occupy the same bed.'[70]

The 1911 Census confirmed the extent of overcrowding in the town. In the cottages of the east end families of eight were not unusual; the Coe family were ten, the Wordinghams, whose household included the 84 year old grandfather, had six children aged from 4 to 18. The west end of the town was likewise poor; the larger families were headed by labourers or maltsters with one or two fishermen's families amongst them, including William Grimes, shortly to become the lifeboat coxswain; there were rather more very elderly folk. In Bolts Close, a former coal house housed seven people.

As for what families ate – another health issue – that would vary through the seasons. Those who had a patch of land on which to grow vegetables would do so. Otherwise it was not unknown for a family to catch and cook sparrows for Christmas dinner, having netted them round a haystack.[71] Stories from elsewhere in the county tell of soup provided after school by 'the Hall'. Protein was in short supply. Winter could be a particularly cruel time.

Security of tenure was often lacking which was, according to contemporary observers, a greater threat to family life even than overcrowding. A family could be thrown out of their home with a week's

---

[70] Revd J Fraser in *Royal Commission Report on the Employment of Children, Young Persons and Women in Agriculture 1867-8* Appendix 1 p.35f
[71] Evans (1970) p. 216

notice. Lord Leicester, who owned many labourers' cottages, was a virtuous exception.

Administratively, the reorganisation of the town's governance at the end of the century brought together the several major local concerns of the community. In 1895 the new Wells Urban District Council emerged painlessly from the Improvement Commissioners – its membership was pretty much the same, its chairman being George Smith, the maltster. Thus it had the power to build new houses, to clear away slum dwellings and ensure that existing houses were fit for habitation; it had responsibility for sewerage, refuse collection, the treatment of infectious diseases and the provision of hospitals, clinics, nursing, mortuaries and cemeteries. The inspection of slaughterhouses, bakeries, etc., of articles of food exposed or prepared for sale and the prevention of various nuisances all lay within its purview. It had power to provide a library and to appoint two managers for the local school; it retained its responsibility for the management of highways, their paving and lighting; for parks and cemeteries; for the provision of allotments; the provision of gas, electricity and water; and a range of other powers over animals, children's employment, factories, fire protection and various licensing responsibilities. It was, in retrospect, the high point of local democracy.

Wells was, compared with many of the new authorities, very small and powers given to larger councils relating, for instance, to pensions and health insurance, were not within its remit. Nevertheless the question for the coming years was how the town was going to deal with its new powers. The machinery of such government required imagination and vision in order to make it work. It lasted until the huge shake-up of local government in 1974, though it was nearly dissolved forty years before that; not only its smallness but the deficiency in its public health provision were causes of its near nemesis.

The parish was in many ways too small an instrument of local government. Public health had long been in the hands of the poor law with its emphasis on deterrence rather than prevention; punishment not provision. The amalgamation of parishes into Poor Law Unions, each with its workhouse, had taken place as long ago as 1834. The local workhouse was in the middle of nowhere between Walsingham and Thursford. The control of disease was in different hands; health and safety at work – to use a modern expression – in yet others. Only by the passing of the Public Health Act of 1875, the result of a Royal Commission, was each district provided with the sufficient means of recording and improving the health of its people. In towns, powers were given to the locally employed Medical Officer of Health. Frederick Taylor was the first such officer in Wells.

Taylor served only two years; his successor, Robert Foot, for several years more. Frederick Long, who had been a surgeon in the town for some years, served out his term from 1880 to his retirement in 1898.

Long had served under the old Improvement Commissioners. He reported verbally each month and annually in writing on the birth and death rates, on the incidence of disease and on the general health of the town. Measles epidemics and the number of fatalities were noted. Diphtheria was an early concern, as were whooping cough, scarlet and typhoid fever. In 1893 twenty children died, eight of them not from these conditions but from 'ordinary causes', whatever they were supposed to be. When epidemics were identified, it lay within his power to close the school to contain them. It was a power he would use. Cholera would be brought in by foreign seamen. It fell to Long to board incoming vessels for inspection before they came to the quay to unload, between the Point and Scolf Beacon. His instruction was to send the sick to Cuckoo Lodge, a mile inland from Market Lane, to recuperate. Fifteen foreign vessels came into the port in 1893. It was decided that a mortuary was needed which was built thenceforth on the quay to accommodate the bodies of sailors who died at sea or while in the port.[72]

He recognised the importance of regular scavenging, the emptying of privies of night soil, as a health measure. In 1894 a horse and cart was purchased by the council to do the job on his recommendation. These vehicles, often called 'honey carts', continued in use in motorised form until the 1960s. Early in the morning, twice a week, the cart would go up and down the yards, lit by two lamps in winter, to shovel the human waste into the cart from the many backyard privies. Some closets consisted of dry earth; others provided a metal pail to contain the waste. It would then be dumped on a piece of land, the midden, just outside the town on the Warham Road, on which the council had taken a lease for the purpose. Long insisted on the disinfecting of the boxes into which human waste was deposited and of the closets themselves with carbolic acid and green vitriol. Some of

Jicklings Yard, Wells – an example of yards not easily accessible to vehicles

[72] *Wells Improvement Commissioners Minutes* (1893)NRO DC18/4/3 p.8

the merchants' houses had water closets, flush toilets, connected either to the brick sewers or to cess pits and supplied by water pumped from a well. Even as late as 1949, there were nearly 600 pail closets in the town. One task performed by the scavengers which was to become more, not less, important was the collection of household refuse, which was to be put in boxes by residents for collection.

The town's drains were another source of disease. The district council seems to have been more energetic in replacing surface sewers by glazed pipes than its predecessor. The power had existed since 1844 but progress had been slow. Many of the old brick sewers in the town had become clogged with rubbish and vegetation, their whereabouts only partly known. When discovered many years later by residents they were often spoken of as being old smugglers' tunnels! They may have served both purposes. The town suffered by being built on two sides of a long hill. Gravity took the flow of effluent down to the harbour on the north side but on the other, only the dyke cut along Church Marsh would carry effluent away to Stonemeals Creek to the east of the harbour. Over the years many proposals were made to improve its flow. In 1905, after inspection, it was recommended that new 21 inch pipes be laid along 127 yards from Church Plain eastwards; but instead the council would only agree to regular cleaning of the culvert. The blocking of this dyke was to be a problem for another half century. Freeman Street had no noticeable fall at all. In that case, the council set about replacing the open drain which ran along the road with 93 yards of pipe to be connected 'to the main sewer' which discharged into the quay.

Little by little street drains were laid, partly to carry rainwater away to prevent flooding, and partly to carry away effluent. The council even took it upon itself to prosecute residents whose property lacked a drain, including Miss Garwood, of the Buttlands, requiring her to make a drain on Newgates Lane, where she presumably owned property. It is hard to know whether her late father, formerly clerk to the Improvement Commissioners, would have been angry or mortified. The council in that case appeared to have been no respecter of persons; it was not always so. In his report of 1896 Long reported optimistically that the general drainage of the town was completed.

Pigsties and cowsheds in the town were another matter. The owner of land behind the Bowling Green agreed to move his pigsty further away from nearby cottages. The owner of a sty in the ruins of the old Ranters Chapel, one Frederick Dyer, was more obstinate, continually moving his pigs and cattle back after an order to remove them. It took years for him to finally comply. Smells were a good indicator of disease. One remedy was clean water. Hundreds of gallons were discharged in flushing out sewers at different times. Another was to clean out and, desirably, to remove cesspits by connecting outlets to sewers.

Water supply was critical. The town relied for its water supply on the many wells in yards and on streets. The water had to be tested for

Old house in Freeman Street, at the bottom of Theatre Yard, now demolished

purity and bad wells sealed. Long noted in 1897 another cause of pollution, salt. The tidal flood of February that year impregnated the wells on the quay and Freeman Street with salt so that they were not usable for some time. From the same cause many houses were flooded, including those on Freeman Street which had underground rooms. Shades of things to come.

Long and his Inspector, William Leggatt, were responsible for dealing with the whole range of public health matters which could impact on the town. Food safety was one issue. He was responsible for ensuring that the dairies in the town and their milk were free from disease, that bakeries were clean and hygienic; that the several slaughterhouses supplied safe meat. He noted that typhoid seemed to originate from shellfish, oysters and mussels, whose lays were close to the sewage outfalls on the quay. He commented that 'Sewerage matter of itself will not generate typhoid but where that disease already exists, sewage matter is then apt to become impregnated'.[73] Shellfish were not the source of the disease, he concluded, but the presence of raw sewage made an ideal culture medium for disease which would infect the mussels, rendering them poisonous. He recommended that mussel beds be placed away from sewage outfalls. The engagement of these officials with public health matters seems to have given them insight into ills which needed attending to but which the elected members of the town were slow to take up.

Long retired in 1898 and was replaced by John Stafford Mellish. Mellish only stayed for three years, but in his short time here he came to recognise another source of disease, the appalling state of some of the houses whose poor condition made it impossible to keep them free from disease. Sam Peel was to be rightly honoured

[73] *UDC Minutes* February 1895 NRO DC 18/4/3

for his concern about the state of housing in Wells years later but there were others before him. Mellish initially recommended, in his 1898 report, that 'some of the worst tenements be done away with and better houses to replace them'[74] which, he thought, would 'attract a thrifty working population in their place.' As to where the present inhabitants would go he did not say; but by 1900 he had recognised the problem. He noted 'the difficulty is that there are no houses for the people if they are turned out,' thus identifying the issue with which Peel was to deal.

Mellish's foresight was not limited to matters directly concerned with health. One of the reasons why improvements were so piecemeal and slow was lack of money. The rating system, which Peel was to challenge years later, charged occupiers, many of them tenants, rather than owners, and then let off the former on the grounds of poverty. The result was a deficit in the town's accounts. Mellish recommended a change to the system so that landlords, not tenants, would be charged; the council even backed him by voting in favour of the necessary Provisional Order, but again and again, pressed by the local Ratepayers Association, they reversed their decision. The town's rating system was governed by the town's Improvement Act of 1844 which no longer served its purpose: it was for the committee to determine who should be excused payment on the grounds of poverty, a provision which had become subject to abuse. Many who could afford to pay were excused by their friends on the council. As a result the council was in debt while pressure was exerted by ratepayers not to increase the rates and therefore not to make improvements to the town. This included allowing the gas works to fall into disrepair and opposing any improvements to the town's housing stock or sanitary provision. The proper financing of the town had to wait for years afterwards. In his last report Mellish stated that the population of the town had decreased from 2,549 in 1891 to 2,491, the number of inhabited houses from 770 to 762.

Mellish's successor, Gordon Calthrop, was able to report a massive fall in infant mortality over the previous ten years, only three under the age of five out of 46 deaths. Long's frankly basic public health measures had clearly begun to have an effect. More ominously he reported a growing incidence of tuberculosis (then called phthisis) and cancer. Of the latter he wrote 'It is much to be regretted that in spite of the large sums expended upon original research and experiments with regard to the cause and cure of cancer that very little progress has been made.'[75] He thought that it was caught by infection.

The Medical Officer of Health was not the only figure responsible for town improvements. The council surveyor, who was also Inspector of Nuisances and Sanitary Inspector, made reports to the council, being responsible for roads and sewerage, for identifying and taking action against nuisances. Ideally the two worked as a team though

---

[74] *UDC. Minutes* p. 244 NRO DC18/4/3
[75] NRO DC 18/4/3 p. 530

the surveyor, unlike the MOH, was an employee of the council, rendering him more vulnerable to pressure. Unfortunately, Richford, the Inspector of Nuisances, who had succeeded Leggatt, fell ill and during his long decline, matters became more serious. Calthrop's report of January 1909 gives us a picture of how limited the sewerage provision was. There was an open southern sewer via Ramm's Marsh and East Sluice, a northern sewer from Freeman Street which turned north along the Run and out to sea; one from the Police Station on Church Plain along Marsh Lane to the Railway Station, joined by another sewer from Nook Lane along Polka Road (first mention) and Standard Road to the quay; and the sewer from east westward along the quay to the Glebe. They were neither sufficient nor safe.

Calthrop continued to report on the regular outbreaks of infectious disease. Back in 1904 he had reported 'it cannot be very long before the market will be practically closed to all oysters, mussels and other molluscs which do not come from waters certified to be free from sewage contamination.'[76] Sewage in those days included not only human waste but offal and other animal parts from slaughterhouses, all of which went directly into the harbour. Finally, in September 1908, having traced an outbreak of typhoid to the proximity of the mussel beds to a sewage outfall, Calthrop banned their sale. Local fishermen protested; the harbour commissioners expressed concern. The council thereupon withdrew the prohibition, 'taking all responsibility for the matter'. The inspector in turn put the onus firmly back upon them and they were forced to renew the embargo. Finally, the authorities in London banned all sale 'so long as the present unwholesome and dangerous condition of affairs obtains'.[77] Shellfish were routinely sold not only locally but also inland. Outbreaks of typhoid in Norwich in 1908 were blamed on Wells mussels though the cases were few and mild. Such an event recurred in June 1914; oysters from Wells were thought to have resulted in a typhoid outbreak in Loddon. The following January Calthrop reported 18 cases of typhoid, three of scarlet fever, and 13 of diphtheria in the town. Pressure was increasing for the building of a sewage works, a very expensive project which predictably was resisted by the Ratepayers Association. Mussels were now only to be used as bait, much to the disgust of local fishermen. Only mussels certified by Calthrop could be sold for human consumption.

[76] NRO DC 18/4/3 (1904) p. 423
[77] NRO DC 18/4/4 (1908) p160; 187; 198; 213

8. In pursuit of leisure

The beach in the early part of the century – tents not beach huts

Leisure had long been the prerogative of a few. Only in 1861 was the working day for all limited to ten hours. Bank holidays came ten years later, an opportunity for day trippers. The health-giving powers of sea bathing were widely canvassed. As long ago as the midcentury the use of bathing machines was acknowledged, and indeed was required by the 1844 legislation.

In practice the first modesty-providing equipment were tents. They were gradually replaced by wooden beach huts. The first person to apply to Holkham Estate for permission to build one appears to have been Mr Dewing (of Dewing and Kersley the millers) in 1902. He gave as his reason that his tent, like many others, had been the victim of the 'disgusting habits' of opportunists who had used the tent 'during the previous night in a manner never contemplated by the owner'.[78]

The quay itself provided its own leisure opportunities. Since the 1840s an annual regatta had been held where spectators could watch sailing and rowing races. The coming of the train service in 1857 meant that large numbers could reach the coast for the day to watch. Even before that, in 1849, delights to be had included trips on the tug *Economy* and in a hot air balloon.[79] The Victorian quest for novelty knew no bounds. The presence of large crowds was, of course, an opportunity for pickpockets, cutpurses and others who would take advantage of those caught unawares. The report of the 1864 regatta tells of those selling worthless items promised to be of value. The harsh economic climate of the 1870s caused the regatta to come to a halt

[78] Christine Hiskey *Notes from the Holkham Archives* (WLHG Newsletter No. 30)
[79] Mike Welland *Wells Regattas* (WLHG archives)

and the revived event of 1882 was an attempt to benefit trade and raise morale as well as provide entertainment. The *Eliza Adams* disaster was clearly in the minds of the organisers. Cycling and running races, the latter across the marshes, were additional to yacht and rowing races down the channel. The day ended with fireworks. In June 1906 a Mr Barnes sought permission to have stalls on the quay. A switchback was permitted to be set up there. So for a while, indeed until the end of the next century, the quay was to be a separate focus of popular entertainment.

Inland, all manner of leisure activities on saints' days had long been common, even after their observance was abolished back in 1834. Good Friday, Mayday, All Saints Day and Christmas Day remained. Bank holidays, of which there were four, were created in 1871, adding Easter Monday, Whit Monday, the first Monday in August and the day after Christmas Day to the calendar.

The Buttlands was the only place where outdoor events could be held. It became a source of dispute. The bonfire, on 5 November 1905 prohibited by the 1844 legislation (which was stoutly ignored), was one source of aggravation to residents. People were using the bonfire as a means of disposing of unwanted items including old

The Buttlands looking north, 1900

clothes and other noisome items. On one occasion children were seen running around with them, such that it took two men with two carts a day to clear up the mess. Stipulations were made that nothing be placed on the Buttlands until the day before the bonfire.

The old Shrove Tuesday Cockfair, so called because it was a venue for cockfighting, now long banned, came into the new century in a more up-to-date fashion. Roundabouts (steam engine driven), gallopers and stalls were the order of the day, booked to take place on the Buttlands. When, in 1907, a Mr Stock applied to the council for permission to hold a fair, Lord Leicester intervened and fearful stallholders refused to pay tolls to the council but instead paid up to his

Lordship's agent, JM Wood. He made firm his claim by demanding that use of the bandstand, put up by the council in 1903 for the use of the town band, be charged at one shilling. Battle was joined: the council stated that no bonfire was permitted on the Buttlands because they created a nuisance, but they had no intention of stopping fairs or of enclosing the land. The Buttlands belonged to the town. His grace's agent replied that his title dated from 1761 by lease and release from a couple called Gooderidge, but that he would lease it to the council for a nominal rent, any tolls to be used for its upkeep. Edward Loynes, the town clerk, kept up barrage of letters and telegrams, demanding to see any instrument of title. The Earl, after a period of standing on his dignity, saying that neither the clerk nor his counsel Mr Gurden were entitled to see any documents, finally let them see the conveyance and it was agreed that the council could lease the Buttlands for a peppercorn rent in perpetuity and which could be enlarged into a freehold after ten years. A goodly sum in lawyers' fees was expended over a matter which was more to do with pride and obstinacy. But the Buttlands, with bonfires, survived.[80] Roundabouts and stalls continued to feature every Shrove Tuesday. Hirers paid £1 a roundabout; stalls were tuppence a foot of frontage and booths, caravans, exhibition shows, tents, coconut stalls and shooting galleries cost a penny per square yard. The Earl finally handed over the deeds to the then chairman of the council, George Turner Cain, on Coronation Day 1937.[81]

The town band on the Buttlands

The Wells Town Band continued to perform on the Buttlands on Sundays when the weather permitted. On occasion, the Primitive Methodists used it for one of their open air revivalist so-called camp meetings. Outdoor gatherings at which hymns would be sung and preachers heard were a distinguishing feature of the group and had been since their foundation in the early part of the century. Fossetts' Circus, a travelling show from Ireland, came, bringing a hundred horses, causing some disturbance when it came to washing them down after the show.[82] The use of heavy machinery such as traction engines put the condition of the Buttlands at risk for which reason the funfair moved to the quay.

Other leisure opportunities became available. The invention in 1874 of the modern or 'safety' bicycle produced another revolution which allowed men and women to proceed along the newly improved

[80] NRO DC 18/4/3 p, 59-96
[81] Jean Stone Recollections of Wells (1988) p.15
[82] NRO DC18/4/3 p. 156

Cycles belonging to those who had come to the beach for the day

roads over greater distances. A less restrictive attitude, not universally approved, towards Sunday observance contributed to the growth of the practice. Some would travel miles inland but it was also possible to use the contraption to get to the beach more speedily than by walking and it was cheaper than the bus. A picture taken in 1905 shows how popular the pastime was in Wells. The formation of the Cyclists Touring Club in 1878 and its rising membership to some 60,000 by 1897 was matched by the desire of local hotels to accommodate two wheeled travellers who clearly travelled many miles. The Crown and The Railway Hotel both encouraged cyclists; The Crown even sported the CTC badge on its front porch.

Football as a national organised game came to assume its modern form with the formation of the Football League in 1888. Wells Town FC was founded in 1903 and became part of the Norfolk and Suffolk League. Its first pitch was at Mill Farm, after which it moved to Market Lane and even played at Stiffkey after the 1978 floods before coming to Beach Road. The sole survivor to date, it was one of a number of teams in the town in the early years. Churches ran their own teams, in part as one way to maintain the allegiance of the young. Sam Peel promoted a team from his Institute which ran in the years before the Great War. After it the Wells Wasps and the Wells Comrades, presumably consisting of war veterans, had a lease of life. Herbert Loynes and Frederick Raven were both supporters and officials of the town club in the 1920s. Loynes was, for a time, its chairman, Raven its treasurer.

Gardens, originally ornamental adjuncts to great houses, became fashionable in the larger houses in the town, small versions of the lavish landscaping which had been practised at Holkham. A garden could be a place to relax but to some it had become a source of employment. Nearly thirty men described themselves as gardeners in 1911, employed to mow the lawns, grow vegetables for the table in kitchen gardens and to tend the flower beds of the well-to-do. Large houses like Bank House (later the Lawn), Mayshiel, The Normans,

Blenheim House and Westward Ho had gardens but increasingly so did those of more modest income who tended their own plots. Allotments had become popular, required by statute to encourage cottagers to grow their own vegetables. The new council houses would have large gardens for the same purpose. In order to service such demands enterprising folk established plant nurseries. On Theatre Road in Wells what for long after was known as the Nurseries was established by Joshua Gales sometime after 1858. In 1888 his son Edwin was advertising vegetable and flower seeds and bedding plants for sale from his greenhouses and walled gardens. Gales left Wells sometime after 1891, leaving the nursery to an uncertain future. However, successive owners over the years were described as nurserymen and market gardeners and presumably carried on the trade until sometime after the Second World War. They were successively Sydney Belcher, James Vinnicombe, Thomas Speller and Leslie Hull.[83]

Even so, the working week remained long, and the quickest way out of town was through a glass or a bottle. For working families life was improving, but slowly.

[83] Mike Welland The Nursery, Theatre Road (unpubl.)

9. Initiatives for change

Sam Peel, elected to the town council in 1913

A new council was elected in May 1913 and among the new councillors was one Samuel Peel. He was to become an honoured citizen of the town, but at that time he was a newcomer, from Cambridgeshire via Wymondham, and as a newly elected councillor, initially an unwelcome one. He had arrived in 1910, a convalescent, with his wife and family, intending to stay with his parents who had retired to Wells. He had been a printer but, having decided to stay, he took a job as a butcher's clerk. Gradually, he began to take an interest in the conditions in the town. The decline of the port had left many men without work; drunkenness was rife; no houses had been built for fifty years; many rented properties were of poor standard; as already described many were insanitary in spite of the efforts of one medical officer of health after another. So shocked was Peel's wife at some of the sights that she described the town as 'the last place the Lord made'.[84]

On election his first act was to demand that meetings of the council should be in public where ratepayers could hear their decisions; hitherto, like the Improvement Commissioners previously, the council met in private. It would meet thereafter in the Friends' Meeting House – Peel was a Quaker – and subsequently the local school. He then requested that the Sanitary Inspector should visit houses in the town which he believed to be insanitary. The inspector at the time, Mr Coles, duly reported to the council in September. He classified the houses he looked at, some 150 of them, into three classes: those needing only minor repairs; those with insufficient closet accommodation or with defective drains; and lastly those which he described as 'dirty', which could only be made fit for habitation by general reconstruction or which required closing orders. It showed the parlous state of many houses, insufficiently drained, filthy and insanitary; with washhouses and closets shared by several houses. Peel proposed the setting up of a housing committee to establish a scheme to build new houses of a regulation standard. Whether convinced by Peel's oratory, the facts revealed in the Inspector's report or by the noisy objections of the public in attendance, the council accepted the report, but with a huge reluctance to act. The conviction held by many of the council,

[84] Susan Wild *Sam Peel – a man who did different* (WLHG 2013) p.9

and among ratepayers generally, that all was well with the condition of the housing stock, was not easily dislodged. In spite of setting up the committee they did nothing.

The following January, referring to the incidence of sickness among the poorer members of the population, Peel declared, 'No wonder the services of the doctor were needed. It is a crying shame that human beings should be permitted to be housed in places such as many a person would not place horses and pigs... It is time that something was done for the labouring classes of today.'[85] He wrote to the Local Government Board requesting their inspectors to hold an enquiry. The board had powers under statute to enable councils to make landlords personally responsible for their tenants' health and to make it illegal for landlords to let property which fell below a standard. Two medical officers of health were sent to examine Peel's claims. He took them on a tour of the town, instancing conditions that varied from poor to appalling: in one case six houses shared one toilet and excreta oozed through the walls; a washhouse was shared by several families; but the problem was general. The board called a public meeting which, according to a later account,[86] verged on the riotous, the councillors leaving the platform at one point in protest; they had to be called to order by the board's inspector. One councillor was ejected for his language and the surveyor had been plied with drinks to prevent him from reporting. Peel spoke in his stead.[87] Finally, the inspector awarded the building of twenty houses.

Resistance did not immediately end there but the pressure was increasing. As if to press home the seriousness of the situation, an outbreak of infectious disease was reported: typhoid, diphtheria and scarlet fever. A special meeting was called to receive a report from Calthrop. A number of possible culprits were identified. Frederick Darley, appointed as sanitary inspector in July, reported that 'liquid refuse is percolating into and fouling two wells'.[88] The following January Calthrop reported 18 cases of typhoid, three of scarlet fever, and 13 of diphtheria in the town. Not only new housing but the building of a sewage works appeared on the agenda. It was a very expensive project and it was predictably resisted by the Ratepayers Association. Calthrop's report concluded by endorsing the need for new housing which was accepted by the council unanimously but again reluctantly.

The reformers would get their way: the houses would now be built, the first of many such projects. Specifications for the houses were agreed and negotiations began for the purchase of a piece of land. Various sites were looked at, one on Warham Road and another on Freeman Street but it became clear that Northfield was the preferred site. Tenders were obtained and a Local Government Board loan sought.[89] From the six tenders, that of Mr Pratt at £3,047 10s

---

85 Wild p. 37
86 Peel recounted the events many years later: NRO SAC 2004/17/9 audio recording
87 Wild pp.40-42;
88 NRO D18/4/3 Dec. 1914
89 Ibid.

was accepted.

The question was how the loan was to be repaid. Peel drew attention to the issue of the rating system raised by Mellish 13 years previously and its misuse by the council. He noted that by September 1913 the council was £6,300 in debt. What was needed, said Peel, was a system by which the landowner paid the rates in all cases and proper accounting methods were used. And when no action was forthcoming from the council he called a public meeting at which he proposed that everyone should withhold their rates until the situation was altered, as he himself proposed to do.[90] The clerk advised that non-payers would be brought to book. Thus, Peel and fifty eight other refusers were taken to Walsingham magistrates court and convicted; but as Peel pointed out, there were in fact one hundred and sixty people not paying rates, excused by the council chairman on what appeared to be a whim. (In fact the number not paying rates was a good deal higher than that, as he subsequently discovered.) The publicity caused the cases against the protesters, which Peel had instructed be appealed to the divisional court, to be dropped. He proposed that all arrears, not demanded, be struck off the rate book and only those who appealed personally on the grounds of poverty be excused in future.

These were only interim proposals. What was needed was for the system to be altered. This could be only done by the council applying to the Local Government Board for a provisional order which would substitute ratings based on buildings with a rating system based on land ownership, so charging landlords not the tenants and permitting council borrowing only with the sanction of the board.[91] To Peel's horror, the council, having agreed to the changes at the meeting of 6 January 1914, once again rescinded the decision two months later. Pressure was exerted publicly by a flow of letters from the Ratepayers Association, headed by GF Rose a local ironmonger. Peel's was the only vote against the rescission of the decision. It would, apparently, be 'prejudicial to the interests of the town' to make the change. Councillors were prepared to continue to submit estimates of expenditure far short of actual outgoings, to borrow at interest on the shortfall and pay interest on debts, some as old as 74 years, simply in order to keep the current rates down. It was the financing of the madhouse. Some, like George Smith, maltster and entrepreneur, recognised this, saying that in future he would pay his full rate! It was a gesture which affected the mood but the repeal of the 1844 Act and its replacement with a modern system of rating would have to wait.

A major item of expenditure was the gas works. Peel had found them to be ill-managed and much of the equipment dangerous. On his election he had been appointed chairman of the gas works committee. The tasks before him were several: the finances of the works

---

[90] Wild p.50

[91] Provisional orders were a means of altering among other things, financial arrangements under the Local Government Act 1875 and were then confirmed by Act of Parliament. This happened in the case of Wells in 1917.

had to be put on a proper footing; no proper system of accounting or even record keeping existed. The metering of gas was ineffective; several gas mains leaked and the very manufacturing process was failing. There was a danger that gas supplies to the town would be halted completely, throwing the town into darkness and bringing machinery on the quay to a stop. The gas manager, who had been expropriating materials, was replaced; various other abuses were brought to light, including the chairman's having had a gas stove installed in his house free of charge. Procedures for ordering goods had to be regularised; the gas purifier was repaired; and the engineer's report of defects written in 1910, made available to the council. This was now February 1914.[92] The report recommended the rebuilding of the retorts – in which coal was burnt in order to produce gas – which was to cost, together with other expenditure, the tidy sum of £1,400. In spite of the damning nature of the report, the council agreed to the expenditure only through the chairman's casting vote. For his pains in exposing neglect and irregularity, Peel was threatened and then physically attacked, thrown off his bike and injured so that he was unable to attend the subsequent meeting of the council. He wrote down his opinions and sent them to the council instead.

The tumultuous events of the immediate pre-war years and the impact of Peel's interventions have been told elsewhere. They are repeated in short order here because of their importance in illustrating the cycle of resistance to change and its overcoming by a combination of stubbornness, persistence, courage and attention to detail. It had happened in 1844 when the Improvement Act was passed in spite of protests in the town[93]; it would happen again later in the century.

That Peel was an outsider made it easier to isolate him but it also enabled him to resist the blandishments of those whose understanding of the need for change was blunted by the persuasions of their colleagues. His use of public meetings to explain the breadth of the problems was probably determinative. Sometimes he is described as a lone voice. This is unfair. None of his proposals would have got anywhere without a councillor to second his motions and enough others to vote in favour of them. Nor could he have achieved anything without the likes of Calthrop, Darley and his successors, officers of the council whose actions as well as their dutiful reports provided the bullets for him to fire. The increased pace of change which Peel instigated can be read in the increased amount of business conducted by the council, such that Edward Loynes, who had been clerk for many years decided, against the wishes of councillors, to resign and hand over to his son. On the other hand, Peel was not always the man of popular myth. As someone who took an interest in so much, he was bound to falter from time to time as we shall see.

---

[92] Wild p.62 ff.

[93] Roger Arguile *Wells-next-the-Sea, a small port and a wide world* (Poppylands 2014) pp.112-113,114f.

Part 2 – From War to War

1. The hostilities

The Great War, as it became known, which Britain joined in August 1914, did not slow the pace of change in the town. In some respects, such as the development of motor transport, it may have hastened it. Its social effects, slow to show themselves, were to be deeper. The war was expected to last until Christmas; instead it was to last for over four years which was to shock the nation.

At first, however, it may have seemed to some to be 'business as usual'. Continental wars were not unknown; the French and the Germans had fought each other in 1870. The British army was, according to the French, merely ancillary to the European effort.[94] There had been hostile incidents between the nations of Europe in the early years of the century and whatever those in positions of power believed, for many ordinary people it only slowly became clear how much had changed.

The first issue was that of recruitment. Young and not so young men were encouraged to volunteer. One by one, teachers from the school, which Raven had built up to an establishment of eight, were lost: Mr Naylor left in September 1914. Mr Peters and Mr Cooper left the following year. A replacement, Mr Rose, who came to the school in September 1915, enlisted the following October. By the summer of 1918 Raven's wife and Mrs Tuck were the total staff of the boys' school. The effects can be seen in the standard of education. Raven was forced to keep 36 scholars in the same Standard as previously because he judged that they had not progressed sufficiently. Other effects were less obvious. The Routine Medical Inspection was put in abeyance. Now it fell to the master to notice such problems as 'defective eyesight, inflammation of the eyelids, earache, gumboils, enlarged tonsils and adenoids, loss of flesh and frequent cough'.[95] Goodness knows where he found the time to undertake this in a systematic manner. All of this was apart from the visitations of whooping cough, diphtheria and, less frequently, scarlet fever and measles. It seems likely that underlying much of the above was poor hygiene and poor diet. Malnutrition appears as a reason for excluding children.

The military effects were minimal compared with the later conflict but they were unsettling. There was more fear than actual danger. Zeppelins, hydrogen-filled airships carrying bombs, were an unwelcome novelty heading overhead towards the port at King's Lynn. Relying upon visual navigation, they appeared to be following railway

---

[94] AJP Taylor *English History 1914-1945* (Oxford 1965) p. 7
[95] *Minor Defects in Children* circular from JTC Nash, chief Medical Officer, Norfolk Education Committee.(undated)

lines; in consequence the signal lamps on the railways were fitted with hoods so that they could not be seen from the air, a very early version of the blackout. Canvas covers shielded the light from engines' fire grates. Railwaymen were, in turn, expected to report any airships overflying by telegraph. The Wells branch was used to transport men, horses and equipment to threatened coastal areas. An armoured train, consisting of an engine, two infantry wagons and two gun-carrying vehicles, patrolled the west Norfolk branch.[96] Zeppelins continued almost to the bitter end of the war so that when, on 5 August 1918, one was shot down off Wells, crowds gathered on the beaches to see if any remains could be sighted.

From an early stage troops were stationed locally at Holkham. The hospital was alerted to their possible needs and it was agreed that in an emergency or in case of accident, its facilities would be made available. On the other hand, carbide lamps which were the means of lighting the hospital, were only to be used during surgical operations because of the needs of munitions factories.

There was some talk of invasion. On 16 December 1914 two German battleships bombarded the undefended Yorkshire seaside town of Scarborough for about half an hour, killing seventeen inhabitants and causing considerable damage to the town and its castle. Lowestoft was bombarded by German naval guns at the cost of a number of lives. The Red Cross were alerted as to what measures might be necessary if there were local casualties. Thought was given to the idea that the Church Rooms might be needed as an additional hospital. Instructions were received as to which roads locals were to take to King's Lynn were there to be an invasion. The rector agreed that the church bells would be clashed as a warning to evacuate. As the initial

Local man Walter Wix driving in France

[96] Jenkins p. 53,58

rush of volunteers to enlist began to abate a request was received from the Lord Lieutenant that Wells men should not hang back. The news from the front was managed and the disaster that was the battle of the Somme in 1916 was reported as being a 'great offensive' which had been 'so successful'. As the battle dragged on there was no disputing the tales told by returning soldiers of the level of carnage. Even as late as May 1918 measures were in hand as to what to do in case of invasion; special constables were to be at crossroads and to be prepared to disable vehicles and destroy petrol in order to hinder the enemy.

But the story of Wells at war can best be told by the memorial to the seventy-six men who died during it which is found on the south wall of the Memorial Institute. No war previously had cost so many young lives across the world.[97] War consisting of set-piece battles and mobile armies on horseback was replaced by trench warfare attended by almost unbelievable noise, destruction and loss of life. Across the channel horses continued to be used even to haul artillery pieces, but motor transport and, in the theatres of war, lumbering and unreliable tanks would make their appearance. Artillery had grown to enormous size and power. Machine guns levelled those who attempted to go over the top and brave the barbed wire entanglements. It was the stories told by those who came home on leave from Flanders that began to make the conflict's horrors known, giving a different picture from that told for public consumption.

Of the names which appear on the memorial, fifty-seven have a known connection with the town. George Smith, son of the maltster, died on the Somme; Frank Southgate, the artist, who was aged 43 at the time, was lost also, dying of a heart attack while at the front. His friend, Pat Cringle, may have been saved by being recruited to bomb-making for the army as a result of his expertise in making cartridges to shoot geese; he made Bangalore torpedoes, a device for blowing up the barbed wire entanglements. The brothers Alfred and Harry Bone both distinguished themselves, Alfred by maintaining wire communications while under heavy fire for four days; he received the DCM in addition to his MM and bar; Harry died of gas poisoning only a couple of days after receiving his DCM for conspicuous gallantry under fire. Overall Wells had supplied 538 soldiers and 82 sailors to the war effort, of whom 41 were recorded as having died.[98]

The land battles in Flanders and the Dardanelles were the most notorious, but many men fought at sea too and Wells contributed its share. Submarines made their first appearance in serious numbers and many crews of British merchantmen were lost. Many men returned wounded. Thomas Kemp's story may stand for many. Born in Walsingham, he was a gas stoker in Wells until he joined the fifth bat-

[97] British and Empire killed were nearly a million; French nearly a million and a half; German and Austrian casualties were nearly three million. A total of over eight million soldiers died across the world.
[98] EB Loynes at a public meeting in the town *Norfolk Chronicle* Jan 24th 1919

talion of the Norfolk Regiment. Surviving the failed invasion at Gallipoli, he was badly wounded in both arms at the battle of Gaza, serving out the war until discharge in 1919. Silver War badges were awarded to those honourably discharged due to war wounds or sickness contracted at the front.[99] Support for the troops took various forms. Men were allowed home on leave much more readily than when the Second World War was being fought right across the globe. In his parish newsletter Revd George Ingle reminded readers that those who were most badly wounded could not be brought home. He organised an egg collection to feed those who could eat nothing else. The parish delivered to his door over two thousand eggs.

The effects on commerce were many and various. One immediate effect which impacted on the malting industry was the increase of 200% in the duty on beer, from 7s 9d to 23s a barrel. The maximum final gravity of beer was fixed at 1036 degrees; opening hours of public houses were cut and discussions even took place about the nationalisation of the entire liquor industry. In October 1916 the government took control of the buying, selling and distribution of all cereals. Maximum prices were fixed for barley. In February 1917 all malting was halted; the capacity of the industry was twice the amount apportioned for wartime beer production and the malting season would have produced far more than was needed.[100] One solution was to export malt. Initially prohibited, licences were eventually issued and malt was sent by coastal barge to France and even as far as Italy. Applications for permission to manufacture malt were made to the Ministry of Food. Smiths applied and received permission to steep 12,480 quarters, a minute proportion of normal production. No reference appears in the Directors' minutes about any interruption in production, suggesting that the chairman, George Smith, prematurely ageing and suffering from excessive drinking, was no longer abreast of events.

The war also had an effect on agriculture. Strikes had become endemic in the years immediately preceding; wages were a third of industrial wages, 15s a week. Initially the hostilities made no difference to the enmity between farmers and labourers and their union. The difference was that the war was perversely to the union's advantage. An early victory just before the war started was a spring strike at seedtime which was quickly settled. Planting could not be delayed. The Earl of Leicester led the way in agreeing a rise of one shilling a week. That summer it was agreed, following the example of the King on his Sandringham estate, that the weekly wage would rise by two shillings. But as the war progressed, more men were lost to the forces so that there were fewer men to bring in the harvest and shortages led to price rises. The workforce fell by 7%. By early 1915 the 1914

[99] A list of recipients exists at the National Archives. Their issue was partly a response to accusations of cowardice made against men who were not in uniform but whose injuries were not obvious. Walter Rix was one recipient from Wells.

[100] Clark p. 138; Letters attached to Directors' minutes 1917.

wage now seemed inadequate. Strike action seemed inevitable. George Edwards, who was in his sixties and, having no role in the union, must have thought his working life to be over, now found himself approached by two farmers requesting a meeting with others, including the Earl, to see if an amicable settlement could be reached.[101] This was the first time that the union had been recognised and by the biggest landowner in north-west Norfolk. The meeting was duly held and a weekly wage of 18s a week was conceded. When some farmers refused to pay, further strike action led to an all-round agreement.

A further problem arose from the Board of Agriculture agreeing to the use of soldiers to assist with the harvest, who were paid more than civilian workers. A West Barsham farmer wrote to the press of the ill-feeling amongst village folk which caused some labourers to refuse to work with soldiers. The use of women was met with equal hostility; men remembered the evils of the old gang system. Boys were different. The County Education Committee issued exemption certificates – in 1915 over a thousand – allowing schoolboys to work on the land in spite of union misgivings. But it was not enough: lack of labour for planting led to reduced harvests; there was a fall in the number of animals raised; the U-boat campaign was threatening grain imports: the union was in a strong position which its leadership was resolved to take full advantage of.[102]

In the event it was not necessary. The war would do their job for them. The supply of bread became the dominant note in British food control. Home grown cereal production became a priority. In January 1917 a Ministry of Food was created, a committee under Lord Selbourne was appointed whose recommendations to government that August achieved what the union had in fifty years failed to do: to provide agricultural labourers with a minimum wage of 25s a week and extra for stockmen, horsemen and shepherds. Fixed hours of working were agreed, thus ensuring continuity of labour. It was still too little: Norfolk men were paid much less than labourers in other parts of East Anglia; but through the mechanism of a Central Wages Board, with regional boards under them, the issue of proper remuneration would be dealt with. Edwards, a long-standing trade unionist, was appointed to the county board which proposed a wage of 30s which the National Board accepted. It was a triumph for the union.[103] The increases seem remarkable but until then Norfolk wages had been among the lowest in the country, and less than half the wage of an industrial worker in Norwich. The effect was to end strike action, to stabilise food production and, as a symbol of the importance of the trade union, to move the union headquarters from Fakenham to London. Edwards and Peel were godly men, both members of the Labour Party, both moderates, good friends despite their difference

---

[101] Noël Edwards *Ploughboy's Progress* (Centre of East Anglian Studies 1997) p.65
[102] Howkins (1985) pp. 114ff.
[103] Howkins (1985) p 117ff

in years; they had achieved much. But the events of the following years, of national impact but focussed in Norfolk, were to test their friendship to destruction.

Not everyone suffered the effects of the war. George Wright took over Mill Farm from his father in 1912, continuing the business of buying and selling animals, mostly sheep but also cattle and, more rarely, pigs. In 1904 Isaac had bought and sold some 400 animals; in 1916, George bought 7,883 animals for which he paid £24,877 16s 2d (and made a profit of £1,391). The following year he dealt with slightly fewer animals, 7,564, but he sold them for £50,811 5s 9d, making a profit of £2,142 4s 3d. The price of meat, some of it to feed the troops no doubt, and in short supply, had soared. Most of them were sold to farms in a radius of thirty or so miles; they came via Fakenham and Norwich markets, some of them from Ireland. He spent over £300 on rail transport that year.[104]

The attention of the country was most likely directed across the channel; home improvements were not to be countenanced. In response to Sam Peel's attempts to improve the condition of local people, the indefatigable Ratepayers Association wrote saying that the proposed housing project should be abandoned 'in view of the war'. In this respect they were unsuccessful. Matters had gone too far. The intention was for the commemorative stone for the new development to be laid by FG Smith as principal ratepayer but in the event Lord Leicester was called upon. The stone was laid in March 1915. Progress was nevertheless slow and initially only twelve houses were completed. What progress there was was impeded by the action of some councillors who pushed down newly erected walls after the

The laying the commemoration stone of the first council houses on 3 March 1915

[104] Mill Farm ledger 1899 - 1937

workmen had gone off site! The police had to be called to ensure that this action was not repeated. The remaining eight dwellings would be added to the stock shortly afterwards.

The houses were a huge improvement, but they were not modern by the standards of only twenty years later. The town had at that time no electricity supply, nor mains water. Wells were dug, more than 22 feet deep, before a good source of water was found to supply the houses. Each house was to have a living room and parlour of modest size, a scullery with a cooking range and washing copper, a large pantry, three bedrooms, a coal store and an earth closet. Each was to have a garden sufficient to grow vegetables. It would be some time before, little by little, they acquired such basic facilities as we take for granted – a kitchen sink, a bath, a flush toilet, electric light, much less the electric appliances of an age after yet another war. It was only by a last-minute intervention, again by Peel, that a gas main was laid to supply them, the contract being diverted from a proposal to re-equip Staithe Street with new gas pipes.[105] There were of course teething problems. The wells supplying the water were not deep enough and the water was subject to pollution; they needed to be deepened. A number of the houses proved to have defective floors which needed to be re-laid.

The solution to the vexed problem of financing on the other hand had been put off. The state of the gas works, and the town supply, was one of Peel's main arguments for the making of a Provisional Order. The auditor had pointed out the loss of income caused by leaking gas mains throughout the town. Only a regulated loan from the Local Government Board would enable the work to be done. The old system could only lead to bankruptcy and stagnation.

Having spent three years trying to convince the council of the need for change, in July 1916 Peel deployed to good effect a stratagem which had worked before. He called a public meeting on the quay. He explained the injustice of the present system and the loss of income from excusals which ran into thousands of pounds: 400 out of 600 houses had not paid rates. The meeting wholeheartedly endorsed his proposals and the council, sufficiently pressurised, agreed to the change by five votes to two with two abstentions at the September meeting. However, three councillors thereupon resigned and were replaced by three co-opted members. At the October meeting, in spite of the adverse votes of the co-opted members supported by two councillors who had not attended for five months, the resolution was endorsed but only on the casting vote of the chairman. Finally, the clerk to the council, Herbert Loynes, was able to put the case at the resulting Local Government Board Inquiry in November. 'The doings of Wells had become notorious in that part of Norfolk owing to the conditions under which the town was governed', he was reported as saying.[106] He pointed out that the process of deciding who

---

105 NRO DC18/4/5 May. 1915

106 *Local Government Journal* November 4th. 1916. (WLHG Archive)

should be excused paying the rate was ineffective and unpopular even with councillors, such that they could only with difficulty be got to attend the meetings. The Provisional Order under the Public Heath Act 1875, placing the town's finances on a proper footing, was eventually passed in 1917.[107]

The threats to the health of the town remained. The issue of the contamination of the mussel beds had not gone away; sewage effluent was blamed, but there were other sources of disease too. Shops, bake houses, slaughterhouses, dairies and cowsheds could all foster disease. All required inspection, but as always there was resistance and pressure from the producers who did not want interference in their ability to run their businesses. In January 1915 Calthrop reported on contaminated milk from the farm of William Hall on Burnt Street. Subsequent investigations revealed other filthy dairies without stone floors, with manure adjacent to milking parlours, and with walls through which effluent permeated. The regulations relating to dairies had been passed by the council back in 1906; but as is always the case, the much more difficult task of enforcement often requires some disaster or at least a serious event for action to be recommended and sufficiently endorsed that it takes place. Darley, the sanitary inspector, reported on the several small dairies in the town, six in all, mostly with small numbers of animals, all of which required attention. The multiplication of sources of disease required the heavy hand of inspection and prohibition whether of the sale of milk or the use of contaminated wells, and lastly the requirement that for instance, well walls should be made impervious, more privies should be installed in cottage yards and refuse heaps should be removed.

The unpopularity of regulation and the expenditure required for improvements led to gerrymandering by some of the councillors who tried to stop staff doing their jobs. Some of it was overt; there may have been a combination of factors at work. The net result was a high turnover of staff. Richford resigned as surveyor and sanitary inspector in 1912 due to ill-health; Coles, his successor, had become ill by May 1913; Clinch, appointed as assistant inspector, stayed only three months, having had his holiday pay docked because he had not sought permission to take leave; Frederick Darley, who was appointed in 1914 and who was deputed to inspect every house in the town and who appears to have been assiduous in doing so, was made to resign in December 1915 for alleged serious financial irregularities, but he was never charged; John Williams, who succeeded him, stayed less than two years though the cause of his departure is not known. The story of his successor, Samuel Bloy, who was appointed in January 1918 and served until 1924, will have to wait, but it tells a similar tale. Whatever the truth of the suspicions, the hostility of council members and others in the town to expenditure and its causes is plain. Herbert Dewing, the mill owner, resigned in April 1916 over the expenditure

---

[107] 7 & 8 Geo.5 Cap. xxxv. (WLHG Archive); Wild p.61

of the town's lighting, and on the annual increments in staff salaries which 'all prove that economy is a thing of the past'. Peel's attempts to reform the rating system as we have seen produced other resignations. It would continue.

Typhoid did not disappear from the town; there were two more cases the following February, but gradually, in spite of opposition to public health measures, the number of cases declined. Unsurprisingly Calthrop was off sick at one point through 'stress of work'. The issue of sewage, on the other hand, never seems to have gone away. Troops were billeted in the town requiring that the council scavengers supply more closets and visit them more frequently.

As the war progressed any energy that the council possessed had slackened. Patriotism had given way to resignation. The threats from outside had become more real. The ending of the war came suddenly after a threatening German push forward collapsed. The sense of relief was palpable. A thanksgiving service was held on the Buttlands on Sunday, 17 November, 1918, presided over by several of the clergy and a war memorial was proposed by Calthrop. It was, he said, to be a living memorial, a club for those returning from war, a working men's club which would provide for the 'social, moral and intellectual welfare of men when demobilised as well as the residents of the town'. Peel wished it to provide a Sunday morning service, a proposal opposed by the rector and others on the grounds that the club should be non-sectarian and non-political.[108] Peel also proposed that the returning soldiers should be found work in the town, something which unfortunately failed to materialise. His intention was that they would work on the defective gas mains and the gas works itself; various street works to improve traffic flow. They would have to wait.

---

108 *Norfolk Chronicle* January 24th 1919.

2. The working environment

George Edwards addressing a crowd on the Buttlands

The ending of the war brought men back home; many resumed where they had left off. For the first three years after 1918 the agricultural employment structures set in place by war continued well enough. But with the resumption of imports after 1920, grain prices fell and the pressure built up to remove regulation and replace it with voluntary conciliation. Wages in the countryside still lagged behind those in the towns though a Wells man might hope to earn 46s (£2.30) instead of the 15s he had earned before the war. Downward pressure from farmers resulted in wages falling first to 42s then to 39s. Then Sam Peel, as county secretary of the National Union of Agricultural Workers, unilaterally agreed to a reduction to 36s and then in February of 1922 to 30s. His action, contrary to the view of the National Executive, began to tear the union and a friendship apart. All that summer across the county, George Edwards spoke at union rallies. In Wells several hundred men came to hear him on the Buttlands, where he reminded them of the years of low wages, bad food and housing and the personal humiliation which characterised much of labouring life. He spoke to their condition. What is more, the mood of farm workers who had returned from the war had changed. Far fewer held to the old habits of deference after their experience of serving under officers, entirely drawn from the well-to-do, at close quarters in the trenches.[109]

[109] Nicholas Mansfield, *English Farmworkers and Local Patriotism, 1900-1930* (Ashgate Press, 2001) passim.

Horse drawn reaper binder

Peel's view was different. He did not believe in strike action; he believed that united action of farmers and farm workers was the way to protect food prices. He believed, as did many of his contemporaries, in a golden age when master and man worked in harmony. Edwards did not. Unlike Peel, Edwards had spent a winter in the workhouse as a five year old, separated from his mother, his father having been branded a thief for taking five turnips home to feed his family; his first job was scaring birds at the age of six.[110] As a youth he had made bricks for a living and had led a team of horses to plough. Never having been to school, he had learned to read from his wife. As a labourer he became a union man, cycling hundreds of miles around the Norfolk lanes recruiting men to the union. He knew what it was to be thrashed by his master for alleged slackness.

Peel's position had become untenable. As lightning strikes began to take hold it became clear that there would be a general strike. Peel secretly laid plans to form a new union. On 4 July 1922, only days after having resigned from the old union, he announced the formation of the National Union of Landworkers. He took sixteen old union members from Wells with him. Edwards was outraged. He believed that Peel had committed a breach of trust, as he wrote to the press in icy but eloquent tones.[111]

As Edwards expected, after the 1922 harvest the farmers pressed for a further reduction – to 25s for a 54 hour week. With winter coming the Norfolk committee, with the exception of Edwards, were afraid to oppose it. Peel's response was to propose that his new union should be 'recognised as the official negotiating body on behalf of the agricultural labourers'. A meeting with the farmers in Norwich Corn Hall was arranged. Only pressure on government from all sections of agriculture, it was argued, would work. In mid January 1923, farmers' leader JF Wright declared that 25s a week was 'impossible with the income of the industry'. Peel agreed that the wage made up

---

[110] George Edwards, *Crow-scaring to Westminster* (Unwin 1922) p. 22
[111] *Norfolk Mercury* March 3rd. 1923

a 'disproportionate part of the farmers' expenditure'. Attempts were made to get the government to intervene. Farmers issued leaflets trying to persuade the workers to accept 25s but for longer hours. The good offices of the bishop of the diocese, Bishop Pollock, were sought. But on 24 March the men struck.

The strike lasted only three weeks but in north Norfolk 905 men came out on strike. Blackleg labour was imported and mass picketing became common and often violent. The Earl of Leicester, among others, was conciliatory and his workers struck for a single day.

By the middle of April some 260 strikers were summoned to appear before Walsingham magistrates' court, on whose bench Peel sat, charged with violence. Many of the strikers were ex-soldiers. What they had seen as well as what they had done in the trenches had hardened their spirits. Most of the bench were landowners; the union thus arranged that a number of sympathetic justices should 'visit' and ensure lenient fines. This did not mollify the crowd waiting outside. They pelted Peel with rotten fruit, orange peel and clods of earth as he left the court, while Edwards attempted to hold back the mob.[112] Peel had gone from being a hero of the movement to being regarded as a traitor. 10,000 men went on strike in April of 1923. The compromise ended with a lower wage for a maximum fifty-hour week, but over 1,200 labourers never got their jobs back. A revived Agricultural Wages Board was set up by the Labour government in 1924. It was abolished in 2010.

The national context of this was the increasing growth of cheap foreign imports, accentuated by promises made, for instance to Canada, that post-war, live cattle imports could resume. Bonar Law, prime minister and himself a Canadian, made it clear that agriculture must stand on its own feet economically. There could be no tax on people's

Farming was hugely labour intensive and whole families were employed

[112] Wild p.85

bread. The sugar beet subsidy and the increasing use of high milk-yielding Friesian dairy cows were to offset these deficits to some degree, as was the creation in 1932 of the Milk Marketing Board.[113] Subsidies on cereals would come.

Harvest on the local farms was still a communal activity involving whole families, indeed whole communities, scything the edges of the cornfields before the reaper binder arrived, still drawn by a pair of horses. There were rabbits to be caught as they ran from the diminishing standing corn. Then the sheaves of corn left by the binder would be gathered into stooks, as they were called. These small collections of sheaves dotted about the fields were left to dry out before being loaded onto a cart and taken away to be threshed. When summer storms laid the corn flat, it had to be reaped by hand. The thick hedges, laid by hand and billhook, were intended to shield the corn from damage. No combines had yet come to empty the fields of people.[114]

Animals were bought and sold at Fakenham market and would be driven along the lanes to and from Wells farms. More routinely, twice a day in fact, dairy cows would be driven to the farmyard to be milked by hand. Vehicular traffic, such as it was, would have to wait. As late as 1939, 90% of the British dairy herd was milked by hand, mostly by women.[115] Flint bought Friesians for his dairy herd and was so successful that he won the British Friesian Society's trophy three years running from 1932 to 1934, thus winning it outright.

Sheep there were still by the thousands across Norfolk, their annual sale being the means of survival of many farmers for whom those years were desperately hard. Sometimes described as 'the locust years', they were difficult times for both farmers and farm workers. Wright's dealings were at a much lower level than hitherto. In 1928, he bought and sold 3,200 animals. Because corn prices remained low farms went over to the production of sugar beet, supported by the introduction of a government subsidy in 1932. Some went into the production of cabbages and sprouts. Much of George Wright's arable production was for his own use as animal feed. Farm work in those days was almost entirely done by hand and hoof.

The first signs of change showed themselves in the gradual mechanisation of equipment. The Alley brothers at South Creake introduced the first combine in the country in 1930 but they were way ahead of their time. Ernest Flint more modestly bought his first tractor in 1928 but used it largely for ploughing; otherwise horses would be used; they impacted less on wet ground. In 1939 there were still over 600,000 horses on British farms as against 56,000 tractors.[116] Agricultural machinery was becoming more and more specialised, though still designed to be pulled by horses. Cornish's foundry at the top of

---

113 Alun Howkins, *The Death of Rural England* (Routledge 2002) pp.50-53
114 Sheila Woods *Out with the Tide* (Poppylands 1989) p.34ff
115 Howkins (2003) p. 152
116 Howkins (2003) p. 122

The Glebe, which produced agricultural implements and which functioned in Fakenham and Walsingham, finally closed in 1936.

It was not just on the land that there was dearth. The period between 1920 and 1929 saw a halving in beer production and the closure of many maltings. F&G Smith concluded that the fall in demand was permanent and closed the Burnham Overy maltings, the mill at Ryburgh in 1923 and in 1929 the Wells maltings.[117]

The matter came to a head following the threat of legal action over the noise produced by the plant. Herbert Loynes, respected lawyer and clerk to the council, objected to the new Crossley steam engine which powered the machinery being started at 4am, particularly on Sundays! An attempt was made to meet Loynes' demands: the engine house was sound-proofed, and an ash-filled trench dug around it. The directors visited Loynes' house to hear the noise levels for themselves. They expressed themselves willing to take further steps to satisfy Loynes but in the interim they were advised by the managers that the capacity of the three branches – Wells, Dereham and Ryburgh – exceeded current and predicted demand. Each branch had much to recommend it but only two were needed to meet likely demand. The decision was made to axe Wells because it was, said the chairman, 'imperative' that the engine start at that time and the board would not entertain the idea of legal proceedings. Wells' efficient working would be 'crippled....and entail further capital outlay' by the effects of the legal action.[118] The board paid little attention to the day-to-day running of the enterprise; they had little interest in the business of malting. Their primary concerns were the level of dividends. Ideas of diversifying into fruit and vegetable canning were rejected out of hand and share capital was reduced by returning proceeds to shareholders. Personal tragedy also played its part: George Smith died in 1917 aged 56; his son GFE Smith died in France in the following year; Herbert Smith died in 1921. Ladas, George's younger son, who was chairman at the time of the closure of Wells, committed suicide in the garden shed of Mayshiel shortly after the closures. He had other troubles and was not well but the loss of the Wells maltings could not have helped his temper.[119] Richard H

Edgar Ladas Smith, in 1927

[117] F&G Smith Feb. 24th 1923 p. 168; the company continued until 1962 when it merged with John Crisp who, in the name of Crisp Malting, are still in business.
[118] F&G Smith, Jan 26th 1929; 25th. March 1929
[119] Wharton p.39, 52. He was buried in the garden of Mayshiel and his body was in-

'Return to Prosperity': Wells quay, 1933

Dewing, maltster of Fakenham, closed his malting in Wells, which seems to have been tied to those of Smiths, at the same time.

Malting in Wells ceased almost overnight following the directors' decision. The buildings were left empty, their machinery cannibalised for other plant. The effect on the town was seemingly dramatic. Even though the number of men working on the maltings could scarcely have been more than fifty, many other men depended upon the work. The council responded by proposing various infra-structure works, which included road improvements and work on the notorious southern sewer which ran from behind the police station on Church Plain to the railway across Church Marsh. An Unemployment Committee was formed which agreed to the building of a concrete culvert. The trouble was that to put men to work required both money and central government consents. Materials had to be bought. A proposal to tarmac the various yards that ran down to the harbour contained the proviso 'as such materials are available'. They would be slow in coming.[120] Another proposal was the widening of the Stiffkey Road where the railway line crossed it. Discussions with the railway company dragged on for years without any progress. The alteration of the corner of Burnt Street with Two Furlong Hill was another; the junction of Two Furlong Hill with Mill Road, a notorious accident black spot was yet another. The sub-committee lacked enthusiasm for the task.

Thus when a contract was made for the supply of sugar beet to the British Sugar Corporation in 1933, *The Times* newspaper, no less, produced a half page picture of the quay with the legend 'Return to Prosperity'.[121] Beet had become a major source of sugar since the war. The first factory, at Cantley near Norwich, had opened in 1912. The beet passing through Wells came by road or rail and was shipped from the harbour mostly northwards to Selby via the Wash and the

advertently dug up when the Health Centre was built in the 1970s. He was reinterred in the same place.

[120] NRO D18/4/7 Oct. 1929.

[121] 8th November 1933

Tom Grange's lorries loading beet onto a barge

Yorkshire Ouse. It lay in huge piles all along the quayside. Tom Grange, who had bought the old Glebe malting, used his lorries to bring it to the town from local farms where it was loaded by chute onto the boats. But the three-year contract was not renewed in spite of pleas to the contrary. Sugar beet continued to be grown but went by rail to King's Lynn.

Some of the former maltings found other uses. Sam Abel opened a garage on the quay and Tom Grange expanded his transport business on the Glebe. The Glebe maltings were, for a time, turned into a funfair with slot machines and dodgem cars under the name of 'the Marina'.[122] Grange took the adjacent property over as a garage for his lorries. Vynne and Everett, corn and feed merchants of Swaffham who had bought into the town some years before and who had premises on the quay, proceeded to buy up various buildings including the Granary and the block behind it consisting of two more maltings, numbers 2 and 6, in 1938 for £1,100. Favor Parker, feed merchants of Stoke Ferry, bought No 1 malting on the west of Croft Yard in 1939. Eastern Counties Farmers Cooperative, whose headquarters were in Ipswich and who had established a branch in Wells in 1935, took over the No 12 maltings on Staithe Street together with a confusingly numbered second malting in 1941 after its Yarmouth plant was bombed – this was probably the now demolished malting on Jicklings Yard. ECF sold grain for local farmers and bought seed, machinery, feed and fertiliser for them at advantageous prices. It even had two cargo vessels at one time. Malting would revive that year when Pauls of Ipswich, some of whose maltings had been requisitioned for the war effort, bought Wells No 18, the biggest in the town, for the knockdown price of £2,100.[123] They used Vynne and Everett's drying facility on Beach Road,

The cargoes that came into the harbour were brought by such ungainly Dutch vessels as the *Cite de Londres* and her sister ship the *Hil-*

[122] NRO DC18//4/8 July 1936
[123] F &G Smith passim and Dec.9th 1939

derthorpe. They brought cattle cake to feed farm animals. Other steam vessels brought wheat for Dewing and Kersley's mill. Thames barges joined them, the largest being the steel hulled so-called *Everards*, all named after members of the owner's family. These spritsail barges graced the channel with their dark red sails, bringing in coal and taking out sugar beet and corn.[124] Subsequently the Everard Company went over to steam and afterwards to motor vessels which visited the harbour. Their names ended with 'ity' – *Agility*, *Amenity*, *Aridity* and so on. They brought in coal to be dealt with by the various coal merchants. Collers, the Norwich coal merchants, had a coal yard on the east end of the quay, from which they supplied the bunkering for steam vessels. They also supplied the gas works, local factories and homes. Yarhams Yard was on the quay itself. Unloading by shovel was slow and backbreaking. So in 1932 a second-hand steam crane was bought to lift the coal out of the holds of vessels using a grab – a wonder of the modern age. Some cargoes had still to be manhandled – lifted out of the ships' holds in sacks and carried on the backs of men across a narrow plank on the quayside. The cross-channel trade had, by this time, completely dried up.[125]

The advent of steam vessels meant that access and egress to and from the quay was much safer but, given the movements of the sand shoals, local knowledge was still essential. Frank 'Tender' Smith, harbourmaster from 1913 to 1956, was one of three Trinity House pilots who guided the vessels in and out, clambering aboard from his dinghy via a rope ladder. His service time was interrupted during the Great War when he served on minesweepers. He was subsequently a lifeboatman for sixteen years and would serve an important role during the Second World War. [126]

Fishing inevitably suffered adverse effects. For four years during the hostilities there had been little fishing and fish stocks had built up. The catches continued to be good for some time, but there was no trade. Prices plummeted. Fish were offered for sale on the quay, taken around the town by pony and trap and taken inland to surrounding villages to sell to working housewives. Sea trout would sell for two shillings a pound, good money in those days.

There was always a problem with bait. Dogfish, known variously as tope or billies, were good for whelks. Then, in the 1930s, when they began to be sold for human consumption under the name of rock salmon, they became too expensive. The problem was perennial; later it would be the cat food market that would hoover up even fish heads to be ground into tinned pet food. Herring and at one time shore crabs, known as gillies, were used as bait.

Many of the fishermen were lifeboatmen too or crew members who came from fishing families: Smiths, Coxes, Grimes, Jarvises and Wordinghams. Billy Grimes was coxswain from 1917 to 1933 and

---

124 Woods p. 41
125 *UDC Minutes* March 4th 1934 NRO DC18/4/5
126 Information provided by Derek and Norman Smith, Frank's great nephews.

Fourteen oarsmen were needed to propel the lifeboat out to sea

when he retired he was succeeded by Ted Nielsen. Nielsen had settled in Wells from his native Denmark early in the century, coming here by three-masted schooner. He stayed and married the daughter of a fisherman, Charles Wordingham, earning his living as a shellfish merchant. The iconic picture of the lifeboatmen in 1920 includes two Smiths, five Grimes, three Wordinghams and two Coxes. John Wordingham was to emigrate to Australia two years later; others would follow.

The lifeboats themselves had changed little over the years; they were, until 1936, powered by sail and oars. *Baltic No 3* which came on station in 1919 was the last of her kind in Wells. Two masts carried three sails, though often only two would be deployed. The main and mizzen carried lug sails much like those used on the fishing boats. Fourteen crewmen manned the oars: main strength as well as knowledge of the sea were essential qualifications; they were known to break the oars in big seas and had to carry spares. [127]

The *Royal Silver Jubilee,* named in honour of the king's jubilee the previous year, came on station in 1936. Powered by a petrol engine

Baltic No 3 *lifeboat, 1920 with coxswain Billy Grimes (left centre) with beard, cap and pipe. To his left is Frank 'Tender' Smith, harbour-master for many years*

the crew were initially uncertain of its reliability and its twin masts would remain available to carry the dipping lug sails borne by its predecessors.[128] She would go on to prove herself during the coming war.

Former Devon lifeboat, Plymouth, *bought by James Jarvis, seen here in Wells harbour. She was later converted for whelking*

[128] The *Lucy Lavers*, of a similar vintage, which still sports her masts, can be seen in Wells harbour, having been restored nearby.

3. Social life

Staithe Street in the 1920s

Houses were becoming more comfortable. Nevertheless they had not, for most people, become the private places they were to become. People were used to meeting and interacting with each other: in the yard, in the street, in the fields, as well as at work. Most people walked to wherever they were going. They would know most if not all those they met. Among the places of meeting were shops. Having little storage space and no refrigeration, most people would shop daily. In the early years of the century Wells' shops met most of their basic needs.

In the years between the wars the three main shopping streets, High Street, Staithe Street and Freeman Street, were still busy. There were shops on Burnt Street. The names of the proprietors had changed over the years but the range of shops remained. On Staithe Street, Wells and Son had two shops, one selling men's clothes, draperies, haberdashery and the other selling furniture; Butcher's clothiers' shop was at the top of the street. There were several shoe shops. It was possible to buy anything to wear in the town. Reeves the grocers had a shop further up the hill; under different names they claimed to have been there since 1777. George Fynn tried out a variety of enterprises including running the Jubilee café on the quay. In the 1930s he had an ice cream shop, made possible by the introduction of an electrical supply. Ernest Flint took on a dairy and ice cream parlour adjacent to the Edinburgh hotel. There were several other dairies in the town, one based on Orchard Farm, the other on Burnt Farm, both of them on Burnt Street. Milk would soon be sold in bottles rather than ladled out of churns from a pony and trap. The High Street still had twenty shops, including Thurgur's at the corner of Church Plain which sold furniture, china and glass. William Thurgur was yet another businessman to become chairman of the Urban District Council. One among several bakers in the town, Rose's shop was on Church Plain.

Between them the streets contained over sixty shops, almost all of them providing for the daily needs of townspeople: not only butchers and bakers, greengrocers, grocers, poulterers and fishmongers, but also tailors and outfitters, glass and china shops, three banks, news-agents, chemists, confectioners, drapers, boot and shoemakers, iron-mongers, a musical instrument shop, a wireless shop, wine and spirit merchants, cycle dealers and a watchmaker. Dressmakers, working from home, some even with apprentices, supplied many needs. On the other hand, if contemporary memory can be relied on, there were until the 1930s no hairdressers: hair was done up in a bun. Men, on the other hand, could get a shave as well as a haircut.[129] There were dairymen, coal merchants, carpenter-undertakers, solicitors, an employment exchange, an auctioneer, a medical officer of health and a tax collector.[130] In 1937 there were eleven pubs. In 1863 there had been over ninety retail outlets, not to mention the numerous trades carried on the town. The telephone altered communications within the town but there were fewer than forty telephones.

Fish was among the many commodities delivered to people's doors. Coal likewise was brought round the streets by horse and cart. Lighter goods like bread would be delivered by handcart. Milk came by pony and trap. Even ice cream would be sold in the street from handcarts. In the evenings a lamplighter would come around on his bike with a long pole to light the lamps; they now burned until early morning.[131]An organ grinder was another common visitor, replete with his monkey dressed in a pillbox hat. Horses still needed to be shod and the forge at the bottom of Market Lane spilled sparks from the anvil and steam as the hot shoes were pressed onto the horse's hooves to be secured with nails.[132] All would soon be gone.

The town was, for a while, to make non-alcoholic mineral waters. Joseph Bullen established a factory on Standard Road in 1903. Having decided to move to Park Road in 1924,[133] he found himself unable to afford to run the new factory and sold out to Robert Claxton

---

[129] Jean Stone *Further Recollections of Wells* (1992)
[130] Kelly's Directories 1916,1922,1925, 1937
[131] Geoff. Perkins *When I was a Young Lad* (2000) p. 24
[132] Woods p.17
[133] The bottles describe the works as being on Park Road; they were on what is now Mill Road. Street names were often changed by local usage.

whose firm continued until 1974, when it closed and the land was sold for housing. Dawson's Mineral Water Factory, owned at one time by Smiths, was in Sun Yard.

Many of the local retailers took an interest in the town's affairs. Herbert Butcher, outfitter, was to be chairman of the council for a number of years. One of the French family, Myrtle, whose family's fish and chip shop operated not only on the quay but on Station Road near the Post Office, was another.[134] Garage proprietor George Turner Cain, Arthur Ramm the butcher and Herbert Jary, boot maker were others. Jack Cadamy, who would take a greater part in council business post-war, was a wireless engineer and ran an electrical shop. George Rose, vocal chairman of the Ratepayers Association, ran an ironmonger's shop on High Street and subsequently a garage on Polka Road. Altogether the various businesspeople exercised influence within the town, not always to its benefit, but it meant that those who took decisions would be seen in the street and would have to answer for their actions.

Public houses were the most obvious meeting places, mostly for men. Regarded by some as places of depravity, people like Sam Peel thought there ought to be other venues where men could meet, relax and even get a bit of an education. Having held open air meetings on the quay from before the war and to which considerable numbers came, he established a Men's Institute and Adult School on Staithe Street. He used lantern lectures intended to educate and entertain.[135] Men learned to read there. Even forty years after the establishment of compulsory education many locals lacked basic literacy skills. When the first shop which they had used for the purpose was taken over by Wells and Son, a drapery business, premises were bought for them by a Quaker couple from Norwich. For a while the Men's Institute ran its own football team.

The needs of ex-servicemen were another concern, particularly for Gordon Calthrop, the local medical officer of health. His proposal for a working men's club as a memorial to the dead of the recent war resulted in the setting up of a committee to raise funds for its building. People were at first enthusiastic. Peel handed over his Adult School Institute on Staithe Street for use by men in the town, subject only to his being allowed to run a bible class on a Sunday morning. Calthrop presided over the raising of funds to convert it for use by men, not just ex-servicemen, from the age of 16. Fundraising was begun and in the meantime, a board with the names of the war dead was erected in the Institute. But by 1927, little had been achieved and the local British Legion branch pressed for the erection of a permanent memorial plaque in the town. The trustees were indignant at the alleged interference with their project but were pressed into action. The Legion offered a piece of land for building on Theatre Road which they had bought from F&G Smith, the maltsters. Fundraising

---

[134] Perkins (2000) (pp.52-57)
[135] Wild p. 24

was resumed and the club opened in September 1933. Calthrop, who had just retired, lived long enough to attend the opening. Its facilities, which included a Reading Room and a place for card games, did not include the sale of alcohol, intended to mollify local pubs but it was a discouragement to those who liked a drink with their relaxation.

Most clubs were for men. A plea that women's welfare should be provided for was met under different auspices. A month after the proposal to set up a men's club, Mrs George Smith, wife of the maltster, called the first exploratory meeting with a view to setting up a Women's Institute. After various false starts, a building was put up behind the Church Rooms on Church Plain, opening on 13 December 1923. It was to provide society and information for its members and to serve the town by raising funds for local good causes. During the war, they raised money for garments for the troops. Jam and Jerusalem came later. The long running Men's Discussion Group was formed in 1931, another of Sam Peel's initiatives. Based on wireless programmes put out by the BBC, it was one of many in the country. Both the Group and the WI continued into the present century.[136]

Seasonal events tended to be arranged in part with tourism in mind. Between the wars the regattas flourished. By the early 1920s they had become a huge success. Crowds from out of town gathered at the quay to ride on the swing boats and try their luck with the many stalls. Tents were erected on the marshes; for a small sum visitors could be rowed across the channel. There were sailing races, rowing races, races on seahorses (whatever they were) - fancy dress obligatory; there were swimming races – for men and boys only - all from the quay. The timing of these events was dictated by the tides which meant that the carnival procession, again in fancy dress, around the streets took place at such a time earlier or later as to fit in with the

Sailing race 1921 regatta

[136] Chris Beale *The History of the Wells Discussion Group* (WLHG Newsletter 44 2010)

Pleasure boating at the Regatta in 1921

water sports. The early boats were undecked single lug-sailed boats like the yacht tenders of the period. They were superseded by new designs. The International 14 foot had a sloop rig, with fore-and-aft sails carried on a single mast; it was very popular. It was replaced in Wells (and in Brancaster) by Sharpies, well known still in Wells. Sharpies were first designed in north Germany in 1931 and were an immediate hit. At over 19 feet overall, gaff rigged, they were much larger than the 14s. The Wells Sailing club had been formed in 1913, Interrupted by the war, by the 1920s sailing races were in full swing. Dr Hicks owned an International 14, *Typhoon*, and had become a very able sailor. At the National Championships for the Prince of Wales Cup, then regarded as the most coveted trophy in the dinghy world, Hicks came third. In local races, he sometimes handed over the helm to his crew, Charles McDonald 'Loady' Cox, local fisherman. [137]

The beach with sailing boats plying for hire

The beach had long been a preferred destination for those visiting the town. It could be reached on foot or by taking advantage of the many vehicles which plied for hire. On arrival there were, according to the 1929 town guide, bathing huts and deckchairs, now provided by the Urban District Council which had rented the beach

[137] Wells Sailing Club Newsletter 1950/Typhoon sailing log 1935

from Holkham. There were boats for hire, including sailing dinghies, which were helmed by the 'expert boatmen who are always in demand as they give their passengers a pleasant and interesting time'. The Beach House, a refreshment house on the south side of the dunes, provided meals, being able to 'seat 150 persons at one time'.[138] More safely visitors could take to the water on Abrahams Bosom, the little lake left by the building of the beach bank just south of the Pinewoods. Opened by Lord Leicester in 1935, the council's Beach Committee provided twelve paddle boats and six rowing boats and a hundred deck chairs. On the other hand requests by local bands to play music on the beach were turned down.

Another reason for coming to the beach was cockling. Visiting families could be seen at West Lake raking for them to take home for tea, struggling down to the station with their haul. With such profusion no one thought of the consequences of raiding a free resource.

Tennis party at Mayshiel 1920s

Garden parties were another feature of the age, allowing ordinary folk to enter the grounds of the great houses of the town while raising money for local charities. Mayshiel, the residence of the Smiths, with its large garden including a tennis court, was popular. The public could enjoy the grounds, take tea and pay good money at the various stalls put up for the afternoon, usually in aid of the hospital, the nursing association or the church. Tennis matches could be watched even if few could participate. The Lawns, another grand house, hosted children's tea parties. Dr Hicks opened the gardens of his house, The Normans, for garden fetes.

A source of entertainment in winter as well as summer was the cinema. The earliest mention of a cinema in Wells is in 1914 when four businessmen, including a Mr Codman from Walsingham, formed

---

[138] *Guide to Wells-next-the-Sea* (Wells Advancement Association 1930 pp. 19,.23)

a syndicate to show films locally. Kelly's Directory of 1929 mentions the 'Electric Palace Cinema (open Thurs. & Sat.)' operating at Oddfellows Hall on Clubbs Lane. The Oddfellows Hall, which had been built in 1885, had been hired out as a place of public entertainment for some years. The films were silent, and Mrs Seeley accompanied the show on a piano. The film stopped when reels had to be changed and when the static generator which supplied the power broke down. After a period of closure it was taken over in 1931 by Cyril Claxton who renamed it the Central cinema. Claxton also took over the Park cinema on Mill Road, an old warehouse previously run by Herbert Wells of Hunstanton using portable equipment. The idea of a permanent cinema providing nightly shows was slow to emerge but the advent of 'talkies' rapidly increased its popularity.

The Regal Cinema, formerly the Oddfellows Hall, on Clubbs Lane

The Oddfellows Hall had long been hired out for large events until 1937 when it sold out to East Coast Cinemas Ltd. who had more than a dozen cinemas in the region. The company quickly applied their trademark name of Regal to the Clubbs Lane premises and set about extending it so that it could seat over 310 patrons.[139] The extension was a huge steel-framed building with block walls and an asbestos roof. The earliest talkies produced sound from discs which were not always well synchronised with the pictures, but sound-on-film technologies were now available as was a mains electrical supply to the town. Carbon arc projectors could be used, providing a much brighter light. Using direct current, they required rectifiers and were very hot and smelly in use. The first sound film shown in Wells, *O-Kay for Sound* featuring the Crazy Gang, was shown in December of that year. The husband-and-wife duo Jack Hulbert and Cicely Courtneidge were early stars. More people will remember the American crooner Bing Crosby who appeared later that month. By the beginning of the war, Technicolor films were shown. As films changed several times a week, the cinemas provided a regular night out.

The rise of the town as a seaside resort resumed after the war with assistance from the railway. Following its welcome to cyclists, The Crown hotel had since 1912 proudly proclaimed itself as recommended by the new motoring organisations, the RAC and the AA.

[139] Mike Welland (WLHG Newsletter 55 2014) the Oddfellows moved to a smaller building on the quay.

Other modest 'commercial' hotels in the centre of town were the Prince of Wales, the Edinburgh, and the Railway Hotel, while on the Buttlands there were a number of boarding houses, so-called private hotels, and an increasing number of 'apartments' advertising for visitors as well as a number of bed and breakfast addresses and four furnished houses to let.[140]

Nevertheless, lacking a promenade and a vista of the sea, the town was more attractive to day trippers from Norwich and Dereham than to staying guests. Paid holidays for working men and women and the advent of the summer Bank Holiday on the first weekend in August, enacted in 1871, gave people more time to travel. Those arriving at the station were met by taxis which would take them from the station to the beach. Days out by charabanc became popular. On the other hand, the town was never developed in the way that Hunstanton and Cromer were. At Hunstanton the L'Estrange family promoted the development of the new resort and at Cromer the Bond-Cabells of Cromer Hall were similarly active; the Cokes were more interested in agriculture. Wells quay was lined with maltings and public houses not hotels and a promenade; it was an industrial town. It may have been for that reason that it was omitted from the maps of resorts advertised by the LNER, the successor company to the Great Eastern, in 1931. The pilgrimage traffic to Walsingham was by then a bigger draw, attracting pilgrims from London and further afield.[141] The line also carried imported potash and exported corn via the harbour and carried quantities of milk to London.[142]

Whatever their length of stay the visitors needed somewhere to eat; fish and chips for preference. In those days few public houses provided food; a sit-down meal could be obtained in the very few restaurants. They also needed somewhere to relieve themselves. A urinal had been provided on the quay since 1907. There was a suggestion that the Jubilee House be converted into wash houses and a public convenience. There was nowhere in the town itself. Thus the council purchased a piece of land at the top of Newgates Lane from International Stores for a set of toilets.

The ending of the war had brought a resumption of wildfowling. Wells was famous, a mecca for shooters, including Sir Peter Scott, later to become a conservationist, who was in those days a fowler. Shooters came from all over England. 'There were shooters behind every tree and hidden all along the sand hills. When the geese did come over everybody fired.'[143] Arguments were often had in the early hours of a winters' morning as to who had shot which goose. The increased numbers began to harm the habitats they came to visit; widespread and indiscriminate wildfowl shooting began to be practised. The numbers of widgeon and pink-foot geese crashed. The causes of

---

[140] Kelly's Directories passim
[141] Jenkins p. 71
[142] Julian Holland *Dr Beeching's Axe 50 years on* (David & Charles 2013) p. 70
[143] Alan Savory in *Wildfowling* p 28

the disappearance of the duck and geese but also the nesting waders were many and various, and not altogether agreed. Disease attacked the eel grass on which the widgeon fed. As the eel grass disappeared, other invasive species of plant began to grow. Then, with the threat of a second war, in 1937 an artillery range was established at Stiffkey, thus making the grazing of sheep on the marshes there impossible.[144] All these things contributed to the desertion of the birds. Only protective legislation and new regimes would eventually allow them to come back.[145]

The division between work and leisure is now one which people take for granted. Though the range of activities had increased, leisure time for the working classes was still a comparative novelty. Fixed hours for agricultural workers were only introduced during the Great War; in any case the demands of livestock could not be accommodated even within a fifty-hour week. Similarly maltsters had to be available when the malt was ready to be turned or shovelled into the kiln. Fishermen worked by weather and tide. Shop workers worked fixed, if long hours, but home workers such as seamstresses could work as long as the light allowed. Leisure was the prerogative of the growing middle classes.

Somewhere in between work and leisure was the church (or the churches). The churches increasingly provided leisure activities in particular for the young but they relied on a perhaps diminishing sense of duty. Back in 1902 a member of the Norwich diocesan conference lamented that 'the clergy have lost the influence they once had over the agricultural labourer.'[146] The idea nevertheless that

St Nicholas church choir with the rector, Revd George Ingle, 1922

[144] Geraldine Green in *Stiffkey with Cockthorpe – a story of Norfolk people* (Poppylands 2013) p. 129, 153.
[145] Pat Cringle *Saltmarsh and Sandunes* (Wells & District Wildfowlers Club) passim
[146] *Eastern Weekly Press* 12th April 1902

children in particular should be trained in the habits of religion was widely held.

At any rate Sunday was a day when all the shops closed, sport was not practised and a good many folk went to church. The town's leading citizens, its councillors, were most of them also leading members of the churches. The Loynes, the Smiths and the Granges were Church of England, the Cadamys and the Ramms were Congregationalists; Sam Peel and Frank Sawbridge were Quakers and the Methodists would see George Edwards regularly in the pulpit.

How many attended depended to some degree on the personality of the clergy though duty still largely reigned. George Ingle was popular. He was fully engaged in the life of the schools and of the town. The church choir still boasted a goodly number of schoolboys – but not girls – in those days. Girls might join the Girls Friendly Society, a national organisation which provided weekday meetings and the putting on of costume dramas. Ingle had a capacious church hall built across the road from the church before the war which was widely used for secular purposes as well as by the church.

Clergy did not retire in those days and his departure in 1929 was due to illness. His successor, Frederick Beddard, was the last rector to have bought his right of appointment (and the Beddards still retain the patronage of the parish). He left suddenly in 1936 because, he said, of the deterioration in his wife's health, leaving his successor, William Moss, to complete and cover the cost of the repair of the tower which, though it had survived the 1879 fire, was in need of further work. Moss, who was a very outward-going man, known as a regular visitor of his parishioners, organised on several years during the 1930s a nativity pageant, depicting biblical scenes with commentary shared between three angels, suitably winged and which com-

Wesleyan Methodist chapel closed in 1936 and opened as the town library in 1949

manded some seventy participants. Running for three nights, the church was filled on each occasion. The church was 'high' though not as high as nearby South Creake, where the vicar during the 1920s demonstrated how promiscuous were people's tastes if they liked the vicar; his introduction of 'high mass' with bells and incense coincided with his more than doubling the size of the congregation. At Wells the Communion service was held weekly at 8am so as to enable those who received communion to do so fasting – before eating breakfast. In some places it was monthly.

The church had an all-male robed choir with about ten men and twenty boys who filled the choir stalls in the chancel, processing up the main aisle at the beginning of the service and returning the same way at its end. Their position between the altar and the congregation made them very visible. Bored choirboys could be seen misbehaving during sermons. Annual outings to Bayfield Park or Cromer were the reward for the many hours of choir practices and services morning and evening. In 1939 they went to Hunstanton by special train which had been arranged to return later than the timetable provided to extend the boys' enjoyment.

The two Methodist churches, Wesley and Primitive, conformed to national agreement to merge in what was an early attempt at church unity in 1932. There were difficulties, including the different political stances of the two bodies – the connection between the Prims and agricultural trade unionism may have died but history casts a long shadow – and also because of the practical problem as to which of the two buildings would be retained. In the event it was the Station Street chapel that would close, its congregation having to migrate to the Primitives' chapel on Theatre Road. For a while, the new minister, the Revd John Cash, held services in both churches until it was agreed by the Urban District Council to purchase the Station Road chapel with the intention of turning it into a library for the town. The war delayed its opening which happened only in 1949.

Consecration of Our Lady Star of the Sea in June 1928

In 1697, the Meeting House, burial ground and a stable were purchased by the Friends from Clement Ives. An additional plot of land, measuring 72 ft by 17 ft 6 inches, adjoining the Meeting House was given to the Friends in 1859 by Joshua Gales. The estate was further enlarged by the purchase, in 1906, of cottages and land adjoining the Meeting House from Joseph Butler of Wells for £325. Expenses of the Meeting House and burial ground were met from the general income of the Meeting and the estate was administered by Lynn Monthly Meeting.

Absentees from this roll call were the Roman Catholics whose religion was viewed with suspicion. The feeling was mutual: one Roman Catholic bishop was recorded as saying then that it was not possible for them to say even the Lord's Prayer with other Christians. The Catholic church in Wells was opened in 1928, the foundation stone having been laid the previous July. Dedicated to Our Lady Star of the Sea, the event was one of great pomp and ceremony as was the consecration of dedication of the church a year later; a presbytery was built adjacent to the church. The building was in the centre of town, the land provided by a local Catholic but for some it was an alien presence. England regarded itself as a Protestant country; services in Wells should be in English not Latin; the major feature of such services was the sermon, not the mass. This new church was different and not altogether welcome. The building was subsequently treated from time to time with graffiti and smashed windows. 'No popery' was both written and uttered fifty and more years after.

4. Clearances and improvements

At the end of the Great War, Wells council proposed to build another eight council houses, to be placed on the east end allotments, having already completed twenty council houses during the hostilities. The 1919 Housing Act placed upon local councils a duty to provide new houses, one which Wells had already fulfilled, but more were needed. Arthur Ramm, who had resisted so much of the modernisation of the town, had resigned as chairman of the council and was replaced by Frederick Raven, master of the school. James Blades, maltsters' clerk, was his vice-chairman. Samuel Bloy, newly appointed sanitary inspector, was asked to prepare a list of overcrowded and insanitary houses as a preliminary to formulating a further scheme. A field north of Park Road, owned by the Southgates, was the preferred site. Pressed by the housing commissioner for a scheme to supply mains water,

Jicklings Yard typical of the narrow passage-ways down which it was almost impossible to take a vehicle

the council replied that houses were the more pressing priority.

The issues of water and sewage went together. Even in such salubrious parts of the town as the Buttlands, the wells on which people relied for water proved to be contaminated with sewage. Down the hill towards the quay matters were inevitably worse. Even the council house wells had proved to be contaminated and had to be deepened. The issue had been first raised in November 1919. It was recognised that this would entail a re-organisation of the sewerage system 'which at present is incapable for taking anything other than slop drainage'. Presumably they were envisaging flush toilets as one of the possibilities realisable if there was a constant supply of water as well as the means of disposing of sewage safely. But the time was not yet. They opted instead to press for more housing which was certainly one way of dealing with the problems of insanitary conditions of life of many people in the town.

Twenty-four houses were to be built at the rate of six per acre to allow for large gardens on Park (Mill) Road. Calthrop had reported to the council in his annual report in 1919 that there were, in the north-east corner of the town, another 180 houses holding 700 people, which needed to be 'reconstituted or re-planned in the near future'. Twelve houses had been served with closing orders but these were impossible to execute owing to a lack of accommodation elsewhere. His report shows how his views on the matter had changed. What had seemed acceptable to him in 1909 was now not so. Work on the sewers was now a matter of urgency.

As for Bloy, his monthly reports to the council show how hands-on was his work. In one report he wrote "the drains on the quay at the cottage occupied by Skinner I found them in a very insanitary

Park Road, (now Mill Road) council houses 1921

condition; the yard was honeycombed with rat runs which were carried under the floor of the kitchen. At the place where the sink discharged over the gulley outside, when the gulley was removed a large cesspit was found full of stinking mud and the bad smells found their way into the house through a hole in the wall under the sink. I took up all the drain which was of all kinds, some bricks covered with wood and some agricultural pipes full of stinking mud. I laid a new glazed pipe drain and connected it with the sink drain and drain from the pump and discharge direct into the sewer which passes through the yard." Existing drains often laid only just beneath the road surface were apt to be fractured by increasingly heavy vehicles and had to be re-laid deeper and concreted in. Bloy's extensive reports to the council indicate how little had changed over the previous fifty years. Moreover, his task was not merely one of repair and remedying defects; it was also one of education. Householders, mostly tenants but including some landlords, had to be persuaded that their standards of hygiene were deleterious to the health of others but also to themselves. Where water for drinking was obtained from wells it mattered that any danger of human waste entering them was avoided. Likewise animal waste had to be kept away from slaughterhouses; this was not easy. There were always those who misused the system. Some, for instance, who had pail closets intended for solid matter, also filled them with garden refuse and even sand and shingle, 'making the pails so heavy such that one man was unable to carry them'.[147] Bloy proposed that they should not be collected.

Writing about the basic problems of cleanliness in December 1922 he noted that at the top end of Mindhams Yard there were only two closets for seven houses, occupied by seventeen people. Two wash-houses served them, one of which was dilapidated. There was no point in serving an enforcement notice on Miss Griffin, the owner, he stated, 'as she does not obey them.'[148] He writes 'She only abused me and said she should not spend one penny on them and the council could pull them down if they chose.'[149] One cesspool was discovered to be eleven feet deep, having not been emptied for years. Such was the immensity of his task.

Some owners were cooperative, recognising the importance of reconstructing the drainage, but not all. The opposition of some councillors continued. Councillor Margetts, horse slaughterer, refused to allow his house to be inspected and shortly after proposed a motion at a council meeting dismissing Bloy from his post. Bloy also reported that Margetts had dumped 'green' horse bones on his paddock. For the moment the majority of the council passed what was effectively a vote of confidence in Bloy, but Margetts had not finished: he tried to prevent Bloy's salary increase from going through.

---

[147] Sanitary Inspector's Report attached to Wells UDC Minutes NRO DC 18.4/5
[148] Sanitary Inspector's Report Wells UDC Minutes December 1922 NRO DC 18.4/5
[149] Sanitary Inspector's Report May 1921 NRO DC 18.4/5

Sam Peel and councillors at the opening of the cemetery

Farm animals were still permitted in the town: pigs, cows and even goats. Bloy reported that a goat fell through an inspection cover on the marsh behind Freeman Street and was drowned. His attempts to remove pigsties from places near to dwelling houses met with mixed success; pigs were being kept in Lion Yard and there would still be pigsties in the town ten years later.

Bloy was also Highways Inspector. In that capacity he had put tarred shingle on roads instead of fine gravel as he had been instructed. This became a cause for his being asked to submit his resignation. Understandably he resisted and, after some discussion, he was given six months notice, expiring in April 1925. However he died suddenly in November 1924, the sixth in office since 1911. He was replaced by George Rodley who lasted two years. Fred Rodwell, who followed him, somehow lasted until 1961. The temper of the times had begun to change.

Work on the Mill Road houses was begun in 1921. Again there were teething problems: the new houses were fitted with gas stoves rather than coal-fired ranges as previously but these proved faulty; the coppers, for washing clothes, were the wrong size to fit their taps. At the same time some of the 1915 houses were showing further signs of deterioration.

The 1924 elections brought the first woman to the council, Miss Curtis Pyle, a retired schoolteacher who had begun her career as a pupil teacher in Wells Infant School in 1871. It also brought a number of shopkeepers, as well as Raven and Blades, Peel and two members of the Smith family, EL Smith and George Turner Cain who had married Jessie, one of Smith's sisters. Peel was elected chairman. The council approved the purchase of land to the south of Theatre Road for twenty cottages, to be called Gales Road, with a plan to build a further seven for owner occupation. Cain opened a garage on Polka

The East End was the most overcrowded part of town

Road. The new cemetery on Market Lane was opened the following March.

The 1928 elections brought Turner Cain to the chairmanship of the council, but he was not re-elected the following year. He was among a solid minority of councillors who serially opposed just those two improvements which would transform the town: the installation of a mains water supply and of a sewerage system. Lacking anyone willing to take on the chairmanship the next year he was elected by four votes to none with seven abstentions. Only after the 1931 elections was the reconciling figure of Frederick Raven re-elected both to the council and to the chairmanship. Raven had just retired from headship of the school after twenty-seven years. Meetings of the council would henceforth be held at the school. Progress would be made. Cain would be re-elected to the chair again in 1937; this time he achieved five votes to none with only six abstentions.

The 1928 elections saw the ending of an era. Herbert Loynes resigned as clerk to be succeeded by WA Williamson. Loynes had succeeded his father, Edward Loynes, in 1914. Edward had been clerk to the Improvement Commissioners and continued when the Urban District Council was formed in 1894. He was the last of the long line of local solicitors, going back to Thomas Garwood in the 1840s. Garwood had been responsible for the 1944 Improvement legislation.

The passing of yet another Housing Act in 1930 gave the council greater powers, combining the existing power to build houses with a more general power to pull down houses deemed unfit for human habitation. Clearance Areas, so-called, could be designated, requiring that all the houses within an area could be demolished either by the owner or, if he refused, by the council. The much larger Improvement Areas, on the other hand were designated on a map by reference to the poor sanitary condition of some houses, overcrowding or narrowness or bad arrangement of streets but which could be improved by the demolition of some of the houses and the repair of others. Having designated the area, decisions could then be made on a case-by-case basis as to which houses could be improved and which needed to be pulled down.

An impetus for further improvement seems to have come with the threat from government to abolish the Urban District Council which was held to be too small. Following legislation in 1929 the County Council was instructed to conduct a review of local government with a view to abolishing and merging authorities which seemed not to be effective. Peel, who was by then a county councillor, argued for the retention of the council. It was an important piece of local democracy, he claimed. At the end of the review process required under the Act, the Ministry of Health reluctantly agreed to Wells continuing as an Urban District Council, noting however that 'public health services in the area were defective'.

Rackhams Yard with pump

That was certainly true. Wells still had no modern sewerage system; its houses lacked a reliable water supply; even its council houses lacked electricity and proper sanitation. Geoff Perkins, who was born off Freeman Street in 1928, described where he lived with its one room downstairs with its iron range for heating and cooking and the stairs up to two tiny bedrooms. Families with ten children were not unknown. Toilets were in the yard and a 'piss pot' at the top of the stairs provided for nightly needs. There being no light, a cautious finger on the rim of the pot was needed to tell whether or not there was room for more.[150] In the morning it might well be emptied out of an upstairs window onto the yard below with the cry 'Gardeloo'[151] to warn bystanders to get out of the way. Kitchen waste, such as potato peelings, would be used to feed pigs which a number of houses kept. Many houses had their own wells, though many more shared a pump in the yard and a washhouse. Latterly some houses had their water pumped from the well into a header tank from which household taps would be fed.[152]

The first serious proposal for the implementation of a water scheme was in April 1930. It made sense for water supply and the replacement of the sewerage system to be dealt with at the same time. Both entailed disruption of the streets with the laying of pipes. But it was not to be. It was opposed, notably by Councillors Cain, Jessop and Williams because of 'the depressed state of the town's employment'. Cain and three other councillors unsuccessfully opposed even the appointment of an engineer to report on the practicality and hence

---

150 Perkins (2000) p. 9

151 Conversation with Ray Smith; the call is French – 'Garde a l'eau – beware of the water. How it came to be used in England no one seems to know.

152 D. Perryman *How they lived* WLHG Newsletter No. 16 (2000)

the cost of such work. A modified scheme dealing only with the supply of water was agreed. Progress was slow; minds had to be changed. Thus in June 1934 did Cain himself propose the consideration of 'the provision of water-carried sanitation in all the houses'. The digging of a huge well, over a hundred feet deep, began on Coe's farm off the Warham Road, the highest point in the town. Supplied with an electric pump to a water tower it was to deliver not less than 90,000 gallons a day to the town. £5,590 was to be borrowed for the works which included the digging of water main pipes down each street to which individual houses could then be connected. The actual cost was £1,100 more. Sinks with taps were to be fitted to council houses and while private house-owners would have to foot the bill to make this connection, the council houses would be provided for at public expense. The possibility of kitchen sinks and baths and even flush toilets lay before them. The Gales Road houses were to benefit from the installation of the first two but not yet the third. As for the sewerage system, the possibility of a treatment plant on the west marsh was at last canvassed. A trial hole on the west marsh was to be dug.

Rodwell's work of identifying further housing need resulted in a proposal to build twenty more 'working men's houses'. The Earl duly offered a two-and-a-half-acre site on which, after a struggle, Westfield Avenue would be built. Initially, because of 'the present financial crisis in the country' the number was reduced to eight. The crisis resulted in reductions in salaries of the staff, a proposal which stopped short of the clerk and the surveyor. There were seventy-eight applicants for the new houses, in which it was agreed, wallpaper would now be allowed. Progress.

At the same time, more significantly, electrical supply was advancing across the county. Until then only a few houses like Mayshiel had their own generators to charge storage batteries.[153] The first poles were erected in August 1932; the council wished cables instead to be laid underground. The East Anglia Electricity company, proactive in promoting the new technology, proposed to supply electric street lights for the ten new Westfield Avenue houses. Given its commitment to gas and its overall reluctance to embrace change, especially if it involved additional expenditure, the council refused. Councillors then agreed to the provision of electrical power but thought it excessive to provide such lights in bedrooms. A single light in the downstairs rooms was enough. A similar attitude was taken to the offered provision of seven lights in each of the new Northfield Avenue houses; the council demanded three lights supplied free of charge otherwise gas would be used.[154] The idea of electric street lighting was another step deemed too far. As late as February 1934 the council turned down the offer by the electricity company to provide it; they did so again the following year. The Northfield Lane houses would get their elec-

[153] F&G Smith 28th June 1930
[154] *UDC Minutes* Dec. 1932 NRO DC 18/4/6

Fire brigade practice using a petrol-driven pump to obtain sea water, 1930s

trical supply only in 1937. The Electrolux refrigerators on trial for use in council houses would not be much use without it.

The advent of electric light brought about a major advance in safety. With the lessening need to use candles to see in the dark, house fires were less likely. Hitherto every house was a fire risk: from candles to ranges to coppers to open hearths. The town's fire engine was for a while stored at the south end of the Jubilee House, the current harbourmaster's office. It was a horse drawn hand-pumped machine drawing water from an onboard tank. Subsequently it was stored in the barn behind Mayshiel, the horses to pull it kept in the adjoining stables. It was only in 1934 that the town obtained a second-hand Fire King steam fire engine, a self propelled machine capable of delivering 500 gallons a minute, which was bought from Holkham Estate at a cost of £100. Though it took fifteen minutes to raise steam, it could draw water from external water sources such as local water pits.[155] On the other hand, it was a 1910 design and petrol driven machines were now being produced. Holkham had got rid of the Fire King to buy just such an appliance.

Developments thereafter were rapid. In 1936 the newly re-formed fire brigade acquired new equipment including a trailer fire pump, lengths of hose and uniforms for the volunteer fireman. Petrol driven pumps were lighter and more flexible in use and could take water from any open source, the most obvious of which in Wells was sea water. The same year as the town got its first mains water supply, it was decided that fire hydrants, seventeen of them, should be installed across the town so that there would be a source of water close to any fire that should break out.[156] The petrol-driven pump would then in-

155 Hiskey (2016) p.385; *UDC Minutes* June 1934;Sept.1936 NRO DC18/4/8
156 *UDC Minutes* Sep 1936 NRO DC18/4/6

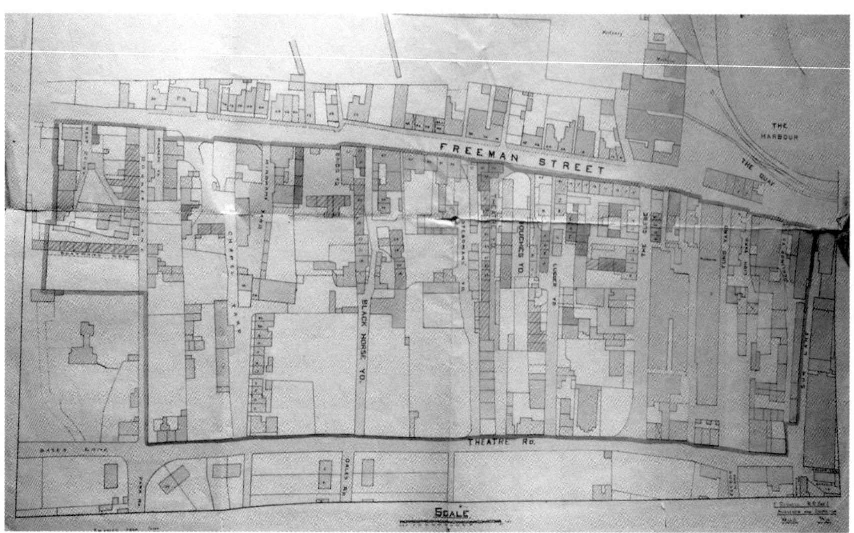

The doomed proposed Improvement Area, 1933

crease the pressure which, however, created some problems of water pressure elsewhere. The council was ahead of 1938 legislation setting up a network of fire stations across the country. That year, the amalgamation of the two Methodist churches in Wells freed up accommodation on Station Road and the fire station migrated once again, this time equipped with a newly acquired Morris Commercial engine and its Dennis trailer pump. Frederick Rodwell had been sub officer, in other words in charge of the station, since his arrival in the town in 1927; he would continue in post as sub officer until 1950.

Rodwell's day job, particularly that part of it which related to housing, continued to absorb his energies. Looking at the yards which ran down to Freeman Street he proposed to take advantage of the 1930 legislation and have it designated an Improvement Area. The initial proposal of 1933 condemned twenty-seven houses, all of them to the north west of the town between just east of Dogger Lane, north of Theatre Road as far as Sun Yard – largely the area which was to be completely demolished in the 1960s. It was the occupants of these houses who would go to Westfield Avenue and Bases Lane. The houses proposed for demolition housed 82 occupants, all of them tenants. Several of the owners wrote to object, promising to make improvements to the houses themselves. Not all did as they promised. Then the council received a communication from the Minister rejecting the scheme, a body blow. It was to set back the development of the Freeman Street yards by thirty years.

Meanwhile various attempts were made to diminish the rat problem, including competitions to supply the largest number of rat tails. A rat catcher had been employed since before the war but the problem of rats was immense. As a result of the competitions, from January 1932 to March 1934, the tally was 7,877, the winner having killed 566 rodents.

The first Clearance Order, one of thirteen, put forward by Rodwell had been proposed in 1933 and was agreed to by the minister in 1936. It was to remove properties on Bolts Close behind the Post Office. Next went cottages opposite the church next to the Bowling Green pub, followed by properties at the bottom of Market Lane. A fourth was on Masseys Yard opposite the church. (It remains as a private yard.) Those remaining affected Burnt Street, Plummers Hill, Jolly Sailors Yard, Staithe Street, the west end of Church Street and where the health centre now stands on Bolts Close. By the time they were agreed in 1939, it was too late. The council would still be attempting to get the occupants of five of the areas condemned in 1955. The war changed everything.

Meanwhile, the impetus for house building was maintained. Even if the redevelopment of yards could not take place better housing could be provided. So in January 1935 the old Ropewalks Field, fronted by Jolly Sailors Yard, was proposed for 16 new houses. Eight houses in Northfield Avenue were sold to help pay for the work at £350 each. Ten acres of allotment land off Northfield Lane were offered by the Earl at £100 per acre, subsequently named Northfield Crescent. Ten houses were to be built there with the proposal for 16 more. He would offer another ten for £850. He was clearly a willing participant in the process.

Over the 20 or so years since Peel's first proposal, the improvement in the life of the town had been substantial and if there was reluctance on the part of some councillors to accept change, much less advance its cause, it was partly due to lack of sympathy for those of whose condition of life they were ignorant but also a prudential attitude towards expenditure. They ran their businesses to make a profit and did not like the idea of some of it being spent on people for whom they did not feel responsible.

5. Health and the hospital

The Medical Officer of Health had a dual role. Apart from public health issues relating to the condition of housing and the supply of food he was, like all of his predecessors, a general practitioner. Gordon Calthrop had been in the town in both capacities since 1903. He moved from a modest home in Burnt Street to the more prestigious premises at The Normans, a large Georgian house on Standard Road, in 1916. There he had his surgery, performing minor procedures as well as serving at the new hospital on Mill Road.

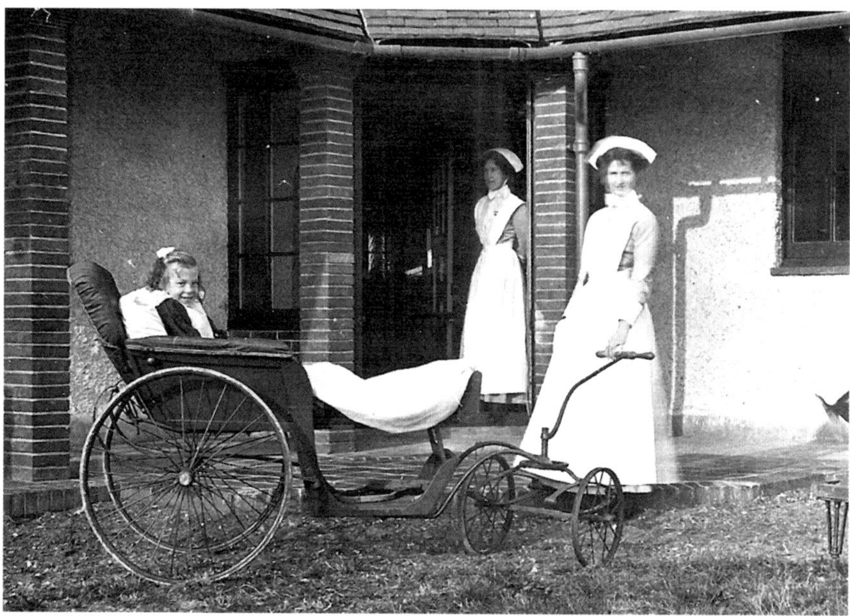

Matron Lucy Crosbie, an assistant nurse and a patient

The hospital continued to deal with surgical cases mostly at the hand of Dr Sturdee. Many of the operations were for the removal of children's tonsils, a procedure which was thought to cure throat infections from which many suffered. The medical staff remained relatively stable. Quite otherwise was the turnover of matrons. Miss Smith, its first matron, was rapidly succeeded by Miss Makin, Miss Makin by Miss Saywell, Miss Saywell by Miss Halliwell and she by Miss Jones. Miss Rhodes succeeded her in October 1920. Miss Rhodes was followed by Miss Rogers who had been initially appointed as a qualified assistant and then came Miss Lucy Crosbie in 1929, a total of thirteen matrons since the opening of the hospital. Several were made to resign for their harsh treatment of subordinates; some suffered illness themselves; one left to marry. Miss Crosbie exceptionally stayed for nine and a half years. Rarely were assistants in any way qualified, though some went on to train elsewhere. They came and went with great frequency. Some, like Nurse Pentney, were asked to return and fill in when departing assistants left the hospital without adequate cover. The first qualified assistant was Sister Rogers in 1923 who went on to become matron a year later.

Finances remained a problem. The deficit in 1926 necessitated the seeking of an overdraft of £150 from the local bank; preferably, they said, without interest. The next year this was raised to £200. Subscriptions fluctuated; the support of village schemes did not keep pace with costs; private patients were a bonus. On one occasion the committee resorted to putting the state of its finances on the local cinema screen to encourage donations. Public support was fundamental to the success of the hospital. Fundraising, whether through subscriptions, collections, flag days, events or sundry donations, made up its entire income which in 1934 amounted to £1,022. The contributory scheme included not merely individuals, churches and local organisations. Businesses with local interests such as the LNER railway company, F&G Smith, maltsters, and Dewing and Kersley, the local millers, all supported the hospital. Patients' fees amounted to just £129 7s 9d. Staff wages took up £266, medical supplies and surgery £37. Endowments, which amounted to over £1,500, provided a

Patients and staff in early days

cushion against future developments. In 1939 overall receipts were £1,203 14s 9d as against payments of £1,289 10s 2d. When the war came the fall in expenditure, especially after they were told to close half the beds, left them in surplus. The number of cases fell from 145 in 1940 to 132 in 1941.

Nevertheless in 1924 an operating theatre was built together with a bedroom for the matron who was effectively on call at all times. Dr Sturdee came into his own. Dr 'Willie' Ernest came to the town in 1926 and became his anaesthetist. Peter Astley Cooper joined the staff in 1933 to be succeeded by Howard Lillie. By 1934 the work had grown so as to include the care of 170 patients whose treatment ranged from amputations, appendectomies, abscesses, hysterectomies, dentistry, intestinal obstruction, tonsils and minor injuries, in other words, invasive surgery of a seriousness that would now be dealt with in a general hospital. Tonsils were removed at the average rate of one operation a week. Another popular demand on the services of the hospital was dentistry, for which the specialist skills of local dentists were called upon; an honorary dentist was a member of the staff. It seems to have been a source of friction from time to time, particularly over payments. Latterly Walter Mudie, a local dentist, was allowed to treat patients in the hospital on payment by the patient of a guinea a day. Operations were performed even on small children, in spite of the prohibition imposed in 1910. It had, after all, two cots.

In 1936 the number of cases had increased to 282. The hospital had, since its foundation, treated over 3,200 inpatients. Most were drawn from Wells or from villages which had contribution schemes but some came from a dozen other villages from Barney to Wighton and a few from out of district. Fakenham was specifically excluded from admissions as was Burnham Market, both on the basis that the

The hospital prior to postwar extensions

hospital would need to be enlarged if their patients were to be admitted and that funds were lacking to embark upon that task.

A clue as to the hospital's interaction with the town was the treatment of injuries to fishermen. Until the advent of synthetics, whelk fishing required the use of hemp or manila rope which easily rotted and so was tarred to extend its life. Without gloves these ropes tore at men's hands as they hauled them up into the boats. Septic hands were a consequence and numbers seem to have been treated. Abscesses were also common. The reason for amputations cannot be assigned but they are likely to have been the result of industrial injuries or undiagnosed diabetes.[157]

[157] *Annual Reports of the Wells and District Cottage Hospital* 1934,1936

Calthrop retired in 1932 to be succeeded by Hicks as Medical Officer of Health; Hicks was to retire thirty-seven years later in 1969. He was the last to hold both roles. He handed over the role of Medical Officer of Health in 1938 to a full timer but continued to perform operations at the hospital. He was to become the honorary secretary of the local RNLI and an Urban District Councillor as well as taking an interest in much else in the town. Widely admired as a doctor, he once 'treated' the teddy bear of a sick child, restoring its sight by dint of sewing back on a new eye, returning it to its owner with its head in bandages, following the 'operation'. He 'vaccinated' the toy tiger of a little girl just to show that it didn't much hurt before treating the child herself.[158] He had what can be described as a relaxed attitude towards alcohol consumption and could often be seen with a whisky glass in his hand and a pipe in his mouth. As a result of his drinking he was banned from driving on two occasions and had to make use of the local poacher as his chauffeur. Having bought it from Calthrope, he too moved into The Normans. The house was also his surgery and he installed an x-ray machine as part of his stock in trade. He lent the machine to the hospital during the war.

The organisation of the hospital was subject to the same forces as were operating in other areas of life. Government now required national registration and the imposition of uniform standards. The idea of a National Health scheme, now taken for granted, first came up for discussion at the annual meeting in 1944. The view was expressed that this 'would sound the death knell of voluntary hospitals'; the board was 'opposed to any interference with the present system'. [159]

Doctors in those days had to be paid by the patient. Thus apart from the school medical services, whose importance cannot be overrated, people were likely to suffer, if not in silence then at least without seeking expert medical assistance. Home remedies such as Syrup of Figs, Gregory Powder and Parish's food were the alternatives.[160] Some of them even worked.

There was however to be a service supplementary to that of general practitioners, that of the district nurse. The idea of such local nurses had originated at the time of Queen Victoria's Golden Jubilee in 1887 but took a long time to spread outside London. In 1914 there were still only 2,019 of them. Wells considered the appointment of a nurse midwife in 1929, deciding only secondarily that she would be allowed to attend maternity cases, which became an important function. She was supported by a separate organisation, the Wells Town Nursing Association. It too relied upon a variety of fundraising events: tennis tournaments, fetes, rummage sales, collections undertaken by volunteers and the support of local organisations such as the primary school, the Women's Institute and the various churches. The nurse's

---

[158] Woods p.16; Facebook - *Down Memory Lane* – Christine Brocklebank
[159] Hospital Management Committee Minutes May 24th. 1944
[160] Jean Stone (1992)

role was to visit people in their homes. In 1936 it was reported that Nurse Wilson had made 3,248 visits including 396 maternity calls and monthly visits to the clinic. This she presumably did under the direction of the doctors. There was also a school nurse paid for by the Education Committee. When she retired in 1937 Nurse Walker had been in post for fifteen years.

6. Children at work and play

Mr Raven, left, with school football team 1927

The Great War had severely dislocated the work of the school. The rebuilding of the staff numbers would take some time. The re-establishment of continuity of teaching would take longer. As late as 1922 the Inspector's annual report noted that the ground lost had not been completely recovered. The death, in 1915, of Miss Taylor, head of infants since 1883, had extended Raven's duties. Her successor, Miss Cutting, left in 1922; her successor in turn stayed for three years; three more following in three years. The building was unsatisfactory: reports noted the poor conditions in which the infants were taught – dark and poorly ventilated – which had been an issue for many years and was not to go away without a radical solution. On the other hand, no difficulty seems to have been noted in getting young children to attend. In 1925, of the 93 infants, 36 were under five and ten were only three years old. This, wrote the inspector, was something to be discouraged. It was only with the firm hand of Frances Rungary, appointed in 1927, that stability was attained.

So-called 'backward' children were much in evidence. The county inspector wrote that 'although the headteacher and his assistants have worked hard it has been impossible completely to recover the ground lost during the period of the war' Subsequent comment was more adverse: 'too little effort is expected from the children; in place of training in self-help they are constantly waited on by their teacher' but the school had 'a happy tone'. The comment continues in 1924: 'a tendency to over-direction' is observed resulting in a 'lack of independence shown by girls'. By 1925 some improvement 'over the last three years' was noticed.

Additional to Raven's other difficulties was the raising of the school leaving age in 1919 to 14. Standard 7, which had been a small group, now became a large class. Pubescent teenagers were a different kind of scholar – larger, more demanding of attention and importantly, lacking much in the way of outlet for their energies. The school had no playing field. Raven continued his predecessor's practice of drilling the boys who would march through the town military style. But he also made efforts to obtain the use of the town football club's pitch for the boys and indeed became a supporter and eventually treasurer of the town team.

The school had been enlarged several times, but it now became clear that the limit had been reached and another site needed to be identified. The nagging issue had been the poor conditions of the infants section. It was thus proposed that a new site be purchased for the infants. The available site, about an acre in size, was some 320 yards away on the other side of the New Road and was owned by Arthur Ramm, erstwhile town councillor, local butcher and grazier. Negotiations dragged on for some time. There were objections to the site on the grounds of cost – the district valuer's figure of £100 per plot was some way from Ramm's demand of £185. Other objections were that it was adjacent to a motor garage and a railway station, was on the wrong side of a busy road and was further away from where the children lived. Meanwhile the suggestion was made that it should, instead be a site for the boys' school rather than an infants' school. The county council agreed. Discussion inevitably took place about toilets: some of the closets would use pails and others the 'dry system'. The site would have a well. Discussion dragged on. Ramm said that he was minded to sell the site for housing in small plots. After much haggling, in October 1927, the sale was agreed at a price of £400. A further difficulty presented itself. The Secretary of the Board of Education pronounced, following local objections and comments from the inspector, that the site was 'high and exposed to winds from the north' which was regarded as putting the children's health at risk. Her own solution was that the greater number of classrooms could face southeast and added the rider that 'probably boys from neighbouring villages may attend and remain for their midday meal'.

The slowness of the process meant that further rethinking could take place. The authority considered the possibility that the building might be used at some future time as a senior school, for those over 11 years of age. The government Spens Report had recommended that elementary education should end at eleven and that thereafter children should be educated separately. Initially, the premises were opened as a boys' school on 16 September 1929 with Raven as its first head. Miss Rayfield had retired as head of the girls' school in 1925 and it was decided that the girls and the infants would be amal-

Pupils at the girls' school, 1936

gamated under Miss Rungary. As the boys had vacated the old premises, their classrooms would be converted for use by infants. It was clear that these were but interim steps.

Raven resigned in 1930, paving the way for the revised proposals from the Norfolk Education Committee which were 'to establish a central mixed school at Wells which would accommodate the eleven-plus boys and girls from Wells school, Wells girls' school, Holkham school, Stiffkey school, Warham school, Wighton school and Binham school'. By 1933 it was estimated that there would be 279 children of that age peaking at 299 by 1935. Two new classrooms, a staffroom, cookery room, a dining room, a cloakroom for girls and 'offices' [toilets] were built at a cost of £5,300. The old school would have the capacity for 330 pupils, the new senior school another 280 places, making a total of 610 places. Finally, water closets (flush toilets), taking water from a well, were to be installed.

The idea of central schools came from government. They were to provide 'an improved general education of a practical character, sometimes with a slight industrial or commercial bias, for pupils between the ages of 11 and 14 or 15'. The school opened on 2 May 1932 and included pupils of 11 and over from the villages. There were now 300 mixed seniors, and 330 junior mixed and infants. Though children were now taught in mixed classes, segregation continued for other purposes. There were to be seven classrooms in the new school.[161]

The first head was John Bolton Aston from nearby Blakeney who managed the change. A pupil of the day described him as exercising 'a quiet and benevolent authority but... allowed no levity'. Another noted however that he made use of corporal punishment; he had an umbrella stand full of canes, both thin and thick ones. Younger boys were transferred back to the old school and older girls arrived. Women members of staff came with them, including Miss Thomson who

[161] NA. ED21/36560

taught cookery and housewifery and was to retire only in 1972. The new school experienced a broadening of its curriculum, including games – it had a sports field – and also rural science, a combination of gardening, and including a botanical garden and a woodwork workshop. Nature study of a scientific character was to be taught. The pupils would make plant propagators and wormeries in one discipline for use in the other. Streaming, by which a year group was divided between faster and slower pupils, was introduced.

The school's importance in the life of Wells can scarcely be overstated. Its main objective was to create literate, numerate and useful members of society; but it also had a health function. Termly medical inspections enabled the identification of patterns of disease, preventing their spread and treating their sufferers. The introduction of an eye clinic and regular visits of the school dentist would benefit generations of Wells people thereafter. Annual diphtheria immunisation must have been the means of expelling the disease from the town. The school was also the means of encouraging friendship networks amongst scholars and former scholars for years.

School was not the only world which Wells children inhabited. Even in school at playtime there was a separate world of games – hoop bowling, marbles, whip tops, impromptu ball games which owed nothing to adults. In the 1920s and 30s the streets were full of children whose world was Wells.[162] Listening to the wireless, as it was then called, required the use of earphones and there were not many such devices in the town; an invitation to listen to someone's wireless was an event worthy of record. The absence of cars rendered the streets safe for playing in. In summer until nightfall children played games in the street, annoying residents whose yards they hid in and on whose roads they played football. Their world included Sunday schools which almost all children attended, with their 'treats', local or

Girls' Friendly Society, 1927

[162] Jean Stone *Recollections of Wells* (1988) passim

latterly, by means of a bus journey, further away. There were concerts in the Church Room.

There was a wider world to explore: in the woods and fields, to Holkham Park and above all the creeks and the marshes whose pathways and crossing points would be well-known secrets. Family outings might include a picnic to East Hills or the beach.[163] The fact that little girls wore long skirts may have made adventurous trips more difficult for them but they were capable of getting them muddied after falling in a creek, only to face the anger of a parent who knew how few clothes there were and none to spare.

The memoirs of Geoff Perkins, local boy-made-good, tell of cockling, picking samphire and digging for clams, or 'babbling' in the dykes for eels. Pocket money could be obtained by offering a ten-year olds' services to local traders, cleaning and chipping potatoes for a local fish and chip shop; of picking up and selling pinecones for domestic fires; of weeding for a local farmer. Gang life was lively, often dangerously playing amongst the railway trucks and piles of beet on the quay or exploring the now-empty maltings, even climbing on the roofs. There was swimming in the hot boiler, a large pool some distance up Sluice Creek left by the outgoing tide. It was warm on summer days but cool in the hot sun and was frequented even by those who could not swim.[164] The two identified parts of the town, east and west, led to street fights between the children.

Family entertainment might include singing around a piano in the front room. Many houses had pianos and piano lessons for girls were popular. When the weather was good, and of necessity, even when it was not, people walked. People walked everywhere. For a small child to walk a several miles a day was normal. Those who lived on outlying farms or in nearby villages would walk into Wells or, if it lay along their path, use the train for part of the way.[165] The Wighton halt on the Wells to Walsingham line was opened in 1924 for just that reason.

This was also a time when children's organisations flourished. The church choir and the Girls' Friendly Society have already been mentioned. The free churches all ran children's organisations and all ran Sunday schools. The Sunday school anniversary was a great occasion for which new clothes were bought so that little girls would be paraded in their finery after the church service and have a picnic on the Buttlands afterwards.

The period saw the rise in popularity of Scouts and Guides, the two major branches of the young people's organisation invented by Boer War hero Robert Baden Powell and his wife Olave in 1914. It proliferated into groups for younger children, Cubs and Brownies. In Wells there were also the Sea Scouts which was a maritime version.

---

[163] Ibid.
[164] Geoff Perkins (2000) p.7,17-18
[165] Jean Stone, *Further Recollections of Wells* (1992)

7. A transport revolution

Steam lorry belonging to Granges

The development of road transport depended on a half-way decent road system, with tarred and gritted surfaces duly levelled by steam rollers periodically hired for the purpose. Little by little the minor roads were tarred. The railway had been the first competitor with cargo vessels, but railways were most efficient when carrying large numbers of people or large amounts of freight over greater distances; they also had limited availability. Whereas every village and every town was served by a multitude of roads however narrow and tortuous. What lay in the hands of authorities like Wells was the improvement of local roads; arterial roads between communities were the responsibility of the County Council.

The first lorries were driven by steam. This form of drive remained long in use, dirty though it was, because it was a proven technology and coal and water were readily available. Quiet in operation with good acceleration, they proved to be very popular. Their drawbacks were their heavy weight and the need frequently to replenish the feedwater which drove them. Tom Grange possessed a number, as did

Steam lorry outside Dewing and Kersley's mill

Dewing and Kersley. Their lorries could be seen carrying grain and flour both locally and to Norwich.

They gradually fell out of favour in the 1930s in favour of vehicles driven by petrol. The Great War had hastened the development of the internal combustion engine. Leslie Barker, demobilised from being an aircraft fitter with the Royal Flying Corps, joined his father in setting up a taxi business in town which quickly developed into a carrier enterprise, picking up supplies from as far away as London. The poor roads and lack of street lighting made this an adventurous enterprise. They once even delivered a corpse for burial in the big city.[166] Coal, as a bulky, dirty fuel, lent itself to transport by lorry and the various merchants took advantage of the opportunity. Because the coal came in by ship as it had done for hundreds of years, coal yards – Yarham's, Collers, Hayhoes and Claxton's – were mostly close to the quay. This trade would develop exponentially post-war. Enterprising hauliers picked up whelks from the whelk houses to take to Billingsgate market in London.[167] Tom Grange, who was to become a major presence on the town council, acquired some of the empty maltings

Sam Abel's Bedford bus used on the beach run

buildings for his lorries, hauling beet, lime and barley to and from local farms. It was estimated that there were up to fifty lorries and trailers, taking corn or barley to the breweries and vegetables to the London markets. Local carrying was of cattle cake from ships, coal and tarmac from the railway. In the autumn beet had to be dug, loaded and delivered, mostly to King's Lynn.[168]

The transporting of people provided new commercial opportunities. Travellers to Wells by train could be taken to the beach in one of the many taxis standing at the station. Larger vehicles, charabancs, or

---

166 Brian Barker and David Lowe *Norfolk Carrier* (2003) p. 15
167 Geoff Perkins, (2000) p.10
168 Perkins (2000) p. 22

buses which succeeded them allowed the transport of larger numbers. William Walden, who was hiring out ponies and traps in 1916, rapidly went into motor haulage and started a bus company. He offered furniture removals as part of this service. Samuel Abel ran a fleet of buses from his garage on the quay. The Dalliston family ran buses from behind Clarence House on the Buttlands. After a degree of haggling and negotiation over the fact that the Beach Road was not a public highway, Abel and Walden were eventually licensed to run a regular bus service from the station.

'Eight Ringers' outing to Mundesley

The advent of the motor bus generated a fresh form of leisure, the pub outing. Many of the pubs seem to have run trips usually to other seaside resorts, down the coast, places with more accessible beaches such as Mundesley and Yarmouth. The town band was taken on some occasions to loudly entertain travellers on board. A darts team might take a coach party. Some but not all were all male occasions well lubricated on the way and at the destination.

Petrol was initially obtained from the Shell depot at Burnham Market but quickly a rash of garages appeared, providing repair facilities

Cain's Garage on Polka Road in 1933

as well as fuel for the small but growing number of car owners. Before long there were several garages in the town.

GF Rose, the ironmonger, built his garage on Polka Road with its ornate frontage. George Turner Cain, down the road a little, called himself a motor engineer. Petrol consumption was poor but the growth in the number of garages, four by 1937, was due to the unreliability of the machines. Ready access to repairers was essential. Leisure driving was a luxury for a small but growing number of townsfolk.

Wells station between the wars

The railway was still pre-eminent. It could carry larger volumes of freight and greater numbers of people than the roads. Nevertheless the many railway companies often duplicated their lines and made long distance freight and passenger movement more difficult; amalgamation suited government which had in any case directed transport during the war. So, in 1923 the government compelled the railway companies to group together. Some of the companies lacked modern locomotives and rolling stock. Some rationalisation of lines and timetables was necessary. The London and North Eastern Railway, which included East Anglia, was the poorest of the 'Big Four' railway companies and the East Anglian lines were the worst served. The gradients on the Wells branch were quite steep, 1 in 77 in places, and required fairly powerful locomotives. The 25-minute schedule to Fakenham suggests that they were lacking. Six trains a day ran from Wells to Norwich in 1921, beginning at 5.55am. Returning in the evening were the 6.22pm and the 7.39pm which took just under two hours. The early train would get a passenger to London by 11.27am but there were no advertised afternoon or evening trains for the return.[169] Freight traffic consisted of two trains in each direction a day, one direct to Norwich, the other to Wymondham. The freight consisted of coal or fertiliser inwards and agricultural products outwards. Agricultural machinery came on flat wagons; fish was transported in special fish vans. Timber, drain pipes and other kinds of freight were transported from rail to road at intermediate stations. At one time an unusual item was fish bait, in the form of lug worms, sent to Yarmouth, Lowestoft and Southwold by passenger train. Barley and malt transport benefitted from the lineside facilities at Wells and Ryburgh. Milk went from Wells inland to North Elmham where United Dairies had a depot. Wells station possessed a loading dock for machinery including cars and furniture, facilities for livestock, horse boxes and prize cattle vans and a crane capable of lifting over a ton. Industrial sidings allowed waggons to be shunted to the flour mill adjacent to the station and to the lime works beyond Stiffkey Road.

Wells was in theory a junction, not merely a terminus; but not until the 1930s was the station rebuilt and the tracks re-laid so as to connect the Fakenham and West Norfolk portions of what had been previously effectively two separate stations on the same site. In the process, the huge arcaded south wall was removed and a more modest train shed built. Even so, there was no real provision for through traffic.

Not all traffic was motorised. Deliveries of goods to the door was still most often made by horse-drawn waggons: coal, bread, fish, cockles, winkles, shrimps, fruit and vegetables, milk, groceries, hardware, even ice cream. The lighter commodities were taken about by hand cart.[170] Children's church treats to the beach were still conducted by waggons lent by local farmers until the late 1920s.

---

169 Jenkins p. 60
170 Perkins (2000) p.23

8. Rumours and war

The idea that there would be another war appears early in the records of the day. Mention of a proposed 'Air Ministry Camp... in the vicinity of Wells' occurs as early as November 1937. Proposals for an anti-aircraft camp at Stiffkey are mentioned the following January. Soldiers arrived by train on a Sunday evening for training exercises and were conveyed there by lorry. By October 1938 the War Office was proposing to lease the Wells foreshore for an anti-aircraft range. The 1938 legislation, creating a network of fire stations across the country, was yet another straw in the wind. By early 1939 questions were being asked about provision for evacuees – children sent from dangerous areas of the country like London to relative safety. The council responded by saying that with an anti-aircraft battery close by and four aerodromes either in place or proposed within fifteen miles Wells was scarcely a safe place for children to be sent. By June 1939 ARP Wardens (Aid Raid Precautions) had been appointed, 12 in number. In August there was a blackout: all the street lighting was switched off. Others took their own precautions. Smiths were advised to sell off their now deteriorating empty buildings in the town because of 'the danger of the international situation' and to take advantage of any offers coming their way.[171] They did so.

Almost in the same breath, in December 1938, the council produced a five year plan for the town which included a new fire station, improvements to the sanitary arrangements for the existing houses, sundry road widening schemes, improvements to the water supply, capital works on the beach, the expenditure of the huge amount of £40,000 on new housing and £18,000 on a new sewerage system. Heavily divided as the council was, both politically and personally,[172] the plan represents a vision of extraordinary breadth. Presumably it was the work of Fred Rodwell, the council surveyor, but it was agreed without demur by councillors. In advance of the larger scheme, the lavatories in the houses on Mill Road were to be converted from earth and pail closets to 'a water borne system'. The houses on Gales Road were to be provided with baths, the water heated from the gas-fired copper in the scullery.

Meanwhile, the 1939 *Guide to Wells* showed no awareness of impending war. It described Wells as a 'natural holiday resort'. It was 'as nature had ordained her, assisted gently and very understandingly by

---

[171] F&G Smith *Directors Minutes* March 18th 1939 (p.148)

[172] George Turner Cain remained popular with the electorate, coming top of the poll, but unpopular with his colleagues on the council. Charles Ramm, son of Arthur, would be similarly adversarial.

the hand of man' although, by way of correction it was 'not too placidly rural': it had a boating lake, a nine-hole putting course, a beach and a cinema! Wells was apparently 'one of the quaintest in a county renowned for its quaint towns'. In truth it depended on which way you were looking.

This combination of plans for modernisation and the promotion of a coastal idyll was brought to a shuddering halt, not only by the war but by its long-term effects. Wells would not be quaint in the same way ever again, all to the good in the view of some. Some things would be hastened by the war. Electrical supply had only recently been installed in houses and already the Electrolux Company had offered a refrigerator on trial for possible purchase by tenants. Northfield Lane would soon get a supply.

Halifax bomber amidst the haymaking

Hostilities impinged upon the town in a quite different way from the first war. The reaction to the news of the declaration was instant if not premature. On 1 September 1939 a Food Control Committee was set up. It was realised that following the earlier war, food supply, particularly from across the Atlantic, was crucial. Children were instructed to carry their gas masks at all times. Discussions were soon advanced for the handing over of allotment land to local farmers. Restrictions on tenants keeping pigs and poultry on their gardens were relaxed. Tenants of uncultivated land would be threatened with the termination of their leases.[173] An instruction was received that iron railings be removed and the metal sent for use in making armaments. The council's initial response was that they had none, but the Schedule of Iron Railings produced at the end of 1941 shows that seventy-eight properties had surrendered their perimeter fences.

Men left for the forces, some of them having been in responsible positions in the town. Leonard Anderson, who had just been appointed as the first full-time Medical Officer of Health, left to join the RAF. His replacement Dr Irene Green, the first woman to hold the post, provided detailed accounts of the condition of the town. Her reports show the vanishingly small incidence of maternal mortality, a great change from former times. She also noted the rise in the incidence of tuberculosis, 21 cases. Henry Aldridge, newly elected chairman of the council, had gone to become a pilot officer. His post was kept open for him for a year after which James Blades was elected as chairman. He returned in 1946.[174] The school bade farewell to three members of staff, Tom Haywood, Alan Drury and Mr Smith, (the first two of whom returned after the war).[175] Some people found

---

[173] *UDC Minutes* Sept. 1939 NRO DC18/4/7

[174] *UDC Minutes* NRO DC18/4/7

[175] *Wells Central School Log book* Dec. 18th.1939; March 1942

Dennis trailer pumps on Station Road

themselves doubly employed: Miss Rungary, primary school head, became First Aid Commandant. More than 150 locals put on uniforms, from the Home Guard to the Observer Corps, ambulance crew and the Auxiliary Fire Service.

The fear of fire from incendiaries as well as from the effects of bombing caused the supplementing of the fire station's equipment with several more trailer pumps. These could be easily transported around the area needed by any heavy vehicle. In fact, they were not much needed. When the whole county was re-equipped sometime after the war, it was found that one of the engine pumps had had only 30 hours service in addition to drills.

The fear of imminent invasion resulted in the setting up of artillery batteries around the coast. Thus at Egmere the 57th Heavy Newfoundland Regiment of the Royal Artillery moved in, setting up two giant 9.2 inch howitzers of WW1 vintage close to Egmere farm. The target areas for these guns were the sea approaches to Wells and Holkham. Practice firings were terrifying and were restricted because of the risk of blast damage to nearby buildings. During one of the few practice firings, a local fishing boat was very nearly hit.[176] After sixteen months the Newfoundlanders left for overseas, being replaced by a British army regiment. It was then handed over to the Women's Land Army before becoming a decoy airfield for Docking.

Not everyone was convinced that the war changed everything. When the Ministry of Health wrote to the council postponing all further house building, Wells council at first resisted, seeking special permission to build more houses, but it was no good. The opposite proposal, to allow the return of families to houses condemned as part of the Clearance schemes, was again resisted but it happened anyway.[177]

---

[176] Len Bartram *RAF North Creake Egmere 1940-1947 a brief history* p.14
[177] *UDC Minutes* Sept 1939 NRO DC18/4/7

Building the air raid shelter on the Buttlands, 1940

In December evacuees began to arrive. There were some 144 of them, all from a Roman Catholic orphanage in Gravesend. Frederick Raven, long retired, was given the job of billeting them with local families. Mrs Dalliston of Clarence House was not alone in refusing to accept them on account of their religion. Some of the children were in poor health. Bed wetting was a problem. They were relocated elsewhere in the country in 1940. Preliminary plans were made for billeting the civilian population moving into the area from bombing. The Girl Guides were deployed to collect waste paper; they had collected over five tons of it by May 1940. Trenches and dugouts were to be dug to provide shelter against enemy bombers for those who would not get home fast enough, as if their homes would be proof against high explosives. More effective were the so-called Anderson shelters, named after their designer, which families were encouraged to build in their gardens from corrugated iron parts supplied by the council. These they could and did self-build and if sunk into the ground and covered with earth seemed quite effective, though they were never put to the test locally. Not a few folk took advantage of the offer. Some even went to considerable trouble and expense in building larger concrete structures in their own back gardens. Another device, the Morrison shelter, was named after the Minister for Home Security, Herbert Morrison. It consisted of a steel box big enough to put a bed in. Both were available free to any family earning less than £350 per annum. In addition a huge brick shelter was built on the Buttlands. It was not much used for its original purpose but instead became a place for illicit assignations by couples, and was latterly made into a static water tank for use by the Fire Brigade.[178] Two so-called trench shelters were built, one on Northfield Avenue, the other on Westfield Avenue. Shelters were no protection against direct hits but sheltering people below ground level would protect them from blast damage. There were blast walls at the entrance to the quay. Another shelter was built at the primary school. Gas masks were issued in quantity. School children had regular gas mask practice. Gas attacks never materialised though they were feared right to the end of the war. One macabre episode, not judged so at the time, was the testing of gas masks by sending 177 children through a gas van, presumably filled with some noxious substance, in order to test the masks. No one knew that gas vans had been used by the Germans to the opposite purpose before the war. The truth was that no one was sure what to expect, how to protect local people and keep them fed or how to resist an enemy

[178] *UDC Minutes* April 1943 NRO DC18/4/8

which might invade, but how and where no one knew.

Even though invasion was not predicted to take place in Wells, pill boxes began to appear at road junctions, to be manned by gunners against the eventuality that the worst might happen. An instruction was issued that no vehicular traffic was to move after sunset except on A and B roads. The pill boxes were built by Royal Engineers, billeted in what is now the Pop Inn at the west end of the quay. They built a pill box by the sluice on the Beach Road and subsequently constructed beach defences, tank traps and barbed wire entanglements replete with landmines.

Winston Churchill visiting the Queen Bee launch site, 1940s

Two six-inch naval guns were brought in and set up on Holkham Meals, peering over the dunes. Their crews, from the 65th Searchlight Regiment (Royal Artillery), were billeted in a camp in the Pinewoods. In the event they were not heavily deployed; they requested from the council a supply of deckchairs for use while not busy practising![179] For target practice they used a number of 'Queen Gull' radio-controlled target boats which were also based in the harbour. Their air equivalents were the 'Queen Bees', radio controlled modified Tiger Moths, which were launched by catapult from Weybourne. They would then be picked up by a coaster, the *Gertruda,* which was stationed at Wells.[180] Nearby, Langham was the base for aircraft towing artillery targets. The regular crump of guns firing at targets from Weybourne, Stiffkey and Wells could be heard for miles.[181] The tubular shaped targets were made of silk, a fabric which was highly enough valued for it to turn up illicitly as petticoats and in local children's clothing. As for bombing practice, the beach was littered with ex-London buses and taxis intended as targets. The need for secrecy both at the time and subsequently meant that there is no record of how often they were bombed but certainly there was a deal of low-level flying over the beach which continued after the war.

War office communications with the harbour ran in both directions. Frank 'Tender' Smith, as harbourmaster, was in receipt of instructions detailing how he was to deny resources to the enemy by the 'immobilization of plant, equipment and vessels'. It was however on the basis that any 'attempt at invasion will be defeated within a short period' so that essential parts should be displaced and hidden but not demolished. Warnings of invasion would be sent via the coastguard officer; port facilities were then to be immobilised, and ships sent to sea. Ships unable to leave would only be sunk in the last resort and only for the purpose of blocking the port.[182]

---

179 *UDC Minutes* April 1941 NRO DC18/4/8
180 Perkins (2000) p. 27
181 Woods p. 47
182 Robert Smith *Crossing the Bar* (Wells Harbour Commissioners 2018) p. 136-7

Wells was in a small way involved in the Dunkirk evacuation in 1940. Lifeboat coxswain Ted Nielsen took eight vessels from Wells to assist in bringing British servicemen from the French coast. Several were found to be too small and unreliable; there was in any case a shortage of fuel for the trip but at least they performed some service by transporting troops from the larger ships into Ramsgate harbour. Three boats, *Bessie*, *ACE* and *Rose* made the crossing. *Bessie* was apparently fitted with a twin Lewis gun and equipped with a bucketful of grenades and a gallon of rum. They were not successful in picking anyone up but Nielson was awarded the MBE for his efforts.[183] *Lucy Lavers*, a lifeboat temporarily based here and now permanently moored in the harbour, also made the trip. After the evacuation, Wells was one of the places to which displaced servicemen were sent.

During the air war that followed numbers of aircrew who had ditched or parachuted into the sea were lost. Of those who were saved, some relied on the lifeboats, though their efforts were supplemented by the four air-sea rescue vessels moored in the harbour. These fast boats, stationed along the coast, enabled several hundred men to be rescued either from certain death in the cold sea or from drowning. Records show that most days three of them would be at sea on both tides, a matter of five hours per tide, requiring two crews for each.[184] Altogether, over 2,000 men were rescued over the course of the war, several of whom came ashore at Wells. One such event took place on 7 November 1941 when six men were picked up out of the sea from an aircraft. The lifeboat crew were often put on standby, sleeping in the lifeboat house when bombing raids were launched from Lincolnshire so as to rescue crews of aircraft unable to make landfall.[185] In July 1942 Nielsen went aboard a Lancaster which had crashed into the sea in search of survivors. For this he received a Vellum award.[186] The *Royal Silver Jubilee* was proving the huge advantage that an engine conveyed.

The war, of course, brought an end to cross channel traffic and few vessels of any kind used the harbour. The only substantial traffic that the war brought was shipments of cement, some thirty-three of them, for the runways of the North Creake airfield in 1943. The severity of the dangers that lay out to sea became clearer as the number of wrecks multiplied, each marked by a green-lit wreck buoy. These were the casualties of raids by E-boats of the German Kriegsmarine which were deployed to attack the coastal convoys. London's power stations depended for their coal on supply vessels carrying it down the coast from the Forth to the Thames; they were an easy target for the E-boats, which were heavily armoured and capable of speeds up to 48 knots.[187]

Many elements of the life of the town continued, albeit under

---

183 Report of Dr WE Hicks 1944 – John Tuck (2014); Smith p. 144
184 Smith p. 138
185 Conversation with David Cox
186 Purchas p. 82
187 Dr WE Hicks in Smith (2018) p. 138

Lugger Yard clearances left to grow weeds

straitened circumstances. Others were left half-done. The houses in Lugger Yard and its surrounds, which had been subject to a slum clearance order, were left derelict and half-demolished; grass and weeds grew long in the yards. Some attempt was made to tidy them up and to demolish some of the empty properties. Other properties were, after some resistance, re-occupied for the duration. If not much could be done to tidy the town up, the bandstand on the Buttlands, which was in a state of dilapidation, was taken down and disposed of.

The local economy both suffered and benefitted. Rationing of most commodities, from food to clothing, meant privation; it also meant the growth of a black market. The building of airfields provided work. Tom Grange's lorries were deployed fetching sand and ballast from Wiveton pit for the runways and perimeter roads at North Creake, Langham and Snoring.[188] Civilian staff were required. Grange's lorries also picked up sugar beet in season from local farms to be delivered to Cantley or King's Lynn. A small boy might spend the day in a lorry cab with his father as it picked up loads from remote farms. At home fuel for cooking and washing was scarce. Coal was expensive. Driftwood was one source of fuel but so were the various coal yards around the quay from which the odd lump or two might be retrieved by small boys and even their parents Engine firemen were known to cast the odd shovelful of coal onto the trackside near a roadway. Great stews could be cooked in backyard coppers, lit early in the day. Butchers for the most part lacked refrigeration and cheap meat might have only the green bits cut off. One butcher was known to hang carcases in his outside toilet. Those who could obtained their meat from the land. 'We never ate butcher's meat in those days,' one fisherman's daughter opined. There were rabbits to be sure but also game of various kinds. Holkham was, after all, close by. What meat there

[188] Drivers included a seventeen-year-old John Tuck

was, of course, might be demanded to feed the troops. It would come on the hoof by train to Arthur Ramm's abattoir on Marsh Lane, and went out again in short order, presumably to the many camps and airfields. Curious children saw it come on the hoof.

Tractors had been in use for some years but in 1942 a combine harvester arrived at Manor Farm, courtesy of Lend Lease, in packing cases to be assembled on site. Flint's pre-war tractor had to be registered when war came; another was allocated for a total of £477 for both combine and tractor. Mechanisation did not reduce the labour force; war time production resulted in its more than doubling. Flint employed nineteen men in 1941, thirty-nine men the following year on his nearly six hundred acres.[189] Some would be taken by Sam Abel's coach to outlying fields as far away as Langham. Some would drive the Manor Farm dairy herd from one end of Wells to the other along Church Street and Burnt Street twice a day and would for many years to come. Later the cows would be milked by machine out of town at the old Field Barn. Flint obtained his first bottling machine the same year, ordering 70,000 aluminium caps for the bottles. They would last him a while. Until the coming of an electricity supply, machinery was driven by coal fired steam engines which would also be used for the sterilisation of the milk.

Apart from livestock, Flint grew wheat, oats and barley, peas and beans to feed the livestock in winter but also potatoes, mangolds, kale, swedes and turnips, clover, cabbage, lettuce as well as grass, both for hay and for summer grazing, all rotated on a four yearly cycle. Sugar beet became a major industry. The roots were to be delivered by train to the factories at Wissington, Peterborough and King's Lynn, returning with beet pulp mixed with molasses as animal feed.

Horses would continue to haul machinery; Flint had seventeen of them including two heavy horses. They drew ploughs, harrows and reaper binders; they were percherons, a French breed of draft horses. Horses pulled carts on the farms and provided deliveries in the towns throughout the war, leaving their manure in the streets. It was a horse town, strangely contrasting with the high technology which droned daily in the skies above. Sheep would be kept on the freshwater marshes to the west of the beach bank. Some crops, like potatoes, were still labour-intensive to harvest. The cutting off of trade with the continent required government direction and strong measures. Cotton was not to be had and flax, the only vegetable fibre able to be cultivated in northern climes was required to be grown. Apparently it could be used for the fuselages of aircraft and parachute harnesses as well as to make heavy canvas.[190]

Labour on farms was short, especially at harvest. Harvest time, which began around the end of July, coincided with the school holidays, scarcely an accident. Boys as young as eight would be employed on the now urgent business of getting the harvest in. Once the reaper

[189] Manor Farm records 1942

[190] Manor Farm Records ibid.

binders had done their job, the sheaves must be brought in and stacked. A nine-year-old boy might sit on a horse whose walking power in endless circles would drive an elevator to carry the sheaves onto a stack, awaiting the efforts of the man with a pitchfork on top of the stack to add to its height. The later arrival of the threshing machine, powered by steam in the early days, would turn sheaves into straw to provide bedding for animals and grain to be turned in to malt or flour.

Women performed many tasks, some of them requiring main strength once thought the preserve of men. Sacks of grain might be transported by sack truck for storage in Eastern Counties' huge bins by women no heavier than they were. The loss of men from farms caused the employment of Land Army girls. Conscription for unmarried girls and childless widows began as early as June 1939. It ended only in 1950. Civilian service on the land was an alternative to military service. Many people, men and women, in and out of uniform performed several jobs as part of a long day: home guard, teacher, transport driver and publican.

Once the Americans arrived in 1943, commodities once scarce to the point of being unobtainable might be traded off the base. Nobody doubted that American airmen died just as horribly as the British but their provisioning was on a different scale altogether. Scarce items such as nylons, chocolate, sugar, cigarettes and alcohol among other things, once off base, could be freely traded. Sam Abel's garage on the Fakenham road not far from the base was a helpful place of exchange. The Americans would stay long after the war and confer on the town an internationalism which would never depart. More of which later.

The schools continued with reduced staffing, an air raid shelter just a yard or two away from the primary school building. Church services carried on as did Sunday schools, to which most children went of a Sunday afternoon whether or not the parents had been in the morning. Sunday school anniversaries were still an occasion for the purchase of new clothes. Some parents would even take the trip to Price's in bomb-damaged Norwich, armed with their clothing coupons to buy a new dress and new shoes. Others would buy locally. A service in church or chapel including presentations for good attendance would be followed by a picnic.

Malting returned if on a limited scale. R&W Paul, whose plant in Ipswich had been requisitioned, took over the No. 18 Malting on the Glebe to continue production. Wells' traditional industries associated with grain and flour milling became more important and both Favor Parker and Vynne and Everitt were required to provide fire watchers to protect their quayside premises from incendiaries. Tourism, on the other hand, simply died. The town had become increasingly reliant on those who came seeking a holiday. Now, it was feared, retailers would no longer be able to pay their rates.

Fishing continued again on a small scale. Many young men had gone away to fight, leaving the fishing to their elders. Those remaining were able to take advantage of the absence of trawlers to engage in long-line fishing for white fish, negotiating their way through the narrow gap in the invasion defences to get out to sea. The beach was otherwise off-limits; the fishermen alone had permits which were inspected by a sentry standing on the beach bank. A few younger men were exempt as being necessary to the war effort, both as lifeboatmen and providing food for the people. So very few people saw Mosquito aircraft practising with dummy highball bouncing bombs off Holkham or the movements of military shipping on the horizon or the London buses and taxis standing incongruously on the beach.

The beach huts, those that had not been dismantled by their owners at the outbreak of war, were confiscated or, left untended, lost their roofs and doors in storms and filled with sand. Unexploded ordnance became a temptation to young children, some of whom, too adventurous for their own good, slipped through the barriers onto the marshes. The more adventurous were lucky to escape with their lives.[191]

Perhaps because of the number of local airfields, north Norfolk

RAF North Creake 1945

suffered several air raids. Air raid sirens were heard day after day. Flares were dropped prior to bombing so that it was as 'bright as daylight outside'.[192] Jean Stone, who wrote down her reminiscences of the war, recorded sirens going off almost every day in January 1941. By February, the number had increased to three or four each day.[193] Incendiary bombs fell harmlessly around the town in August 1942. Bombing, possibly intended for the railway station, was frequent and damage to houses caused by shrapnel, though mostly superficial, was clearly frightening. Low level dog fights were observed close at hand; a machine gun post was set up on the quay. The following year, three

---

191 Perkins (2000) p. 40

192 Lesley Jarvis (WLHG Newsletter) Nos. 72/3 an account of the effects of the war on Wells by Helen Lucy Hayes

193 Jean Stone (1988) p. 24

bombs were dropped on Market Lane, apparently without doing any damage. On 18 August the harbour was brought to a standstill by a raid deploying so-called butterfly (antipersonnel) bombs. A team led by Captain Edward Bourne detonated thirty-one of these particularly unpleasant devices, doubtless saving the lives of those who might be attracted by their brightly painted colours. Bourne was awarded the George Medal. His sergeant, Fred Fisher, was awarded the BEM.[194] Bourne was not the only man to be decorated.

Frank Taylor DSM, subsequently harbourmaster from 1956-74

Frank Taylor, whelk fisherman from early years, joined up and was awarded the DSM for his exploits with the Naval Intelligence Department. His job was to land French resistance fighters in occupied France. On one occasion, escaping capture, he had to be smuggled back to England via Algeria. After the war, he first served as a Trinity House pilot in Wells for five years; then in 1956 he became harbourmaster and second lifeboat coxswain – in which capacity he was awarded a bronze medal. Taylor retired in 1974. Charles Platten got the DCM after having walked 250 miles across the Libyan desert dressed as an Arab where he was able to observe enemy positions. Billy Butters got the MM as did Robert Churchill; William Deeks got the DFC; Graham Cawdron got the DFM; Robert Turner Cain, son of George, got the DSO; Margaret Flint, who joined the ATS at the age of 18, was made sergeant-in-charge of a platoon of drivers and vehicles and was employed by Royal Engineers Eastern Command in charge of invasion defences; she was awarded the BEM. Others were mentioned in despatches.[195] David Coke, second son of the Earl, died, shot down over Libya in 1941 having survived the Battle of Britain, and was awarded a posthumous DFC.

In all, thirty-three men of the town died, including Ted Nielson's son, Theodore. Another was the head teacher's son Harry Eggbeer, a RAF navigator, whose Short Stirling was shot down in 1943. Three were buried by the Burma railway; six died in the navy. It was to be expected that from a seaport many would serve afloat: over 60 did. Two brothers, Norman and Kenneth Barrett, died on board ship. Kenneth died when his destroyer the *Curacoa* was sliced in two by the liner *Queen Mary* while escorting her in an incident that was to be hushed up for years. Such were the perils of warfare when safety was sacrificed to the need for secrecy (and the perceived need to maintain morale). George Grimes was killed on board the Everards merchantman *MV Aquiety*. Many men served in the Far East of whom

---

[194] Supplement to *London Gazette* December 23rd. 1943; www.royalengineersbomb-disposal-eod.org.uk/george_cross.html
[195] Geoff Perkins *Some more Wells people* (2009); *Heroes and Fighting men and women of Wells-on-Sea* (undated)

thirteen are known to have been made prisoners of war after the fall of Singapore, four of whom died.[196] Billy Burgess served in both World Wars and survived.

Of the several airfields the nearest was RAF North Creake, which was actually at Egmere just up the road from Wells. From being a decoy base in 1941 it became operational in December 1943 when it passed into the control of No. 100 (Bomber Support) Group. Its important function was the operation of radio counter measures to reduce the escalating losses of RAF night bombers due to the ever-increasing effectiveness of the German air defence system. The story is worth telling.

Allied bomber losses were becoming unsustainable due to the development by Germany of sophisticated radar tracking devices which enabled both anti-aircraft guns and night fighters to identify and destroy bombers. The aircraft of North Creake were deployed to reduce that threat. They did so by scattering small aluminium strips known as Window to simulate, on German radar screens, a force of bombers heading in a quite different direction from that of an actual raid, so diverting fighter aircraft from them. A small number of planes flying backwards and forwards in a creeping pattern could simulate a much larger force. The other device, known as Mandrel, was a bulky jamming system carried on board which prevented the Germans from knowing the dispositions and intended destinations of much larger numbers of actual bombers. Both Window and Mandrel were used to dramatic effect on D Day when the destination of the D Day landings in Normandy was concealed while spoof squadrons created the effect of large numbers of aircraft setting off for Calais. During the base's short operational life seventeen aircraft were lost, eight Stirlings and nine Handley Page Halifaxs. The Halifaxs, more powerful than the Stirlings which they superseded, could carry bombs as well as radar equipment and were able to remind the Germans of our capacity to inflict damage by air.

There was accommodation at the airfield for nearly 3,400 personnel who were dispersed around the perimeter of its three intersecting runways. The airfield buildings bestraddled the Fakenham Road which nevertheless remained open to the public, except when a Halifax ran off the runway and caught fire when it hit a tree.[197] RAF North Creake ceased operations at the end of the war. Though the runways were removed, the control tower still exists, having been converted inside into a 1940s period house.

The influx of troops was not always a blessing. The council reported wanton damage in the town in January 1942 caused by troops billeted in Holkham who had come into the town for the evening. While admitting their vital presence, a protest was made. Later the council was

---

[196] Perkins (Undated) The book contains the records of over 400 men and women from 'Wells who served during the War as well as group photographs of the various uniformed home services.
[197] Bartram passim.

asked to participate in a scheme for the treatment of venereal disease. Drunk soldiers caught fighting in one of the local pubs were banned from the town. A deserter living in a disused van outside the town was apprehended for burglary. [198]

It is impossible to know at what point people began to lose their fear of losing the war. Government propaganda created an impression of inevitable victory which some believed. The impression given was that everyone could do their bit. The Spitfire Fund raised £275 9s 1d in January 1941. A year later, following Warship Week, the town was asked to adopt *HMS Rockingham*, a US vessel which had been transferred to the Royal Navy. Unlike the spitfire, the warship was elderly, unseaworthy, saw little action and was sunk not long afterwards. Likewise, with government encouragement, even as early as April 1941, plans were being made for the reconstruction and redevelopment of the town 'to be implemented after the termination of hostilities'. Produced by the recently constituted North West Norfolk Joint Regional Planning committee, a draft planning scheme for Wells was presented to the council. It proposed the zoning of land in various categories. There were to be private open spaces (mostly land belonging to the Earl of Leicester), public open spaces such as the Buttlands and Church Marsh; land zoned for different densities of housing development across the town; industrial zones and land on which building would be permanently restricted: in short a comprehensive delineation of development. Interestingly, within the last category, areas not to be built on were the two entrances to the town, from the Egmere and Burnham directions, both of which were developed in recent years. [199]

Like all plans, what happened was not quite what had been proposed. On the other hand, council housing was now seriously on the agenda. By the autumn of 1943 the council was already in negotiations with Holkham for the sale of fourteen and a half acres of land adjacent to Northfield Lane for building. Sixteen houses were proposed, which rose to thirty. By the following January, the proposals were being formulated for 'Post-war Reconstruction' and in September a committee was formed to coordinate the building of sixty council houses including forty 'pre-fabs', the long awaited sewerage scheme, new street lighting, replanning the beach and playing fields, new gas provision, an industrial area, an extension to the cemetery and new refuse collection arrangements. A new Fire Station was proposed, to be built between the Polka and the Flour Mill. The adoption by the County Council of the 1944 Education Act was noted with approval. The Act raised the school leaving age and re-organised secondary education.[200] The council seemed to have become a different creature from that which had opposed or fought over almost all improvements to the town no more than half a dozen years earlier.

---

[198] Lesley Jarvis (ibid)
[199] *UDC Minutes* April 1941(insert) NRO DC18/4/8
[200] See below p. 149

As D Day drew near convoys of American army lorries supported by tanks would arrive, driving down the quay, chewing up the roadways with their tracks, their crews throwing packets of gum to eager local children. The girls, it is said, had never had so much choice; the Regal cinema became a mecca for off-duty servicemen. The story goes that on the eve of D Day, many of the service personnel from Egmere were in the cinema and a message was flashed onto the screen requesting them to return to the base immediately[201]. Earlier in the war the manager succeeded in emptying the place by interrupting the film with the news that German paratroopers had been dropped at Blakeney. The Park Cinema, which functioned only intermittently, sought a reduction is its rates because of its winter closure, without success. The presence of troops was bound to create problems from time to time.

1941 plan showing proposals for the comprehensive redevelopment of the town

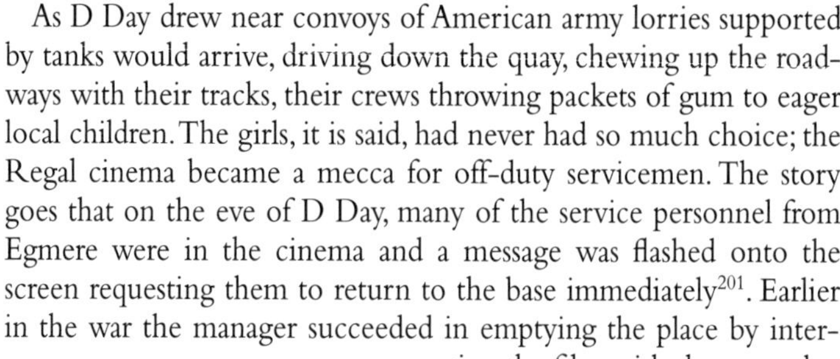

Following D Day the council proposed the fixing of street lights 'as soon as present lighting restrictions be released'. In September the Reconstruction Committee was set up with its huge agenda. Remarkably in retrospect, though the war in Europe was still not won – the Ardennes counter-offensive by the German Wehrmacht took place in the winter of 1944-5 – and though the country was bankrupt, spending plans were laid for the remaking of the town and their implementation in short order. In February 1945 the East Anglian Electricity Supply Company was asked to quote for the provision of 79 electric street lamps in the town. It offered a seven-year contract at £327 6s, the lamps to be lit from half an hour before sunset until midnight. The estimated cost of the sewerage scheme, including connection to every house, was £12,670 – though toilets, inconveniently, were to be downstairs! The final figure was to be almost four times this amount. A contract was made for making good the street surfaces following the sewerage

[201] Bartram p. 19

works, at a cost of £2,155. A county scheme for the implementation of the 1944 Education Act was circulated.[202] All of these works required long-term loans but this seemed not to deter the council.

House building entailed the biggest investment: almost on VE day, the council formulated its detailed proposals for the new houses: there were to be ten each of three-bedroomed, two-bedroomed and two-bedroomed pensioners' bungalows on what would be known as Northfield Crescent. The original forty pre-fabs were reduced to twenty, and subsequently to ten. In the meantime the council concerned itself with the under-occupation of its properties and with empty houses. Government, both central and local, did not fear to impose its priorities on people's domestic arrangements. A government circular drew attention to the requisitioning of unoccupied houses; eight properties in the town were requisitioned. A number of tenants whose houses were too big for their needs were required to exchange and given notice to quit, under a Victorian statute now repealed, if they refused.

Looking to the future, and in early anticipation of the tourist season, the council fixed new fees for the beach car park and charges for the boating lake. A beach manager with staff was appointed. A bus service to the beach was arranged.

With the same object in mind the council showed its dismay that the Air Ministry continued to use the air space over the beach for aerial exercises. This would not encourage sunbathers. The official reply was to the effect that no other exercise area could be found, that they would take place only over a stretch of beach 400 yards long and on forty-eight hours per month but that these would be divided into one and a half hour operations in morning and evening, in other words, four times a week. The council sent a telegram requesting that 'no further exercises shall take place pending further correspondence.'[203] It demanded that East Hills should cease to be used as a firing range.

There was real enthusiasm for all marks of war to be removed. Barbed wire was taken from areas of the marshes and, with assistance from the personnel of High Cape RAF camp, the beach was to be cleared of barbed wire as soon as the War Department released it, which should be 'as soon as possible'. A request that a mine sweep of the beach be conducted by the War Department was denied. A notice on the beach denying liability for injury would have been of little consolation. Fortunately the mines which had been laid in the early days of the war were removed by the Royal Engineers Bomb Disposal unit. Because the maps showing their location had been lost, the task was hazardous. In the event two men, Corporal Amos Henshall and Sapper Josiah Potter, were blown up on Holkham beach in December 1944 by these mines.[204] The sudden closure of the RAF camp in Au-

---

[202] See p infra. p149
[203] *UDC Minutes* ibid. 24th July 1945 NRO DC18/4/8.
[204] http://www.roll-of-honour.com/Norfolk/NorfolkCoastalMineClearance

gust 1945 left the council once more responsible for beach clearance. POW labour was used at first. A local company was asked to quote for the removal of the tubular steel tank traps. The road block, one of a number, at the west end of the quay was also to be removed.

In dribs and drabs demobilised service personnel began to return to their jobs and resume their lives. No one talked in those days of post traumatic stress disorder but plenty of them must have found it very difficult to adjust. Jack Jordan, who fought with the Chindits in Burma behind Japanese lines, was haunted by his memories for years afterwards. He had been left for dead behind enemy lines and owed his survival to local native people. His daughter told how he would wake in the night at home, still fighting in his dreams. Many others would live with their dark memories, refusing to talk about them. Dennis Frary was captured in the abortive Arnhem raid. Dennis Hewitt was among many men of the Norfolks who were captured at Singapore and worked first on coal barges and then on the Burma railway. Latterly he worked on a dysentery ward, routinely burying his comrades until Hiroshima, after which his captors simply left and he was forced to fend for himself until relief arrived. He died in 2001. Tom Haywood and Alan Drury resumed their duties at the school. Then there were men like Chick Smith who had served as merchant seamen both before and during the war and who resumed their seafaring lives, in his case working for the Everards line thereafter. He had been the captain of the *MV Sedulity*, delivering high octane fuel and troops on D Day. He would one day return as harbourmaster.

The war changed many things. The building of the airfields changed the landscape, taking land out of production, dislocating rural roads and bring large numbers of service personnel from elsewhere, including the United States. These changes could in theory be reversed. The war also introduced much more centralised ways of taking decisions. Mechanisation on farms and the development of road transport would significantly mark a break in the notion of the traditional village. Small town life would be more and more influenced by urban ways of thinking. The war had stopped some things, such as television transmissions. But Wells would no longer be an agricultural community or even, though few could foresee it, an industrial town. It would fight hard to retain its identity.

Part 3 – The making of the modern town

1. Managing the peace

The war had fostered the growth of a massive bureaucracy controlling most aspects of people's lives. The incoming Labour government, with its tendency towards direction, simply took advantage of the system which the wartime administration had created. Control of housing was one aspect of this. No housing developments could take place without the approval of the Ministry of Health. Underoccupied houses could be requisitioned by the council for allocation to needy families. Labourers could not be recruited from one area to another whether for defence works or for housing building without government approval. This constrained local initiative but did not prevent it; some decisions were made which would now be regarded as harsh. Tenants could be made to move if they were under-occupying a property. So, a resident of Westfield Avenue was made to move to a smaller property on Bases Lane even though she had cultivated her garden in Westfield Avenue and the house had been recently redecorated. It is possible to understand the pressure on the council to find accommodation for families but also the importance of tenants' feeling that the place where they lived was their home. Another example of this was the directive from the Ministry of Health that 'isolated properties' which had been declared unfit and were due for demolition should be taken down 'only where it is essential'. Post-war austerity bit deeper. Street lighting was discontinued in 1947 'during the present emergency'. It would gradually be restored, but only in winter for some years.

Plans are just words on paper; when decisions have been taken still nothing has yet happened. It must have been a relief for people to see the building works begun on Northfield Crescent; originally planned in 1937, it was nine years late, now with its own sewage treatment works. These new houses, still pretty basic by our standards, were of a different order from the cramped cottages so many still lived in. As the Medical Officer of Health, Leonard Anderson, reported, newly returned as he was from the war, the previous proposals to remove unfit and often verminous housing from the stock in the 1930s had only very partially been implemented. Of the 44 houses proposed for demolition since 1936 only 16 had been demolished; 11 stood empty while 16 had been re-occupied. In addition in January 1939 a further 35 houses had been declared unfit, most of them north of Theatre Road and yet a further half dozen houses were thought to be unfit for children to live in. Thus, Anderson proposed to undertake a survey of the whole housing stock of the town, which reported in the June of 1946. He noted not only the presence of grossly insanitary houses but also empty houses which constituted a danger. Enough was known for there to be no need for further delay. Thus, new houses were allocated even before they were complete and the year saw yet further proposals for houses: 10 more bungalows on Northfield Crescent at a cost of £9,050; four more houses were proposed later in the year; then a further 16 houses on the south side of Northfield Lane and 10 more houses on its north side, including six four-bedroomed houses. The council even experimented with a different kind of prefabricated house, the so-called Airey house, constructed of concrete slabs, set ship-lapped to form the exterior envelope, of which six were ordered to be built on what would become Northfield Waye.

The building of numbers of houses as a single project was conceived as being the role of local government. The idea that houses might be built by private developers at no cost to the council now began to be spoken of. Central government would not consider the idea. A proposal to allocate a plot of land east of Ship Cottage on East Quay was rejected by the Ministry of Health 'at the present time' when application was made. The priority was for public housing. So, in December 1946, the council agreed to the acquisition of land for 20 more three-

Building council houses on Mill Road

bedroomed houses in Northfield Lane and another 20 four-bedroomed houses. This total would shortly be increased to 50 in total.[205]

The achievement was impressive. A press report noted that in four years Wells had built 120 new bungalows, flats and prefabs and re-housed 140 overcrowded families – a new house for every 18 of its population, which was compared with London's record of one house to 81.[206] The scale was of course very different. Altogether, since the passing of the 1890 Act, the town had built 206 council houses. It was to build nearly 150 more. It was a remarkable effort, but it produced its own growing pains. The sewage works for Northfield Crescent was designed for 30 houses. By 1947 it was already serving 64 houses and a further 70 were planned. Plans had been laid long before

205 *UDC Minutes* March 1947 NRO DC18 /4/8

206 *Sunday Express* August 28th 1949.

for the building of a completely new sewage works; now the need was immediate. Likewise, the water works, built 12 years before, could no longer deliver the amount of water required for the new town. Wells needed to be connected to a 'regional scheme' of water supply. Fred Rodwell's report proposed new mains, some of them duplicating existing mains and others providing a means of getting water to the new houses. The underlying theme was that, important though local democracy was, there were practical problems which were only susceptible to solutions on a wider scale.

The council again pressed the case for private housing. The minister's contention that such plots 'would be required in connection with the council's future housing programme' was met with a proposal to allow private development 'having regard to the number of houses already built and the fact that there were various people in the town needing accommodation which they were willing to provide free of expense to the Exchequer or the rates if a licence to enable them to do so is granted'.[207] Arthur Ramm, possibly in anticipation of further development, had bought land off Mill Lane which he proceeded to turn into a small close of houses. It was to be the first of many, some much larger. Having laid down the roadway for a close of houses, he sold it off in plots, one to Mr Dalliston whose bus company was run from nearby.

It was now 30 years since the first council houses had been built. The first houses were now pretty antiquated and poorly provided for by current standards. Those built in Gales Road in the 1920s seem not to have been well built from the start. Lacking electricity, food had to be cooked on a coal-fired range and washing done in a brick copper. Now piecemeal requests to turn ranges into open fire grates and to convert brick coppers into gas-fired ones were granted. The provision of electric cookers meant that a better electricity supply was needed; it was nevertheless agreed to in all new houses. The new prefabs were to be equipped with refrigerators. Thought was given to providing every council house with a 'fridge'.

The town's first telephones had been installed 20 years before but few private individuals owned (or rather rented) one. The request went out for public kiosks to be installed, one at the beach, the other at the railway station. Two more, one by the Post Office and another by the Buttlands, followed. Emergency use was all that was envisaged.

Among the many things that had been suspended or delayed during the war was the democratic process. The elderly James Blades had taken over the chairmanship of the council when Henry Aldridge was called up in 1939. The council was to remain in being for the duration, observing Blades' 80th birthday in 1946, until the elections of that year saw a sea change in membership. Apart from Blades, Sam Peel did not stand. He was to devote his attentions to the work of the County Council. The controversial George Turner Cain was to return

---

[207] *UDC Minutes* April 1948 NRO DC18/4/8

as chairman; he was almost the only councillor from pre-war years to serve. He retired in 1949 after 24 years as a councillor. Ernest Flint had been elected to the council in 1943 on the death of Butcher. Harry Farrow and Henry Aldridge were the others. Flint was elected as chairman in 1947, remaining until 1951. He died in 1957.

The new council would have to deal with further changes, some the result of changing technology, some the result of the growth of government. There was the economic future of the town to consider. The provision of electrical street lighting was now being implemented across the town without controversy. The proposed nationalisation of the gas industry was less well received, particularly as it left the council with a deficit which was to have been covered by future profits and would now have to be covered by a rate increase. The District Auditor was tart in his comments. The beach and its adjacent marshes, which had been wrecked by the work of the various arms of His Majesty's forces, were to be the subject of vigorous reclamation. A beach sub-committee was appointed; the leases from the Earl of Leicester were to be renewed; the playing field, which had been ploughed up for agriculture, was to be returned to the town and laid out as grass; the golf course was to be levelled and its greens reseeded. The council was to order the repair, renewal and replacement of the refreshment facilities at the north end of the Beach Road, to organise the re-letting of the beach hut sites, to put the boating lake back into use and obtain boats for use upon it. A camp site was to be opened and Sam Abel's bus service from the station to the beach was to be resumed.

Given the lack of accommodation for visitors in the town and its general condition, the emphasis on the recovery of areas adjacent to the beach was understandable, as was the continuing reluctance of the War Department to take responsibility for the amounts of rusting metal that remained, stretching from the lifeboat station to the western boundary of the town. While the council was now reluctantly getting on with the job of removing the various beach defences, the mines required professionals and Eastern Command was contacted for their assistance. In the event, unexploded ordnance would be uncovered more than fifty years later.

A honey cart in Litcham

For all this, without a doubt the replacement of the town's completely inadequate sewerage system was the biggest enterprise, after housing, to be undertaken. The sheer cost, now raised to an estimated £51,000 (£1.76 million by today's values), gives an indication of its scale. It would be borrowed on long term loan. The plan was to replace the present 'combined' system by which, at best, waste water and solid matter were led into the harbour, either by pipes or open channels, by what was called a 'separate' system. Sewage was still collected from soil or pail closets or found its way to cesspits. Only the sewage from the council estate was treated in any way. The new 'separate' system would allow rain water to empty into the harbour while foul water and solid matter would be taken to a sewage treatment works to be built to the north of Freeman Street. A pump on Knitting Needle Lane would be built to take the waste from the south side of the town over the hill. This, it was hoped, would end the bi-weekly night visits of the 'honey' carts and, more important, raw sewage would no longer be discharged into the harbour.

The first stage was the building of the sewage treatment works on the west marsh which was not without problems. Perhaps because of the nature of the ground, settlement occurred up to eighteen inches (nearly half a metre) in the works, no doubt improving the fall but threatening the stability of the works. The second stage was laying of new sewage pipes to replace the nineteenth century brick sewers, many of which were partially blocked, if not by rubbish, then by vegetation. The new system was to reach every house in the town which was, of course, much smaller than it was to become. But finally the individual houses were to be connected to the street sewer, beginning with the council houses. It was determined that toilets would be downstairs and located in the coalhouses of their properties. When it came to private houses most householders, though not all, were keen to take advantage of the new provisions. The landlord of the Eight Ringers on Church Plain only reluctantly agreed to be connected; others were to concede years later. As connections were made for each street the consulting engineer, Vernon Maslin, reported it to the council. Cesspools and septic tanks were by-passed and removed. The hope that all houses would be connected by 1952 was however, vain; it would take until 1966 before the last of the pail and earth closets were replaced by water closets. The night cart was sold for £20 but had to be replaced by a motorised vehicle and a pump for emptying cess pits. The hoped-for completion of the system suffered another delay when the 1953 floods submerged the pumping station up to the roof. Many houses were forced to revert to the pail system. The major works were finally signed off in May 1953, at a cost of £44,329 an overrun of £2,154.[208] After further delay it was announced that sewage waste

Laying sewer pipes Burnt Street 1951

[208] *UDC Minutes* May 1953 NRO DC 18/4/9

would no longer be discharged into the harbour but for a short while effluent from the slaughterhouses would continue to be so. Not everything could be done at once and the cost of replacing earth and pail closets over the succeeding years would never be computed.

To take the story further, by 1965 many more houses had been built and the predicted summer increase was a third of the winter population, as a result of which the treatment works were said to be overloaded. The costs of an upgrade were then estimated at £48, 000 to £50,000.[209] Subsequently, it would require a two million pound investment in 1993 to cope with the predicted trebling of the population in summer and to rebuild the treatment works which were in such danger of overload that it was feared that there was danger to safe beach bathing and to the ecology of a sensitive and important area of biodiversity.

The process of regionalisation and its consequence, the reduction in the powers of the council, continued inexorably. Wells had only just pre-war had a full-time Medical Officer of Health. It was now decided that Wells would become part of No. 8 District whose full-time officer would cover Docking, Walsingham and New Hunstanton, though the office would remain in the town. Dr JC Johnson was appointed to the post. Standards were undoubtedly becoming higher and with some reason. A report on the slaughterhouse in Staithe Street noted that the slaughterman's apron was 'filthy putrid' and that the bodies of two animals had been found left on the floor of the slaughterhouse, one having suffered from peritonitis and the other from tubercular abscesses.[210] All good fun!

As the town got its gas lamps replaced by electric street lighting, little by little the houses did so too. Gas was inherently dangerous. In 1948 the gas works rather spectacularly exploded on 1 December, nearly killing the gas manager. He crawled out of the wreckage while townspeople imagined that they were being bombed. The gas leak was plugged and the supply was rapidly restored but the works now provided much less for light and more for cooking and heating. The cooking and heating requirements would increase.

Some signs of the war lingered on. The Stiffkey AA Battery continued until 1948, causing complaints from cockle gatherers and worm diggers at the restrictions imposed upon them because of the needs of firing. Langham RAF station closed in 1947, though it was re-opened during the Korean War.

The ending of the war meant that the risk of fire was much reduced but the organisational changes made would be permanent. The county council took over the fire service. Some items of equipment at Wells were recalled and the station was left with a trailer pump and a towing vehicle. Later the station would be equipped with a water tender on a Commer chassis. Rodwell, who had been sub officer since 1927, retired in 1950 and was replaced by Harry Gorringe. He

209 *Wells Urban District Council – Report on the Sewage Works.* 29th December 1965
210 *UDC Minutes* July 1947 NRO DC18/4/8

was in charge when a large fire occurred at Stratton's Granary on Standard Road. It was also during his time that the Brigade was called out to the fire at Walsingham church.[211] The station moved to Burnt Street in 1966. Gorringe was replaced by Stanley Pett in 1960, he by John Porter, and he by Peter Walsingham. The fire service, like the lifeboats, continued to call on the voluntary efforts of local people.

With war had come rationing; the peace did not bring it to an end. Wells people were much better off than many in the country because of the presence of game and fish. In the fields around about were pheasants and partridge, some of them legitimately obtained; rabbits were obtainable at any time of the year. Fishing restrictions were lacking. Most people kept their own chickens and some kept a pig. Poaching continued. Groceries were a different matter and presented both opportunities and problems. It was wise to keep in with the shopkeepers.

Almost nothing was pre-packaged in those days. Most commodities came in bulk: sugar came in sacks, butter in tubs; cheese, flour, lard, dried fruit, oats, pulses and spices came likewise in sacks, tubs or crates to be cut up or weighed out and packed by the shop. Vinegar came in huge bottles. Bacon came as a side. Before the age of polythene, everything was wrapped in paper or sold in so-called sugar bags. Candles were needed for those in council houses who had no electricity upstairs; blacking was required for cooking ranges. Regulations governing supplies meant that only a certain amount of each commodity was supplied to cover the ration to which each person was entitled: two ounces of butter, eight ounces of sugar per person per week and so on. Inevitably there was some slippage and some bartering: petrol in exchange for sugar; pipe tobacco for fishing boat fuel.[212] The ending of rationing in 1954 brought about the gradual opening up of shopping; but the habit of keeping in with shop owners to secure commodities, which were often still in short supply, continued. Home delivery, once almost universal, by bike and by van, continued for many years.

Like every other part of Wells life, and that of the nation, developments in education, long envisaged, had come to a standstill during the war. Teachers were called up to fight. Those who were left behind had heavy expectations outside of school placed upon them.

Mr Eggbeer, who had taken over as head of the secondary school in 1940, was now faced with a new educational regime across the country, the creation, as a result of the 1944 Education Act, of a divided system of education. This would make of Wells a modern secondary school, as it was first called, designated to receive pupils from nearby village schools as well as those from Wells who had not passed the scholarship examination for entrance to the local grammar school in Fakenham. Hailed by some as the brave new order, in the view of others it condemned those who failed the 'scholarship' to leave school without any kind of qualification while those who passed could go on to obtain

[211] Nicholson p. 36ff.
[212] Alison Christmas interview with Derek Styman November 2001

certificates with which they might enter university or teacher training college. The raising of the school leaving age to 15 by the same Act meant that village schoolchildren could no longer be contained in their local schools which had no room for an extra year; they must go to Wells. So in 1946, twelve 14 year olds arrived from Blakeney. In the following September 33 children between 11 and 14 arrived from Cley and another 77 from other schools.[213] In 1948 94 children were admitted, 17 of whom were unable to read. The HMI report of 1949 was critical of the school and of the head. Of Eggbeer it said disparagingly that 'his leadership should also be more definite and inspiring'.[214] He was known as a head teacher who latterly rarely left his office; he was often seen with his leg up, the result of chronic gout. Of the children the report said that 'it was difficult to discover whether what was so well recorded in the notebooks was known to the children.' The inspector recorded that by now ten village schools sent pupils to Wells at 11 and a further five 'unreorganised' schools sent pupils to the school at 14.

The concern of Miss Rungary at the primary school was that her charges should, as many as could, go to the grammar school in Fakenham. For this reason, she would each year select a small group for extra coaching that they might improve their chances. Not all held such high ambitions. Many boys were wanted for work on farms and in the absence of compulsion would not be in school much after 13. In the 1950s, the truant officer, Mr Hawke, made his weekly visits to the houses of those for whom education presented no open door to the future. One girl who refused to go to school even at the age of 14 found herself sent to a children's home, not simply for the duration until she reached the age of 15 but for three years, way beyond the term of compulsory education. Such were the mores of the education establishment.

There was also a resistance in some families to sending children to a school in another village. The transfer at 14 from village schools which lacked the capacity to keep them longer was a compromise widely practised across the country. There were now 281 pupils on roll.[215] As to the quality of the teaching RE (Religious Education) came in for adverse comment; the act of corporate worship was 'perfunctory'. The subject would increasingly be taught by non-specialist teachers such that it became marginalised. But the work of the teacher responsible for 'retarded children' called for special mention; under her 'kindly and sympathetic guidance the children make steady progress'. The school's teaching was streamed between A and B, there being between twenty-five and forty in a class. The Inspector must have been somewhat fearsome, commenting that under oral examination children were 'strangely silent and tongue-tied'. As in earlier days teachers were described as 'over-directive' not allowing for enough

---

213 *Wells School Log Book* 1946
214 HMI Report Wells Secondary Modern School May 1949
215 NA ED109/9010/5

free expression.

In the year following the report the school population grew from 281 to 364 which, in eight classes, meant an average of 45 pupils per class. There were in fact 108 in the top two forms. In spite of the lack of space Eggbeer created three extra forms and managed by 1952 to have built three extra classrooms. In 1960 North and South Creake were added to the list of feeder schools making twelve in all.

The division at eleven was held by some to be unduly harsh, fixing the career chances of children on the basis of a single examination. Mr Eggbeer and Miss Rungary's successor, Mr Clarke, was to oversee the implementation of a series of modifications to the system. In 1952, the first stage of the 'scholarship' had 41 candidates entered, of whom 17 took the second stage. Twelve were successful, ten of whom went to Fakenham. As for those already at the secondary school, some were judged to be 'late developers' who could take an examination to allow entry to the grammar school in each of their first two years; those who were borderline were allowed a second or third chance with further tests. Those who made the transfer were in single figures and those who did so lost a year, being placed in the first form of the grammar school. Children might also transfer at 14 to King's Lynn Technical College in order to continue their studies. In 1953 eight pupils passed the College's entrance examination.

In one extra-curricular subject a qualification was obtainable. Mr Rounce, who was appointed in 1951, had a passion for bee-keeping. He was permitted to establish six hives at the bottom of the field by the railway line. A bee-keeping club was founded which flourished for some years until his departure in 1958. Its members might obtain a national qualification. The enthusiasms of other teachers can be evidenced by the existence of other clubs: an electric club; a geography club, a sketch club, a chess club, a history club and a brass band. The school took part in inter-school sports which raised standards by raising aspirations. One pupil, Carol Lee, distinguished herself as a sprinter at several of these events and went on to be entered in the All-England School Sports representing Norfolk.

Communications in Norfolk had always been something of a problem. A problem with bus transport was the weather. 1941 was a bad year for snow but, even without anything else falling out of the sky, 1947 was worse. The snow began to fall on 7 February and, even with the high proportion of children living in the town, the attendance had fallen to 24. There was some relief by the 18th of the month but snow fell again and it was not until 12 March that the roads were completely clear; the last bus to make the journey was that from Walsingham. Until then, even when some of the roads were open, school would finish at 12.45pm to ensure that the children got home. There would be other winters when drifting snow would defeat bus drivers. 1958 was another one such. A later head would lament the fact that whether the school remained open was in practice made by the bus companies rather than by himself.

2. The port – opportunities and disasters

Like much else the harbour had suffered neglect during the war. The quay wall adjacent to the old lifeboat station was badly eroded; some of the stone blocks needed replacing and the wall outside the old lifeboat station needed to be built up. The harbour commissioners' derisory income, partly derived from car parking charges and partly from harbour dues, was barely sufficient to pay for necessary repairs. The harbour tramway appears not to have been much used. The horses had gone. Instead, their wheels were eased along the track with long rods. Negotiations were even begun for the removal of the rails and the making up of the roadway; the council did not expect to contribute to the cost but neither did the railway company: another impasse.

Ex-US army lorries in service on the quay after the war

Meanwhile, coastal traffic was slow to resume: three coasters in 1946, six in 1947, two in 1948. 'Foreign ships seldom enter Wells harbour' wrote the Medical Officer of Health in 1949. Some wheat went to Scotland and barley to Suffolk. Exports were all grain. Eastern Counties Farmers and Borough & Strattons both had granaries in the town. Grain was barrowed on a narrow plank from the quay onto the ship in sacks, the contents then emptied into the hold; it was a precarious and sometimes dangerous occupation. Between September and December, when fertiliser came into the port, the quay was a busy place. The fertiliser came in hundredweight paper sacks to be lifted out of the hold by crane. Kainit, a salt-based fertiliser which came from Wismar in East Germany, normally arrived in bulk and was lifted from the hold by Tom Grange's crane equipped with a grab. He hired local fishermen and bait diggers to load or unload the holds.[216]

[216] Richard Seeley Coaster: *Photographs at the Port of Wells-next-the Sea* (Wells undated)

The last steamer to come into Wells harbour

Everards' spritsail barges were gradually replaced by diesel coasters. Wells pilot Frank 'Tender' Smith's last job was escorting the coaster *MV Assidity* out to sea on her way to Antwerp in January 1956. There were still occasional visits from steamers. The *Vic 55*, an early visitor, had been built during the war as a supply vessel for naval vessels; steam was the logical choice of power at a time when coal was readily available while oil was in very short supply. She was probably the last steamer to enter the harbour.

The recovery of the town's commercial life received an unexpected

Loading bagged grain by barrow in the 1950s

blow in the form of the east coast floods. Wells had always been subject to flooding; the great storm of 1897 carried vessels onto the harbour tramway. Tides are the work of the mysterious forces of sun and moon, of wind and weather. Spring tides, as every sailor knows, come not seasonally but every fortnight when the twin forces of sun and moon in alignment pull the seas more strongly. If coupled with strong northerly winds, a tidal surge down the narrowing length of the North Sea exposes the Norfolk coast to the risk of sudden and severe flooding.

The most devastating of such events in modern times took place on the night of 31 January 1953. 307 people died in England and many more were saved by the heroism of rescuers. In Wells the west bank of the channel was breached in three places, while floodwaters came also from Burnham Overy where the banks were breached; the sewage treatment works were put out of action as a result.[217] The *Terra Nova,* a wartime air sea rescue boat which was used by the Sea Scouts, was left high and dry on the quay wall. A breach in the east bank let water up the old creek, flooding the railway station, past the church and as far as Two Furlong Hill. The largest breach was where the old channel used to flow out to sea from Holkham. Houses and shops on Freeman Street were wrecked; hundreds of pine trees were uprooted and many of those which remained died from standing for days and sometimes weeks in salt water. Hundreds of farm animals drowned, their bloated bodies lying on the sodden fields and on the marshes for days afterwards. Grazing of animals on the marshes had ceased during the war but had resumed thereafter. Mr Harrison of Warham had three hundred bullocks and four hundred sheep there.

Tom Grange (left) directing operations after the 1953 floods

[217] Letter dated 17th. Feb. 1953 printed in WLHG newsletter 26 p. 4

Terra Nova being tipped back into the quay after the surge had set her down on it

Warned of the impending high tide, he was too late to save them.[218] The golf course and the playing field were lost, as was the boating lake.

Tom Grange, who was also chairman of the Urban District Council at the time, set about organising the repairs to the beach bank which was undertaken with the help of Dutch engineers. Armies of people lined the bank armed with shovels trying to fill the gap but each tide washed away much of their work. The town was brought to a halt, including the school. Alan Drury, craft teacher at the school, who was a local town councillor, took time off school to do salvage work in the days immediately following the inundation, clearing up the mess and recovering what household goods could be re-used. For months afterwards the school became a distribution centre for foodstuffs, among them oranges and lemons, sent by the Italian Red Cross. It is a reminder that the homes of the school's children included some houses left awash and stinking and their parents lacking in food as well as reasonable habitation to sustain their lives; and this for months after the tragedy. A Flood Relief Fund was set up which, by October, had raised and spent the sum of £16,995 distributed to householders who had lost their belongings, small traders who had lost their stock, and for the redecoration of houses and repairs to business premises.[219] Insurance companies do not feature largely because most folk, including probably all the tenants, were uninsured. The *Terra Nova*, which had been left on the quay for some weeks, was finally slid into the water but her timbers had dried out and she sprang a leak. Rapidly towed to the East End and beached, she was left to rot slowly into the mud having never sailed again. According to Dr Hicks it was months before the breaches were finally stopped up and more than a

[218] Tom Grange in *A Wall of Water* (Masque Community Theatre 1985) p. 26
[219] *UDC Minutes* Oct. 1953 NRO DC 18/4/9

year before the bank was fully restored.[220] A tide level recorder was installed by the quay which stands to this day. High tides combined with adverse weather continued to cause problems. The 1968 winter tides severely damaged beach huts; the summer tides of 1969 caused less damage but were still a matter of concern. It was feared that the beach bank would be overtopped so that consideration had to be given to raising it.

MV Antelope *unloading fertiliser, September 1961*

The revival of the harbour's fortunes in the 1960s owed much to the change in agricultural practice post-war.[221] There had been an exponential growth in agricultural production, both dairy and arable, very much dependent on artificial fertiliser and animal feed which could be obtained cheaply from abroad. Barkers, who had opened a ship brokerage in King's Lynn, set up in Wells, taking over the handling of these cargoes. Favor Parker likewise had bought the Granary in order to go into importing animal feed. Kainit was a rich source of potash useful for treating both grassland and beet fields; it came from East Germany. In September 1964 the *MV Nederland* arrived in Wells with 380 tons of the stuff intended for Seamans of North Elmham; it then loaded at Favor Parker's wharf 400 tons of barley intended for Hamburg. The market had found a niche which Wells was to exploit over the next nearly thirty years.

Coasters double banked in the 1980s – EDP

[220] *Wells School Log Book* 1953; Smith (2018) p. 204ff
[221] See chapter 5 infra.

That year 34 ships brought in fertiliser and animal feed, taking out grain. In 1967 the number of vessels doubled to 73 ships bringing 5,000 tons in and taking out 3,000 tons. Kainit was used for the sugar beet; fishmeal more widely. Incoming bulk cargoes were unloaded by crane and grab directly onto lorries into Barkers' temporary storage at Great Snoring or to Favor Parker's feed mills at Stoke Ferry.[222] For a short while outgoing vessels carried peas and sugar beet pulp but latterly ships mostly left in ballast, that is, empty. Any grain to be exported was delivered on board ship in bulk via elevators, or else via Favor Parker's suction hose. It would have been dropped into a pit behind the Granary and poured into its bins.

In the first six months of their brokerage operation Barkers dealt with 64 vessels. Of those only two carried cargoes of barley outwards, one to Kirkwall in the Orkneys, the other to an unnamed port. Animal feed and fertiliser continued to be the mainstay. By 1982 the trade had increased yet further so that there were that year 258 inward movements, almost all departing in ballast, or empty. At the height of the trade as many as eight vessels lay in the harbour, double banked. Locals were employed in unloading; some became crew. The Fleece on the quay was an effective recruiting agency; some went on a single trip, others for a number; men would join the crew of vessels headed for Dutch and Danish ports: Rotterdam, Hirtshals, Kiel, Thyborøn or Wismar, mostly across the channel, a complete change from the pattern at the beginning of the century. Less well known was the requisitioning of vessels to carry armaments for transhipment to Ireland for the MOD. Local seamen were recruited for the task but

Bill Newstead, 'Boy' Court, Capt Francis Moeller, Brian Barker and Myrtle French celebrating fifty inward trips by the Danish vessel Tramp *into Wells*

[222] Records of Barker and Sons Ltd.

were not allowed to assist with loading or unloading.

Ports are liable to be volatile places. They suffer the frequent arrival of seamen from different parts of the world seeking what pleasures they have been deprived of at sea. Some of those who stepped off the boats in Wells were from Germany, Holland or Scandinavia; some were from the former Portuguese colony of Cape Verde; others, of course, were locals. The deaths of two visiting sailors who had stayed too long in the pub, drowning in the harbour as they sought to rejoin their vessels, was not widely advertised. The babble of foreign voices could be heard late at night, often combined with the sound of breaking bottles, and even heads. People avoided the quay at such times. Contraband of different kinds could be purchased. The oldest profession was practised; some were brought in by bus.

Some ships became old friends. The *Tramp* out of Thyborøn in Denmark visited the harbour so often that its fiftieth visit was marked by a presentation by the mayor, Myrtle French. Its captain, Francis Moeller, became a familiar figure in the town. He married a lifeboatman's daughter. In all *Tramp* would visit Wells eighty times until she was lost in the north Atlantic in 1983. Happily her crew were saved and Moeller would occasionally bring his new vessel, the *Othonia,* to Wells. The Sully brothers' fleet, all with names beginning with Subro then adding names beginning with V – *Viking*, *Venture*, *Valour*, *Vega* and so on – were frequent visitors. Based in London, they most often made the short crossing to and from Rotterdam.

Harbourmaster Chick Smith with Function

The flood of January 1978 found the town better prepared than in 1953. The flood itself was a fraction lower than it had been in 1953. More important there was no loss of life along the coast; but the devastation was still considerable. Many vessels were lifted onto the quay, smashing into each other, including the 300 ton coaster *Function*. One fishing vessel, *Strandline*, was carried through a breach in the bank and came to rest in the fields beyond. The North Point Bank which had been breached in 1953 came within an ace of being breached again; it held – just. The beach bank was severed in two places just where the old creeks had entered the channel.

This time it was Charles 'Chick' Smith, son of Frank, who as harbourmaster was to take charge. The difference wrought by technology was dramatic. In 1953 men were employed weaving withies into hurdles against which lorry loads of clay were dumped. One lorry fell into one of the breaches and was never recovered. The making good of the bank took months as we have seen. Now RAF helicopters were deployed carrying sandbags from the lime works, some 70,000 tons, supplementing the work of the lorries. An impediment was the arrival of crowds of sightseers, 'ghouls' as some locals called them, who came to see the show; their presence was not welcomed. Horrendously strong winds hindered the helicopter trips, their work being initially undone by each succeeding tide which opened the breach again; several barges were sunk into the gaps. It was a Dutch dredger hired in for the purpose which pumped thousands of tons of sand from the main channel that made the difference. From there several bulldozers pushed the sand into appropriate mounds to create the new bank. Once the water had been fully excluded work could begin on rebuilding the Beach Road which, amazingly was completed by the Whitsun holiday. Over £1.6 million was spent on the repair of the damage. Looking somewhat bleak, the Pinewood caravan park was open for business by the summer tourist season that year. [223]

Rebuilding the west end of the quay, 1982

Lifting *Function* back into the water constituted a major logistical challenge. Smith hired one of only two cranes in Europe capable of lifting her back into the quay. However, the weight of the huge sixteen-wheel crane, in addition to the weight of the vessel, had damaged the quay, causing subsidence. The works to repair and improve the quay included the digging out of the surface and filling with reinforced concrete. Plans were in place by October to extend the beach bank by some means across Freeman Street using a movable steel gate. A proposal to build a six-foot-high wall joining the east and west banks was thought to be too damaging to the commercial and visual amen-

[223] Smith (2018) p. 204ff

ities of the area. The low retaining wall had been erected in 1961. The flood gate was put in place in 1979. Then, in 1982 the quay wall, built in 1845, was extended using steel piles northwards to the harbour office. More steel piles were sunk to form a new wall running southwards along Beach Road and a moveable barrier was built to protect the west end of the town from further flooding. In 1987, the other end of the quay, Tug Boat Yard, would be tidied up by the rebuilding of the quay wall and the laying out of a grassed area for sitting out, replacing a much more ambitious scheme for providing extra moorings on the quay because of growing concerns about sewage emanating from leisure boats moored in the channel. The money was found by the district council. [224]

The near loss of *Function* did not deter the trade, but there were other problems more routine and of longstanding. One was the silting up of the harbour which made entry and departure difficult. Vessels ran aground for several reasons: some skippers would arrive a day or two early while the tides were still small; or southerly winds would hold the water back; sometimes skippers were known to lie to the pilot about their draught because they wanted to get into the harbour at all costs; some were plain unlucky. Sat on the sand they were mostly re-floated by the next tide but sometimes it could take four or five days before they could get away.[225] Because the harbour entrance was so difficult, and constantly changing, the port's pilotage was very important. Several locals assisted the Trinity House pilot Albert 'Boy' Court in boarding incoming vessels to bring them to the quay.[226] They had then to be turned around to tie up facing seawards. This could be achieved by driving them into the beach bank by the old lifeboat station so that the still incoming tide would carry the stern round until the vessel lay parallel to the quay wall against

Coasters stranded in the channel waiting for the flood tide; it was a frequent occurrence

[224] WTC Minutes Sept 1987 The cost of Tug Boat Yard rebuilding was to be £36,000.

[225] Richard Seeley *Coaster: Photographs at the Port of Wells-next-the-Sea* (Dawrich undated)

[226] Albert 'Boy' Court. a sprat fisherman from Kent, was assisted by local boat builder James Case, fisherman Tony Jordan and John Crook, chandler of this parish. Case subsequently became the pilot.

which it would be tied up. The old alternative was to rely on a post sunk into the edge of the marsh to which a bow rope would be attached to achieve the same result.

For the pilot to board an incoming vessel as she came over the bar remained hazardous. In heavy seas reaching the side of the vessel safely, much less climbing the rope ladder lowered over the side, could be a matter of life or death. Trinity House ceased to maintain a pilot boat after the loss of its vessel in the 1978 floods. The *Sea Quest*, privately owned by Tony Preston, was replaced in 1989 by the remarkable steel boat *Ni-Tricia*. She was built by her owner Nigel Hingley in his back garden in Chesterfield, and brought to Wells by road. With her powerful engine, she was able to act as a tug to tow vessels in or sometimes to push them off the sand into deeper water when they got stuck. Hingley subsequently bought an old coaster, *Wallbrook,* which sat in the channel for some years, that he used for dredging shingle to be graded onshore and sold as aggregate. Occasionally when another coaster ran aground, *Wallbrook* would come alongside and unload part of the coaster's cargo so that the now lightened vessel could make the quay.[227] Hingley also built a boat trolley which ran on rails and which could be hauled up by means of a diesel engine above the water level when work needed be done on a vessel's hull. It meant that fishing boats could be maintained and repaired locally instead of being taken to Yarmouth or Fosdyke. The boat trolley's usefulness declined, its engine was removed and it was finally cut up in April 2019. Vessels are now lifted out of the water by the harbour's hoist.

Increasingly the process of unloading and loading became mechanised. The suction hose attached to the gantry of the Granary enabled bulk cargoes to be emptied into the many bins inside, but it often be-

Sheets put up to minimise dust created while unloading, 1980s

[227] Alex Tuck (ibid)

came clogged and, in any case, could only work on one vessel at a time. The company's two cranes would deal with the rest but had the disadvantage that they produced clouds of dust which blew up the roads to the inconvenience of locals. Huge tarpaulins were rigged on steel posts to contain the dust with some degree of success. Methods of loading and unloading continued to improve. To deal with bulk cargoes a bobcat, a small, motorised truck with a shovel attached, was lowered into the hold to push the cargo into piles where the grab could pick it up. When cargoes came in sacks as in the case of fertiliser, they could be stacked on pallets which could then be moved by forklift truck. These improvements speeded up the process of unloading which was particularly important in a port with a limited tidal window when vessels could enter or leave. Time was money and the quicker unloading was achieved the better, though it reduced the number of stevedores required. The storage facility at Snoring was another source of employment for local men. It was said that more money was made from storage rather than from unloading ships.

The 1984 miners' strike brought an unexpected disruption. Wells, like a number of other small, non-unionised ports, experienced a short-lived growth in the coal trade that year, in this case by a third.[228] However, miners' pickets arrived to confront local men, casual labourers, who were unloading Dutch coal from coasters arriving at the quay. The encounter was violent but short-lived; one vessel was turned away, leading to the cancellation of the shipping contract. The vessel went instead to Mistley.

The ending of the coastal trade came quite quickly and took the port authority and indeed the town itself by surprise. In truth the problems were becoming insuperable. A joint meeting of the various

Albatros *unloading soya in 1995*

[228] Tony Lane, *Foreign Fuel, Foreign Ships and Disorganised Trade Unions an alternative interpretation of the Defeat of the Miners in 1984-5* Work, Employment & Society vol.10 (1996) p.68ff

parties, the Nature Conservancy, Rivers Authority, the County Council, the harbour commissioners, and four members of the town council was presented with the problem that as boats were getting bigger the task of dredging the channel was becoming more difficult; there was no way of disposing of sand and mud dredged and no money to do a proper job. The income of the harbour commissioners would not cover the cost of major works. Whereas they might find £7,000 or £8,000, the estimated cost of the work was in the region of £300,000.[229]

It was a combination of changes in regulations, the economics of small vessel transportation and the unavailability of the harbour to larger vessels that brought about the demise of the trade. Most of the vessels were broken up; a few went to ply their trade on inland lakes abroad. Barkers ceased operating as shipping agents in 1988. By 1991 only fifty-five vessels came. In March 1992 the *Othonia* was the last motor vessel bringing cargo to Wells, leaving the *Albatros*, a Dutch sailing barge now familiar to Wells visitors, to continue until 1996.[230] She was to return, at first offering leisure trips and subsequently as a floating pub and restaurant. She had first come to Wells in 1986.[231] Another sign of the times was that in 1939 almost all the vessels carried a British flag. By 1954 most were Dutch. German, Dutch and Danish vessels predominated by the 1960s.

The 1990s were to be a quiet period in the life of the harbour. The cost of road haulage precluded the revival of the coastal trade even if the problems of siltation could be overcome. The possibility of attracting vessels working on the North Sea oil and gas fields lay open should finds be near at hand. As a fishery harbour it still maintained full port and harbour functions but was now used mainly for leisure boats, sailing and motor cruisers. Its income from these and from car parking enabled it to improve its buoyage to a standard exceptional for a port of its size.[232]

---

229 *WTC Minutes* Sept 11th 1989

230 PR Jarvis *Port of Wells Shipping Register 1939-1996* (unpublished)

231 She was due to return after a refit in 2022.

232 Christine Abel in *The Turn of the Tide* (ed. Ian Scott (2005) p. 56

3. Lifeboatmen and fishermen

Lifeboat Cecil Paine *with Ted Nielsen, coxswain, and crew*

Ted Nielsen saw out his service in 1947, having taken over the new twin-screwed Liverpool type lifeboat the *Cecil Paine*, which came on station in 1945. The *Cecil Paine* was the subject of an abortive escape attempt by seven German POWs who stole a lorry, broke into the boathouse and tried to start the engines. Realising that they had no chance of launching her, they abandoned the attempt and were arrested as they returned to the lorry.[233]

The new coxswain of the *Cecil Paine* was Billy Cox. For his part in rescuing five men from the Turkish steamer *Zor* he received the thanks of the Institution on vellum. On 18 May 1955 *Zor*, which was making for Hull with a cargo of timber from Finland, rolled in strong winds causing her cargo to shift. She began to list badly, causing baulks of timber to cascade into the sea and leaving the lifeboat in danger of being holed by them. *Zor* ultimately sank, having had the rest of her crew saved by the Sheringham lifeboat. Lifeboats often worked in conjunction with each other. [234]

The two lifeboats were to work together the following year when the collier *Wimbledon* began taking on water into the fore-hold thirteen miles off the Norfolk coast on her way to London from Sunderland. The major part of the rescue was performed by the Sheringham boat, but having lifted eight men from *Wimbledon*, including the dead captain of the vessel, the assistance of the Wells boat was called

---

233 Robert Maltster *Saved by the Sea* (Terence Dalton 1974) p. 241-2
234 *Wells-next-the-Sea Lifeboat* – a history (2001) p.12

Lifeboat crew who went to the aid of the Savinesti

for to bring the doctor and the dead man ashore and to take extra fuel to the Sheringham boat, *Foresters Centenary. Cecil Paine* came out again to escort *Foresters Centenary*, now somewhat storm-damaged, into Wells harbour.

In 1965 a new boat, *Ernest Tom Nethercoat,* came on station. David Cox, nephew of Billy, had been coxswain since 1960 and was to continue in that position until 1986. During that time the lifeboat was engaged in call-outs, 'shouts' as they were called, which tested her to the limit. She was the last open boat to be stationed at Wells, though latterly she had a collapsible canopy over the cockpit. Exposed to the weather, her crew stood off the *Sea Gem*, a collapsed drilling platform, for 21 hours, attempting to rescue crew members who it was believed were trapped below in their now sunken quarters.

Not all shouts ended happily. A helmsman would stand at the wheel, often washed by continual breaking waves, navigating only with a compass and a watch. Only in 1977 was radar first fitted. It mattered a good deal that the crew were all fishermen who knew the waters well. In 1978 the lifeboat went out to the motor fishing vessel *Pilgrim* in danger of breaking up while under tow at the mouth of the Wash.

The next February the call-out was to stand off the Romanian freighter *Savinesti*, which had lost power and both of her anchors. The weather was appalling: forty-foot breaking seas, a force 12 hurricane, and a snow blizzard. The lifeboat remained on station for eleven hours, ready to take off the crew should the *Savinesti* founder. Finally relieved, she turned for home. Sailing in such seas with a following wind risked being broached – turned around to lie abreast of the waves and so liable to be capsized. A drogue was deployed to slow the boat down as she slid down a wave to be released as she climbed up the next. Without radar – it had been damaged by the sea – she

Six members of the Cox family and a Stephenson (first from right) – lifeboat crew 1960

overshot Wells, finding herself off Brancaster. She eventually got back to Wells and as she came towards the bar her crew found a lone fishing boat, John Ward's boat *Strandline*, with all its lights on, awaiting them in order to guide them into the harbour. The crew could scarcely walk when they disembarked and it was several days before some of them could make proper use of their fingers. The *Savinesti* incident was a stark reminder of the essential community spirit in the lifeboat service and the considerable risks taken by volunteers in a boat sometimes dwarfed by mountainous seas.

The deceptively dangerous nature of the sand shoals was revealed the following April with the loss of the fishing vessel *Concord* on the west sands at Blakeney. In spite of the efforts of both the Sheringham and the Wells boats, five lives were lost.

The lifeboat crew, having run out of Grimes, who had all of them retired, were for a while mostly members of the Cox family, brothers,

Old and new – Ernest Tom Nethercoat *was replaced by* Doris M Mann of Ampthill *in 1990*

fathers and sons.[235] The last two cousins, Alan and David, retired in 1986. David was succeeded by Tony Jordan who had been his number two for a number of years. A fisherman too, his boat was the former Grimes boat, *William Edward* and before that *Sally*, after whom he named his daughter.

His term of office however was cut short by his reaching retirement age and in 1989 he handed over to Graham Walker, another fisherman, who was to take on the replacement boat in July 1990, the slightly larger but much faster Mersey class boat *Doris M Mann of Ampthill*. Her arrival necessitated the reroofing of the station. *Doris Mann* was the first vessel to have a covered cockpit. As lifeboats had become faster and more sophisticated, so the advent of GPS and other electronic aids made call outs to large vessels less frequent. It became more likely that leisure craft, fishing boats and even walkers cut off by the tide would be the subject of shouts. In 1981 it was the *Sarah K*, a fishing vessel off the Woolpack buoy. In 1992 it was the yacht *Cerealia* which was saved. In 1996 it was the fishing vessel *Remus*, which, having run aground, had to be taken in tow in gale force winds. In 2000 a family was rescued from the yacht *Candy*. Allen Frary was by this time the coxswain. Another fisherman, he retired to Scotland in 2018 after nearly twenty-one years.

The launch of a lifeboat was at one time a heart-in-mouth occasion for the families of the lifeboatmen and also a very public event in the town, announced by the letting off of a maroon rocket. When few men had cars, they ran or more likely cycled down the Beach Road, wanting to be among the first seven who would form the crew. If a regular crewman arrived after a reserve he would displace him if he arrived before the launch. For townspeople, hearing the hiss of a maroon followed by a dull boom as the warning device exploded lifted all eyes to the heavens and out to sea to where the breakers formed an unbroken line of surf on Wells bar. The maroon launches were brought to an end by the advent of radio pagers so that no longer would anyone know that there was a shout other than those around the crew who would run off even in the middle of a council meeting. There was no question that they would go.

William Edward, a *wooden whelker, in full sail*

The sea however has not changed. Dramatic rescues still happen and people can drown very easily; fishing boats can run into mechanical difficulties; leisure yachts can be

[235] Audrey Cox – film interview for Rescue Wooden Boats (RWB archive)

threatened by worsening weather. Anyone can run out of fuel.

Most of the lifeboatmen were fisherman or were from fishing families. But if the lifeboats had changed so had the fishing. The war had disrupted the fishing, allowing stocks once again to recover. Some of the boats had been built pre-war and some had scarcely seen the water. *Bessie* had seen service at Dunkirk but others like *Sally*, *William Edward*, *Knot* and *Harvester*, big wooden whelkers, bought respectively by the Grimes and the Coopers, came into their own. Some had a dipping lug sail; *Harvester* was a gaff cutter.

The whelks themselves were still caught in baited hexagonal pots made with tarred rope woven onto iron frames. Shanks were longer each with thirty-six pots which had to be brought aboard, emptied, re-baited and stacked before being dropped back over the side. Each trip would entail the hauling of six shanks. It was a three-man job. Hand hauling, which was hard on the hands, was increasingly replaced by the use of mechanical haulers originally using separate engines; Austin 7 car engines were favourite. Later hydraulic haulers were driven from the boat's engine. However, the capstans that they drove were at the stern of the boat and the lines easily became entangled around the boat's propeller, entailing the dangerous task of climbing overboard to free them. Whelks were bagged at sea and brought onshore using wooden yokes. Later they would be loaded onto trolleys and taken either to the whelk houses, there to be boiled,[236] or they were shipped live elsewhere. After boiling they would be removed from their shells at the various little facilities in the town, notably at Grick's factory, behind the Bowling Green or shipped to Boston or King's Lynn.

Preparing whelks for sale

Whelks found their way by railway inland to Manchester, Birmingham and Leicester, many of them to Billingsgate market in London.[237] Some were used as bait by the long-line fisherman along the coast and were sold to them as such. The closure of the railway brought lorries into use to take them to the nearest railhead but it was easier to drive to London directly. Then EEC regulations required that they be taken elsewhere for processing rather than boiled locally. It may have been more hygienic but it could result in a long delay before they could be transported to King's Lynn for processing. The sheds found other uses, in-

[236] Deryck Featherstone *Wells, a kind of paradise* WLHG newsletter No. 41 p.9
[237] David Cox – conversation.

cluding the keeping of lobsters in vivaria prior to sale; some took on more gentrified uses by local artists.

The boats, still made of wood, were larger than crab boats, between twenty-four and thirty feet long. Built by Emery's or Johnson's of Sheringham their double-ended wooden hulls were made with oak ribs, larch planking and a mast of spruce. Some of the sails were made in Wells by a member of the Grimes family. Some carried more than one sail, a foresail and a main, a dipping lugsail. Shallow and broad-beamed, they were good sea boats designed to be hauled up shingle shores. Even when engines came in many fishermen could not afford them or preferred sails and oars as more dependable. Engines entailed a modification of the design with a heavier stern post to accommodate the Belfast Barker motors. Wells boats had not much changed in design since the days of their predecessors which had undertaken the Dunkirk trip. They had just become bigger and not necessarily safer for all that. Lacking electric power and any aids save a compass and a watch, even engines were hand-cranked. No-one had a radio. Thus

Unloading whelks from Spero II *on East Quay*

when his boat sprang a leak from a plank cracked by savage seas only a bilge pump or a bucket saved whelker Lawrence Money from the loss of the catch, the boat, his own life and that of his crew. Judging the best course against the combination of wind, tide and sea conditions would add or take off an hour and more to or from the duration of the trip home and whether the crew would get home at all.[238]

But they were almost the last in the line. Emery's last wooden boat was built in 1957; *Harvester*, his last boat for Wells, was built for Sid 'Custard' Cooper in 1951. They were superseded initially by decommissioned lifeboats of which there were several in the harbour. *Ann*

---

[238] Written account by Lawrence Money

Isabella, a Liverpool class lifeboat, served as a whelk boat for 'Diddy' Cooper for some eighteen years.[239] The Coxes had *Anne*, *Elizabeth* and *Spero II.* Other larger lifeboats proved unsuitable.

The predilection for nicknames was widespread though it didn't apply to everyone. The Coopers sported names like 'Custard', 'Diddy' and 'Demon' but grandfather Russell never acquired one. Only 'Loady'– Charles – Cox got a new moniker among his family. The origin of such names was sometimes obvious, sometimes obscure.

Cortina*, one of the newly arrived trawlers from Faversham*

'Blucher' Jarvis apparently went about waving a toy sword as a child. 'Spitter' Hubbard's name – he was an engine driver – speaks for itself.[240] And just as those families had come from elsewhere more than half a century before, so new men, new families with new ideas, would come to join the fishermen: Leggatts, Courts, Nudds, Wards and Fulfords among others.

Alf and George Leggatt, brothers from Whitstable, came in their wooden trawlers seeking the errant shoals of sprats which seemed to have deserted their home waters. Their vessels, *Romulus*, *Remus*, *Cortina*, *Faustulus*, *Sea Hawk* and *Leona* became familiar in the harbour.[241] One of their skippers, Albert 'Boy' Court, was to become a lifeboatman and pilot. Using electronic aids and otter trawls, they achieved some 400 tons of fish a year pair trawling – two vessels sailing side-by-side with the trawl net between them. This was a method pioneered by Alf Leggatt for which he had received the MBE in 1956, long before he came to Wells. The fish were boxed in ice and mostly sent off for canning 400 miles away in Scotland or back to Whitstable; some

[239] Alan Cooper – filmed interview at Rescue Wooden Boats archive. Cooper worked in partnership with 'Sonny' Warner another Sheringham man.

[240] Geoff Perkins *A Town and its People, as it once was* (1996) p. 101

[241] The *Remus* ended her days at Brancaster. The *Romulus* had been broken up some years before. The *Cortina* sank in heavy seas off Skegness in 1968 https://leggattfamily.co.uk/fishing_years/

were taken directly to Grimsby to be made into fish meal. In winter they fished for whitebait to be processed in Lowestoft. Wells boats also trawled for skate and thornback rays, known locally as roker, which were mostly sold locally. They were to be found on the coastal strip between Thornham and Blakeney. Shrimping was another kind of fishery, requiring huge nets hung over the side on long beams; it too came and went. As a result fisherman had to supplement their income as stevedores and even as crew on the coasters. While some remained as fishermen throughout their lives, others changed jobs frequently, working inland, driving lorries, even returning to the sea if good sense and good money seemed to suggest it. When times were hard, and often in winter, men went worm digging, carrot washing or sprout picking.

Long-line fishing, an ancient but highly labour-intensive practice, had been carried on during the war but it was not popular in Wells. It was not dissimilar to the practices off Iceland long ago when hundreds of baited hooks were attached to a line held to the sea floor with anchors, upwards of half a mile long with hooks every seven or eight feet. Onshore before each trip, each hook was baited with a whelk or a lugworm at the end of a short length of twine called a snood, as many as three hundred of them in a pack or line. The intended catch was cod and as late as the 1980s a hundred stone (over half a tonne) of them might be caught on a good trip. On the other hand the size of the catch could be derisory so that it was not an economic fishery.[242] Allegedly, Wells didn't go in for lining: 'they were too busy whelking!' Wells' fish and chip shops, it was claimed, were supplied from Sheringham.[243] Later the fish came from much further away.

Crabbing and lobster fishing began in earnest only in the 1980s by which time the trawling had ceased. The two didn't go together. Trawling would pick up the shanks of pots, dragging them over the sea bed and destroying them. Already by the 1970s it was regarded as the major culprit in destroying fish stocks. Crabbing on the other hand had long been practised in Cromer and Sheringham.[244] There, on the long chalk shelf offshore the crabs would spawn; indeed it was once thought that only between Weybourne and Mundesley was there a worthwhile fishery.[245] This was the official line propounded by government. However, after the 1978 floods, some fishermen, notably the Frary brothers, looking for whelks off Sheringham Shoal found crabs in their pots. Crabs eat whelks. They also migrate, mostly but not always westerly along the coast. Moreover, Wells had what the coast to the west lacked, an accessible safe harbour. Instead of small boats having to be hauled up the beach by manpower or tractor, they could sail up to a quay wall and find safe mooring even in severe

242 Fran Weatherhead *North Norfolk Fishermen* (The History Press 2011) p.104
243 Weatherhead p.107
244 Weatherhead pp110-111,152
245 *The Norfolk Crab Fishery* (MAFF 1966) p. 2

Allen Frary, onetime lifeboat coxswain, digging for worms

weather. *Black Beauty* was the Frary's first crab boat, bought from Sheringham. Their use of pots laid on the sea floor and their eventual stringing together into shanks of twenty or more pots anchored to the seafloor was a comparatively recent innovation. Hitherto, single pots, so-called swummers, had been used.

Unlike whelk pots, crab and lobster pots were bigger and rectangular, but because lobsters were adept at escaping, so-called parlour pots, which had two sections, were invented. Once in the second chamber, the animals were trapped. All made originally of wood, hazel was popular; eventually they were replaced by metal framed pots. At one time local blacksmiths had made them up but they had gone by the 1980s.

There would be further developments in the boats, both in their construction and their equipment. The use of a wheel rather than a tiller, and the subsequent installation of a wheelhouse, were followed by the use of electronic aids, of which the VHF radio and radar were among the first. Wooden boats, whose construction had been an art rather than a science, but without plans, were now displaced by GRP. The first GRP boats might be made from moulds taken from their wooden predecessors. Thus Tony Jordan's old wooden hulled boat *William Edward*, which had begun life in 1949, was used to make the mould from which *Blucher* was built in 2000. The first 'plastic' boat was *Isabel Kathleen,* a whelk boat commissioned by John Nudds some years earlier. She would be followed by others, some of completely new design, intended to be faster to travel to the more distant banks where whelks were to be found. Bigger vessels, sometimes twin-hulled, carried more pots. *Pathfinder* was the first of these, followed by *Two Brothers,* owned by the grandson of 'Blucher' Jarvis, Andy McCallum, who had also built *Blucher.*

The fishery is always subject to the variability of the catch but also its value. And the dangers of over-fishing remain as long as men want a good catch this year whatever the consequences for next year. Men able to find work in a warm lorry might not find the work inviting but it is said that anyone willing to work hard can make good money. For some the freedom of the sea is a major attraction; for others it is a pain. But in any case, the increase in regulation made one trade after another more difficult to practise. Whelks could no longer be boiled locally; stern trawling became illegal; one species after another was declared to be at risk so that catches were limited. Netting from the shore, while still legal, had become entirely uneconomical because of catch restrictions.

Worm digging declined for different reasons. It was less profitable and unendingly hard work but it required only a fork and a bucket. Well within living memory one could see upwards of a hundred men out on the sands between Wells and Blakeney digging for worms or raking for cockles. Lugworms, which inhabit the sands, were dug by fork and cast into a bucket by the thousand; the famed 'Professor' Coe, longstanding bait digger, reckoned over a lifetime that he had dug thirty-five billion worms. Some were packed up and sold to leisure fishermen inland but their original use was as bait for long-liners. The worm diggers were, many of them, peripatetic, working along the coast during the year but the decline of the cod fishery and the sale of farmed lugworms have brought about their virtual disappearance. The tell-tale worm casts show that there are still a great many worms out on the sands but a solitary bait digger has become what one is likely to find. The erstwhile practitioners have died, retired or turned to less arduous and more profitable activities. In their day they sometimes compared unfavourably with real fishermen who needed an expensive boat and tackle; [246] but in truth the work was hard, demanding of concentration, always being aware of the imminence of the 'gov'nr', the tide, whose swift advance could endanger the unwary.

If there are still worms in quantity, the same cannot be said about cockles, once raked from just beneath the surface by local people and holiday makers alike, traditionally by women. Wells West Lake just beyond the Pinewoods was a favourite place; another to the east of the Wells channel was on Bob Halls Sand. Gangs would go out together, lugging the sacks home at the flood tide. The sacks could weigh up to a hundredweight (fifty kilos) and it was a long walk over the soft sand to the shore. Horses and carts were used at one time, then as numbers reduced the sack would be laid over the crossbar of a bicycle for the last part of the journey home. If the cockles have not gone there are far fewer of them and the competition from wading birds has increased with protection. Their decline is often blamed on the depredations of holiday makers who took them away with them in huge amounts. It was, in any case, a hard job bringing small rewards compared with what could be gained as a crew of a

[246] Sally Festing *Fisherman* (1999) p.85

whelker. Selling door-to-door in the surrounding villages, once profitable, ceased to be so as women's work patterns changed and many villages were depopulated as houses were bought as second homes.

If lugworms and cockles live in sand, mussels need mud. The parts of the shoreline where mud and shingle predominated were rarer, best where the various streams ran at low water draining the marshes. Mussels were once in high demand and mussel lays were rented from the Commissioners after closed bid auctions. Over twenty lays extended from the lifeboat station as far as the whelk sheds on east quay.[247] Mussels require tending if they are to thrive during their three year lifespan. To prevent them from being choked by sand they have to be turned with a fork. Mussel flats, small boats propelled by a pole, or quant, would drift out to the mussel beds on the falling tide, and be filled by hand with mussels, ready to drift in with the next flood tide. There are few mussel beds now. The inshore beds silted up. Whether they have benefitted from the cleaning up of the harbour following building of the sewage treatment plant is a moot point. Allen Frary, one time longshoreman and lifeboat coxswain, contended that the mussels tasted better in the old days when offal poured into the harbour. Public health professionals might not agree.

The world of fishermen and lifeboatmen overlapped in life and in death. The Shipwrights Arms on the East Quay was a place of meeting for most of them of a Saturday night or a Sunday dinnertime; inland visitors were an unwelcome intrusion. The noise was that of loud voices and the clack of dominoes, the air full of cigarette smoke and the floor the routine destination of spent dog ends. Its closure in the 1980s was a sign of changing leisure habits.

Poignantly they came together in death. The deaths of Raymond Money and Cyril Everitt on 30 January 1952 while fishing on board the *Tony* was the more tragic because so sudden. Fishermen came from Brancaster, Sheringham and Cromer to the funeral; the cortege was said to stretch half a mile from the church. The coroner raised the question of safety since the men had neither lifebelts, lifebuoys nor lifeline. Now as then the inconvenience of such accoutrements in a working environment was the predominant factor. The loss of the *Concord* made clear another deficiency; the standard of buoyage in those days at the entrance to the little harbours along the coast was poor. Even much later the sea would claim its victims. When William Cracknell, not a fisherman but a boat builder and Sharpie sailor, was drowned with his friend, Lionel Fortescue, at almost the end of the century, one could scarcely move in church. Such is the solidarity of seafarers. The church's modest congregations were multiplied tenfold when such as Tony Jordan and Graham Walker, both lifeboat coxswains who died ashore, were brought into church to be honoured, remembered and sent on their way.

---

247 Smith (2018) p. 106

4. The last years of the council

Slum clearance is an expression which has disappeared from the language; in Wells, in spite of the building programme, no action could be taken to implement the pre-war Clearance Orders until 1954; because of the national housing shortage, government refused to permit it. Thereafter, the District Surveyor, Fred Rodwell, sought to make good the deficiency. Most of the clearance areas, of which five remained untouched, were small scale, but the yards to the west of the Glebe were rabbit warrens of cramped dwellings and unpaved yards whose piecemeal clearance before the war left areas of dereliction only slowly repaired. The expectation was that those whose houses were demolished would be housed locally. The current building programme for the Northfield estate, which would be completed by the end of the decade, did not meet the need and plans were laid in July 1948 for the building of Northfield Waye. Meanwhile the estate was to be provided with its own parade of shops on Northfield Lane, a grocer, a butcher or greengrocer, a fish shop for both fresh and fried, a draper and general store and a post office. The idea was that everything would be provided within the estate.

Stearmans Yard running down to Freeman Street

There were now over 350 council houses. The council thus enquired of the new Ministry of Local Government and Planning whether the ministry would consider a scheme by which the council would build houses for sale. The ministry replied to the effect that it would prefer that land be sold for private individuals to build on. Further council houses were built, the emphasis now being the building of bungalows for the elderly. Eleven two bedroomed bungalows for Northfield Waye were proposed in 1957 followed by 20 bungalows for Church Marsh, subsequently renumbered as part of Northfield Crescent.

The most ambitious plan was for the old pre-war Improvement Area to be revived. The idea was to clear the land to the west of the Glebe and to drive a new road from the quay directly to the 'dry road' (B1105 to Fakenham), giving easy access to large vehicles from the south and west of the town to the quay. Several dozen new houses would be built following a new lay-out. Originally a fur factory was planned to provide employment.

Demolition could only take place once the residents had been rehoused. Of the 174 houses declared unfit in 1955 there were still 86 on which no action had been taken.[248] Rodwell retired in 1960 after 33 years in post to be succeeded by Arnold Rogers. Rogers was regarded as a serial moderniser who wished to remove as many older properties as he could. He recommended to the council that the area which included all the yards from Freeman Street to Theatre Road and as far west as Dogger Lane be for residential and light industrial use stating that 'a very high standard of layout and design of buildings would be required as the site is conspicuous not only from the proposed new road but also from the foreshore some half a mile away'.[249] Demolition began of the vacant houses on Theatre Road and Stearman's Yard in June 1961. The Freeman Street houses were demolished in November. Little besides the Methodist chapel, Warren's Garage on Theatre Road and the Glebe itself were to be spared. The road was to cut across the space taking in part of the garden of Blenheim House so as to join up with Park Road. While the demolition of unfit houses could be pushed through, the raising of wider issues resulted in opposition. It was, in any case, a complicated scheme. Delay was inevitable.

There remained pockets of unfit housing around the town. Referring back to the 1947 survey, Rogers' report to the council at the end of 1963 showed that there were still 102 suspect houses where no known work had been carried out and fifty which were the subject of further clearance proposals which he proposed to implement.

Looking round for further building land, the council identified a number of open areas within the town envelope but at the other end of town. One of these was already in its ownership, the land on the south side of Mill Road which had been given over to allotments. It had been bought from the fourth Earl of Leicester for that purpose in 1948. The Earl had imposed a covenant on it that the land should not be used other than for allotments and smallholdings. It lay con-

---

[248] *UDC Minutes* March 1961 NRO DC18/4/10
[249] *UDC Minutes* April 1962
UDC Minutes April 1962 NRO DC18/4/10

veniently between two arterial roads and the railway line, forming a neat triangle and demand for allotments was falling. A second proposal was to build on part of the old Orchard Farm, a field running down from behind the first part of Mill Road to Burnt Street. This required the purchase of the land from five different landowners as well as the development of access from Mill Road; it would take some time to implement. A third proposal proved to be the easiest to implement. Though it required access via the narrow Gales Road, the land behind the council houses on the north side of Mill Road was purchased for what was to become Gales Court. Twenty-four bungalows intended for the elderly were built in several blocks, some at right angles to the road.

The Gales Court development was limited by surrounding houses. The west end allotments on the other hand offered a much larger prospect, to which attention now turned. There were still unfit houses to be taken down and the post-war prefabs had long exceeded their design life. Government approval for the appropriation of ten acres of the land out of a total of nineteen was obtained; Lord Leicester was to be asked to release the covenant. Twelve months' notice was given to allotment holders; sheds were to be removed and no new sheds were to be erected – in fact, the area was peremptorily cleared; only eventually it was cleared of rubble and laid down as grass. The remaining allotments were reduced to ten roods in extent.[250] Detailed street plans were drawn up for the whole 19 acre site. A Leicester firm, HJB Plastics, was invited to set up a factory on the site and, in anticipation of the success of the venture, obtained temporary premises at the bottom of the High Street. It was to be 60% owner-occupied, with old people's bungalows and a children's play space.

The Earl, who had inherited the title in 1949, was not wholly opposed to the idea of releasing the covenant for part of the land. He wrote to say so to the council in October of 1963; he wished to look at the proposed layout, he said. The council refused. It sought and obtained planning permission, and contracted with a Cornish firm for the building of the roadways and services, all this in spite of the Earl's solicitors writing to say that 'the trustees are not prepared to consent to the general release of the covenant but only for housing subject to their approval of the plans'. They suggested two fields east of the railway station and west of the lime works, which they owned, for industrial development. The council again rejected the idea of a partial release of the covenant and of submitting the plans for the approval of Holkham.[251] They wanted a general release, voting down an amendment in favour of the Estate's request; nothing else would do. HJB Plastics notified the council that it would be returning to Leicester. The process dragged on, delayed by a shortage of finance and arguments about housing density; the contractors for the roadways withdrew. The decision was taken to sell the site for private housing.

---

[250] *UDC Minutes* October 1963. NRO DC18/4/11
[251] *UDC Minutes* November 1965 NRO DC18/4/12

Desultory discussions with Holkham continued, which again offered 'modified terms on which a negotiated release' would be considered, once again rejected.[252] Finally, however, in May 1972 the Earl took the matter to the High Court which found in his favour. Afterwards he commented that 'I agreed I would release half the land, about ten acres, for building provided they built bungalows with gardens, the kind of places bank managers and such people would like for their retirement. I wanted half the land nearest the allotments to keep building and noise away from the hospital.... in view of the outcome they probably wish they had accepted the offer at that time.'[253]

During those years attitudes towards house building had changed. If councils could build whole estates, so could building companies, even individual builders. The council had long suggested the building of houses for sale to government which had earlier opposed the idea as we have seen. Dalliston, who ran buses from behind the Buttlands on Mill Road, began a small development which became Southgate Close in November 1960. Behind it lay three acres which were developed into a close of thirty-three bungalows and dormer bungalows designed for the retired; they proved popular with incomers[254]. A similar proposal came from Mr Wilcox, head of the firm of Waveney Developments Ltd. He proposed building sixty-five bungalows behind Burnt Street, having purchased the land from its town owners, Mary Kitson, owner of the Edinburgh and William Thurgur, former shopkeeper. The houses would be built by local builder, John Acock, who was also a councillor. It would be called Waveney Close. The site works, roadways, sewers, water mains and so on, were begun in October 1964, accessed from Market Lane.[255] Unlike the council which was able to borrow large sums, local private developers would build a couple of houses at a time and, having sold them, would seek permission to build more. The firm unsuccessfully sought to buy the Freeman Street site and were to offer to share in the allotment development, an offer which the council refused.

However, the entrance via Market Lane was problematic; it led from Burnt Street, the A149, which was the main road through the town, which had its own problems. The whole length of the road from its entry to the east to its junction with the 'dry road' was too narrow to be suitable as a modern arterial road. Various proposals were made to widen it by demolishing houses on the north side. It seemed as if Waveney Close might be accessed also from Church Street further east which likewise was narrow; the decision was taken to block it off. The junction of Market Lane and Burnt Street would be improved. The access via Church Street was made into a footway. However for all this the major east-west road through the town contained several pinch points which remain to the present day, only

[252] *UDC Minutes* October 1968; the voting was 8 to 3. NRO DC18/4/14
[253] *EDP* May 20th 1972
[254] *UDC Minutes* Nov. 1960 NRO DC18/4/9; Dec. 1962 NRO DC18/4/11
[255] *UDC Minutes* Oct. 1964 NRO DC18/4/12

partly alleviated by the imposition of a 20 mph speed limit.

Private housing was to continue to be built. The following year Charles Platten got approval for the building of ten chalet bungalows at the west end of the town off Bases Lane. He had originally proposed it as a holiday camp! He proceeded to build a couple of houses a year until completion. In 1971 Mary Kitson, now council chairman, was to state in her annual report to the council that 25 private houses had been built with another 29 under construction; many of which would be built on derelict land.

Meanwhile, much of the existing privately owned housing stock in the town lacked even basic kitchens and toilets. The Housing Act of 1949 had provided for grants towards the modernising of houses whose cooking facilities mostly consisted of solid-fuelled ranges, and which lacked other means of heating water, bath and wash basins. The implementation of the Act took some time following the installation of mains sewerage but after a while the treatment of applications became routine and a maximum grant of £155 became the norm. By the late 1950s scarcely a council meeting passed without some application being made. Ranges became open fires; baths were fitted, some of them even upstairs; flush toilets were now supported; water cylinders with immersion heaters were approved; kitchens acquired gas or electric cookers: all were the object of grant applications. They continued to be applied for into the 1960s. As another sign of the times, three old cottages in Honeymoon Row which might once have been demolished were instead converted into one residence. This would happen again and again. Buildings dating back five hundred years which might have been lost were thus preserved.

As the stock of council housing increased in number so the task of maintenance, not merely of the older houses, also became a preoccupation of the council. Improvements included the wholesale installation of gas Ascot water heaters. There was also concern over the upkeep of tenants' gardens. It was a matter of stick and carrot. Tenants were reminded of the conditions of the tenancy which included the cultivation of gardens.[256] Competitions were held for the best kept garden. The incentive failed to improve the upkeep of some of the gardens so the council resorted to tidying up overgrown plots and charging the tenants. A proposal that tenants of under-occupied houses should be required to move was defeated.[257] Attitudes had changed since the war.

If new land was hard to find, new houses would now be met by infilling. Ten bungalows were to be built on the west side of Knitting Needle Lane, necessitating the shortening of gardens of houses on Northfield Avenue. Tenants asked for and were given compensation for their loss of crops. Fifteen more bungalows were to be built on the east side of the lane.[258] Further infilling took place with the

---

256 *UDC Minutes* May 1960 NRO DC18/4/9

257 *UDC Minutes* May 1962. NRO DC18/4/11

258 *UDC Minutes* January 1967. NRO DC18/4/13

building of what became known as Nielsen Close, named after the onetime lifeboat coxswain. Built in two phases, 31 houses were to be added to the stock, enabling the rehousing of the pre-fab dwellers. In time, these 31 houses were to become 47 dwellings.

In-filling was not confined to council property. Mayshiel and The Normans were very visible but not the sole examples of houses with lavish gardens whose owners sold them off for development. In 1961 Mayshiel was divided into flats, part of its garden being turned into a parade of shops. The Normans, sold by Dr Hicks on his retirement in 1969, was acquired by builder Walter Gould to become a square of town houses, named after other invaders, some of whom, like the Scots, had failed in the attempt!

The priority at the beginning of the century had been for social housing to replace slum dwellings; that process had taken fifty years. Private developers became significant players after the Second World War whose purchasers would be private individuals. This rise in the number of property owners was a feature to which the early post-war governments paid no attention, discouraging the sale of council houses. This was to change. Initially sceptical, and understandably so given the housing shortage, by the 1960s the council began to look favourably on the idea of selling some of its housing stock. By 1971 it had sold nine houses (including one of its 1919 stock), and the sale of eight more was in prospect.

The energetic efforts of the council so described could not conceal its anomalous status. As one of the smallest Urban Districts in the country its continued existence had been under threat at various times by central government, before the war and again in 1954. The council responded to the threat by saying that its finances were sound; it maintained 4.51 miles of main roads and 4.881 miles of district roads; it had built more than 350 houses and was maintaining 294 so that there was no need to abolish a council which was working well. That it survived until the wholesale local government re-organisation of 1974 may be thought a tribute to its energy and effectiveness. But it was certainly anomalous. It was surrounded by Walsingham RDC which, as a Rural District whose headquarters was not Walsingham but Fakenham, had fewer powers than did Wells. Walsingham had a population in 1951 of over 22,000 compared with Wells population of not much more than a tenth of that number. This may account for the slight impatience on the part of Walsingham when it came to the provision of water to Wells. The water supply engineered twenty or so years before was no longer adequate for Wells' needs. Groundwater levels had become dangerously low so that by the mid 1950s it was supplementing its supply with water from Walsingham. Negotiations for additional supplies from Houghton and Egmere were protracted. The Rural District was not keen to come to the aid of Wells.

The supply of water was to continue to be a source of concern. Water consumption had increased in the ten years after the war from under three million gallons a month to more than twelve million gallons. A year-round hose pipe ban was introduced. The building of a storage water tank on Theatre Road was proposed but was thought to be too small. Instead a cement reservoir holding 500,000 gallons was built adjacent to the bore hole on Warham Road to be filled at night initially from Gunthorpe and then from the Stiffkey valley. The lifting of the hose pipe ban increased consumption by 30,000 gallons a day. Clearly some greater degree of coordination was needed and the creation of a North West Norfolk Water Board was mooted.

The issue is a subject in its own right; demand constantly increased and new sources had to be found. It was another issue on which an individual authority could not hope to find the solution, raising the question as to the viability of the then structure of local government. The creation of the Water Board removed the responsibility for the provision of the town's water on 1 April 1969; an agency agreement ran for another year. Likewise, the running of the gas works had been handed over to government following the Gas Act of 1948; public health had, since before the war, been more centralised - the offices were to move to Fakenham in 1961; the fire service had become a county responsibility before the war; responsibility for the lighting of county roads was transferred to the highways' authority in 1966 (though initially delegated back). It was not all one way. Onetime chairman of the council, Jack Cadamy, noted the doubling of the workload of councillors since the war.

Planning was an example of the increased demands following the Town and Country Planning Act of 1947. The Act had put in place a system of planning control operated by the County Council but by which applications, in most cases, had to be approved by the district council. Issues such as the placing of advertisements and signs by local retailers would come before the council. As petrol stations proliferated the oil companies offered illuminated signs to be placed

Church Plain with Thurgur's shop

outside them. Initially, the council was reluctant to grant permission. Of 51 applications in January 1963, 44 were objected to; but the tide was against them. Housing development and the enlargement of houses was brought before them.

Wider issues such as the so-called Road Pattern Plan came up for consideration. Just as traffic flow had been aided by the building of Polka Road in 1845, so now the case for the new road to run from the quay across the newly demolished housing from the Glebe to Park Road was being pressed. The issue of east-west travel had not been solved. One alternative put forward was the idea of converting into a roadway a section of the old Heacham railway line which ran around the back of Wells from the Warham Road to meet the Holkham road at the boundary of the town.[259] The county council responded that it was better as a footpath between the two schools.

The council included a cross-section of the town's people. There were farmers, there were hauliers, and there were teachers; there was a retired maltings foreman and a railway engine driver; several shop owners: many of them owned land in and around the town. The council consisted almost entirely of men. Rachael Chamberlain was not the first woman to be elected to the council – that honour belongs to Miss Curtis Pyle – but Mrs Chamberlain was scarcely a newcomer. She was the eldest daughter of George Smith and consequently sister-in-law of George Turner Cain. She was vice-chairman in 1966. Council meetings were often lively and occasionally boiled over. In a small town where individuals were liable to undertake a number of roles, conflicts of interest were inevitable. In 1954 six councillors resigned, including the newly-elected chairman Henry Aldridge. Fourteen people stood for election to fill the casual vacancies. Stability was obtained by the election in 1955 of Dr Hicks as chairman. He was to be re-elected every year for nine years following.

From 1962 the sub-committee system was made more effective. There were now seven sub-committees: Housing, Public Health, Finance, General Purposes, the Beach, Publicity and Allotments. Although only seven members could attend any one sub-committee it meant that the full council meeting was reduced to endorsing or, occasionally, questioning the sub-committee reports. The council also re-introduced the principle of excluding the public from certain items, unknown since Peel's early days. It was applied to such varied matters as the appointment of the new camp site manager, the provision of land for new housing, the state of individual houses, housing allocations and the redevelopment of Thurgur's now empty shop at the bottom of High Street – the council wanted to buy it as council offices and stores.[260] Since 1954 the council had met in the old Park cinema, converted into offices, before which it had met in the secondary school.

Conflicts arose particularly in relation to property. Charles Platten,

[259] *UDC Minutes* June 1961 NRO DC18/4/9
[260] *UDC Minutes* Jan 1962 public excluded NRO DC18/4/10

Sun Yard, now part of Platten's fish and chip shop

war hero, who had come home to worm digging, had been opportunistic in picking up derelict land and empty premises wherever he could. He had bought up a granary on the quay which he intended to convert into an amusement arcade, espresso bar and restaurant. The latter, which was styled a Milkobar, was adjacent to Sun Yard, one of the many yards that ran down to the quay. In September 1962 it was reported that Platten had closed off Sun Yard by building on it; he was at that time a member of the council. He duly made a planning application for the formation of a new kitchen 'adjacent to the existing archway' which was granted on the understanding that 'it did not constitute permission to obstruct a public right of way'. This he ignored, building doors which entirely closed off the entry to the yard. The council proceeded to face both ways at once. At the elections of May 1964 Hicks stood down both as chairman and as councillor to be replaced by William Thurgur; Platten was not elected. Legal proceedings were proposed against him but a recommendation that the law be upheld was defeated by seven votes to five in full council. He was eventually fined £2 but a motion to extinguish the right of way through Sun Yard was accepted, again by seven votes to five. Leslie Cox and Myrtle French were among those who were in the minority. Cox, who had been a councillor for nine years, resigned in protest – he returned to fill the casual vacancy thus created only weeks later. Never shamed, Platten proceeded to complete the closure of Sun Yard before getting planning permission. It did not help that the advice of the relevant government department was to the effect that there were a number of yards leading down to the quay and that Jicklings Yard was adjacent and more convenient. The right of way was extinguished.

Platten was not the only person to excite controversy. Charles Ramm, scion of the family of butchers whose father, Arthur, had opposed mains sewerage pre-war, fell out with Rogers the surveyor. The dispute was over the repair of 30 Church Plain whose roof had fallen in (while the tenants were watching television) and which Rogers reported should not be occupied until necessary improvement works were completed. Ramm pronounced the report 'a lot of lies'. Other councillors sided with their officer but Ramm was unrepentant.

Ramm found himself on the side of losing arguments time and time again, challenging the surveyor's salary increase, various rate increases and the manner of the council's conduct of its business. At almost every turn he opposed council expenditure, falling out with both his fellow councillors and officers, such that his regular attempts to regain the chairmanship were frustrated. In November 1970 he proposed that Wells be amalgamated with Walsingham, arguing that a penny rate in Wells produced £332 while in bigger Walsingham it raised £2,222.[261] In this case he had a point but the council was not convinced: Wells had its own sewage plant and its council houses were in better condition than those of Walsingham. The numbers did not, in its members' view, count.

For its size the council was very ambitious. Encouraged by its surveyor it continued to worry at the issue of infrastructure, in particular the clearing of the various yards running down to Freeman Street and the building of an access road from the quay to the Fakenham Road which had been in abeyance. Following the demolition, part of the site was sold to Bullards the brewers who built the Ark Royal pub on the site, replacing the nearby Ship Inn. The intention now was to clear the remaining yards westwards as far as Dogger Lane[262]. Mr Loasby, the council's new architect, presented a detailed plan of the site proposing the building of 67 houses, four flats and 65 garages[263]. Again the idea was to take in part of the garden of Blenheim House in order to accommodate the access road. Clearly there was opposition, not only from the owners of the Ark Royal. A modest revision, leaving more of the existing houses in place at least in the first stages and retaining some of the existing yards, was referred to the county planning officer. He saw things differently. Attending a council meeting, he told the members that it was no longer considered 'that traffic requirements should take precedence over other considerations...and provided adequate routes exist or can be provided, heavy traffic should not be taken through a residence area... and if the proposed road is not proceeded with it would be possible to plan a comprehensive re-development of the whole site either by clearance or rebuilding or by clearance coupled with improvement of existing buildings.' Modified plans were produced proposing a two-stage pro-

[261] *UDC Minutes* Nov. 1970 NRO DC 18/4/15

[262] Rackhams Yard, Bouches Yard, Lugger Yard, Theatre Yard, Stearmans Yard and Magness Yard were all knocked down.

[263] *UDC Minutes* March 1967 NRO DC18/4/13

cess by which the majority of existing buildings would be temporarily retained. Eventually, after nine years of discussion and a number of proposals, in January 1970 an amendment in the name of Mary Kitson, seconded by Myrtle French, proposed that 'all former proposals for area action' should be abandoned 'leaving the area as it is'. Dogger Lane and its environs would be saved, the proposal to create 108 car parking spaces off Theatre Road could be implemented without hindrance; and the long- planned scheme which had caused the loss of houses, many of which could have been saved, was abandoned.[264] The council noted that an additional 76 dwellings had been built since 1952 and all 152 pre-war houses had been modernised.[265]

Another issue which might have seemed peripheral to the council's concerns was the matter of town twinning. In a letter to the council in March 1967 the idea was mooted by the Wells United Christian Council that the fostering of international goodwill might be furthered by a link with a European town. They suggested that a likely candidate might be the West German town of Laubach in Hesse. They had been in touch with the burgomaster of Laubach who was receptive to the idea. For some this was a step too far. The local press were appalled and said so in strong terms. The council's response was to take the matter out of the hands of the churches and to recommend that a Dutch or Danish coastal town be approached and that the implementation be handed over to a locally convened committee, not the churches whose views on peacemaking were evidently unacceptable. The fact that one of Laubach's influential citizens had written a detailed refutation of the views of the Nazis, in a ten-volume diary subsequently published, was probably unknown to them. But it cannot have done Anglo-German relations much good. The Danish town of Blaabjerg was to be approached but nothing came of it. In the event the council's initiative died, along with much else following local government re-organisation, and when the idea was revived some years later in 1982 it was at the initiative of the French town of La Ferté St Aubin, south of Orleans, from which a request was sent to the town council. The council engaged the schools and set up a sub-committee.[266] The first official visit was in 1985.

Mary Kitson had been a councillor since 1967. She and her husband had owned the Edinburgh hotel since 1921 and had acquired the land on which Waveney Close was built behind her house on Burnt Street. As chairman from 1970, the first woman to hold the post, she presided over the collapse of the bid to develop the west end allotment land, and the completion of the children's adventure playground and the building of a number of private houses. She was also the last chairman of the council.

The abolition of the Urban District Council in 1974 took place

---

264 *UDC Minutes* March 1967, Sept. 1967; NRO DC18/4/12; Jan. 1970 NRO DC18/4/14

265 *UDC Minutes* April 1970 NRO DC 18/4/14

266 *WTC Minutes* Dec. 6th. 1982

not because of its anomalous status but as part of a countrywide reform. Local government reorganisation was mooted as early as 1967. The original proposals included the idea that there would be a unitary authority for the whole of Norfolk. A revised plan proposed two levels of government, County and District. If Wells was to be part of a larger whole the council expressed the view that it should link up with King's Lynn, an ancient maritime alliance.[267] The proposal that the council would lose all control of its amenities by the loss of parish status was a battle that was to a small degree won but it was to be a shadow of its former self. Thus, the council went into mourning at its last meeting in March 1974. The Local Government Act of 1972 came into effect on 1 April and made Wells a part of the North Norfolk District Council, which would comprehend three other former urban districts, all much larger, and three rural districts, based on Cromer. Wells parish council, though called a town council, was to be an amenity body with responsibility for street lighting and the care of a few pieces of public land, losing without any compensation not only its housing stock but most of its assets including the old railway station site and the maltings which it had only just bought from Eastern Counties Farmers Cooperative. Even the records of the Urban District would have been lost to landfill but for the efforts of Myrtle French who collected them from the skip.[268] Just to put the tin lid on it, North Norfolk District Council's own minutes were not safe. Those from March 1993 to February 1999 have been lost.[269]

[267] *UDC Minutes* June 1971 NRO DC 18/4/15
[268] The 1813 Enclosure document found its way to Cromer where its survival owed to another piece of local initiative.
[269] *EDP* September 24th 2018.

5. Farming, industry and tourism

Most of the industries in the town had been agriculturally related: malting, milling, horse-related metal manufacturing and harness-making. The ploughing up of grazing land and even woodland during the war had massively increased production of corn; imported chemical fertilisers would further increase yields. Post-war subsidies would protect that production. The use of Friesian dairy cows, begun pre-war, had more than doubled milk production. But in some respects, even until 1950 the activities in the fields would have been recognisable to people seven centuries before. Though Fordson tractors had been imported before the war to 'speed the plough', many ploughs were still hauled by animals; cows and sheep were still driven to and from local markets along lanes narrow and broad, even as far as Holme marshes. Cattle bought in Norwich market would be driven from the railway station up to Mill Farm in considerable numbers. The fertilisation of the land was still partly dependent on 'tathing' with sheep dung. The thinning out of seedlings was still done with hand tools. Harvesting of some crops such as beet, potatoes and brassicas was labour intensive. Norwich still had its cattle market until 1960; so too did Fakenham if on a lesser scale.

Temple's carrot wash, 1984

Nevertheless, the post-war change can be evidenced in a variety of ways. Numerically, between 1945 and 1960 the number of agricultural workers nationally fell by 20%. Within another twenty years it had fallen by a further 50%, to a mere 314,000. In Norfolk as a whole, in 1931 44% of the male working population was involved in agriculture in one way or another; by 1971 that had fallen to 13%. Manor Farm's figures were even more dramatic: from 55 on the payroll in 1947, to five in 1972. The 1947 figure included ten Italian prisoners of war and 22 members of the Women's Land Army. The workforce was to operate a mixed farm: dairy cattle, beef cattle, pigs, poultry, ducks, together with arable land devoted to the provision of animal feed and bedding, to the growing of oats, wheat, barley, rye, broccoli and cabbage for human consumption, and beans for stock feeding. That year Flint employed a contractor to plough and harrow some of his acreage. The following year, he went in for pig rearing and grew more vegetables for human consumption – brussels sprouts and cauliflowers. Milk production, which had been a mainstay during and after the war,[270] continued after his death in 1957 but at a much reduced level: the Friesians, nearly 200 of them, were sold off in 1962 and the smaller herd of Jerseys were sold in 1971.[271] Rising health standards and the predominance of pasteurised milk in any case caused him to hand over the process to Seamans, a dairy company based in King's Lynn, who had a plant adjacent to the farm. Thus, when his grandson, Rodney Crafer, took over the farm, admittedly a smaller tenancy, he was engaged entirely in the production of wheat, barley, oats and sugar beet. A mixed farm had become an arable farm.

Mill Farm, which had employed 22 men in 1956 and had six horses that year when George retired, was taken over by Val, his son. Val had been farming in Norwich and was used to more modern methods. He in turn continued to keep beef cattle until 1995 when his son Desmond Wright took over. Cows simply did not make money at that scale. This pattern was not everywhere followed but mixed

Eastern Counties' yard in Staithe Street 1950s

farming became less and less common and dairy production was to decline dramatically throughout East Anglia over the years.[272] Some farmers would keep a few hens and a cow for milk and butter but that would soon cease too.

On New Farm the change was wrought by the decision of the County Agricultural Committee, the successor to the so-called War Ag., to turn its tenant, Tom Coe, off the land for poor farming practice. The Committee was not known for being decisive so this was unusual. Probably it was Holkham Estate which precipitated the termination of the tenancy. The new tenant, who took over in 1950, was John Temple, whose family had farmed on a modest scale round Wighton.

---

270 The total cattle herd in 1950 was 335 beasts: Manor Farm records 1936-2004
271 MAFF returns 1962/1971 Manor Farm Records 1936-2004
272 Dairy cows in Norfolk numbered 44,981 in 1945; in 2016 they numbered 6,123

Temple found himself faced with a huge task in order the make the farm work and pay: everything needed to be done, from cleaning out ditches in which animal skeletons were found to removing turkey muck which reached up to the window sills. Coe was left with a single field behind the midden. As was the almost universal practice it was a mixed farm, bigger than either of the other local tenanted farms, at one time over a thousand acres. In 1962 he started keeping

Percy Phillips leading his flock up Standard Road 1980s

sheep. Initially numbering several hundred, they were kept on the various reclaimed marshes. Not himself a sheep farmer, one of his workers, Percy Philips, himself the son of a shepherd, took them on and continued to do so until his retirement in 1995. He did the lambing, he did the shearing almost single-handedly. He led the flock from the marshes through the town, assisted by his dog. Temple's major interest was in cattle which he reared for beef, bringing in calves by train for fattening. Dairying continued at Wighton. The arable land required improvement for which reason he concentrated on roots, peas and three-year leys, but also on brassicas. He kept chickens, in such numbers as to enable him to sell the eggs to Sainsbury's.[273] Mechanisation came quickly. By 1958 the remaining two horses had gone. His machinery included six tractors, plus a crawler, and two combines, hauled by a tractor and able to deliver threshed grain to a lorry via a chute. Some older practices remained, such as building and thatching a haystack, but machinery was again used for most of the tasks. Straw yards were built. Unusually, Temple was still employing 30 men as late as 1975.

As manpower numbers fell, machinery represented an opportunity

[273] New Farm Census returns 1958-1975; Farm Study Scheme No 7 Association of Agriculture 1962

but also a necessity. All farms might use a tractor. Arable farms needed new kinds of plough, seed drills, grain dryers and combines which were now replacing the once ubiquitous reaper binder. Horses, of which there had been twice as many as tractors immediately post-war, had by 1960 simply vanished. In fact, as early as 1951, the Ministry ceased to require a return as to the number of horses on a farm.[274] The number of horses was such as not to require their recording. And whereas the carting of dung from farmyards to the fields had been the norm, artificial fertilisers, which had been imported since before the war, had now become an essential item of expenditure. Those who had animals would manure some of their fields, but many had none.

The pace of change was assisted by the presence in the town of Eastern Counties Farmers Cooperative (ECFC) which continued to sell grain on behalf of local farmers, to sell seed, to process and supply animal feed and to supply the new kinds of farm machinery from its Fakenham depot. It also milled wheat and barley mixed with high protein soya and coconut, to be made into pig and cattle food; it obtained chicken feed from Ipswich for local distribution. It brought in grain from local farms in its lorries to the grain store on Staithe Street for onward sale. Sometimes grain was bought from local farms, ground into animal feed and then returned to the same farms. Five lorries were stationed in Wells. Very little came by sea though malting barley went out by ship from time to time.

However, the limitations were that the Wells premises were never large enough to meet demand. Promises from Ipswich of modernisation were never fulfilled; Wells was at the end of the road, bounded by the sea. As lorries became bigger, access to the plant even via Theatre Road could only be achieved by knocking down properties in Hamonds Square. The Wells works ceased most of its activities in July 1970 and it was bought by the council for £6,000 the next year with the intention of turning it into an Arts Centre. ECFC continued to supply farm machinery from its Fakenham depot and to pick up grain directly from local farms for processing elsewhere. It was to go bankrupt in 1994 in circumstances which did it no credit. In what appeared to be an attempt to shore up its finances, lorries were sent to local farms to pick up all the grain they could lay their hands on. When they went into receivership shortly afterwards, the hapless farmers received only 10p in the pound.[275]

The road haulage trade post-war had initially confined itself to general carrying. Then the nationalisation of road transport in 1948 left small carriers like Barkers unable to carry parcels to and from Norwich which was more than the maximum twenty-five miles allowed for private carriers. The limit was subsequently lifted and Barkers resumed its wide-ranging parcels trade, providing a daily service delivering anything from drain covers to wheel hubs, tyres, bi-

[274] Manor Farm records 1936-2004
[275] Whey Curd Farm, Wighton accounts 1994

cycles, carpets, school books, rolls of barbed wire, oxygen cylinders and seed potatoes; anything that was requested.[276] They established a depot in Norwich. Barker's major competitor, Grange's, had bought ex-army American trucks left behind by the departing troops which he proceeded to update with British and, increasingly, European-made vehicles, transporting agricultural produce. His enterprise, being much larger than Barker's, was nationalised and his premises both on the quay and the Glebe were taken over. Tom Grange was employed by them in their Norwich office. With de-nationalisation in 1953 Grange was able to buy back his assets at advantageous prices. Barker's business as a general carrier began to decline meanwhile. With the improving reliability of motor vehicles, and the increasing replacement of components rather than their repair, specialist repair shops were no longer needed. There were further changes in the licensing system and the decline in specialist industries in the city. Seeing how the market was changing, in the 1960s Barker's went into long haulage, carrying anything from bulk potatoes to baked beans all over the country.[277] Barker's lorry fleet increased from four to nine vehicles. Bureaucracy was everywhere in evidence: it was necessary to prove 'need' on the part of a customer in order to obtain a licence to carry goods and Barker found himself routinely opposed by Tom Grange when he applied for one. It was the testy rivalry of old friends whose families had been in business since way before the war.

Vibrator at Leicester lime works

By 1972 Grange had ceased trading and the various granaries had begun to close. Barker's began to make contracts with local farmers for the export of produce but largely for the import of fertiliser and animal feed (which was how they came to enter the ship brokerage trade). They had closed down their haulage business in 1970 after a strike. Hitherto they had run a fleet of eighteen lorries and a staff of thirty, carrying all over the country, but were experiencing financial problems. In order to put the business on a better footing, an agreement was reached to pay drivers on a piece-work basis instead of an hourly wage which latter, they said, was unaffordable. The drivers rejected the agreement and went on strike. After eleven weeks of strike action, and a failed attempt at negotiations, Barker's decided to close the business, a bitter blow for many in the town.[278] They turned to shipping, to their filling station and the building, in 1980, of a storage facility on the old Leicester lime works which had closed the previous year.

The closure of the Leicester lime works in June 1979 was another blow. It had been a big employer in the 1950s. Finely crushed lime-

[276] Brian Barker and David Lowe *Norfolk Carrier* (2003) pp29ff,
[277] Barker p. 56ff
[278] *Eastern Daily Press* December 24th 1970

Grange's garage on the quay

stone was sold to local farmers to sweeten the soil; it was particularly good for sugar beet. In its day, it provided employment for local lorry owners. A rotary kiln turned it into lime mortar for use in building though this was being replaced by Portland cement. Owned by Holkham Estate, it was sold to Thomas Moye in the 1950s who in turn sold out to Charringtons, the coal merchants. They had no real interest in the works but had bought it because it ran a coal business as well. Its closure left another gap in the town.

Smiths the maltsters had long gone. At their remaining plant at Great Ryburgh they had begun to use more mechanised, less labour-intensive, methods of manufacture. The huge pneumatic maltings installed at Ryburgh were from a different world; Smith's themselves formed a partnership with a new company, Crisp Maltings, which was ultimately to take Smith's over.[279] Many of the buildings given to other uses, such as grain storage, were eventually demolished and replaced by houses. Paul's of Ipswich, who had come to the town at the beginning of the war, experimented at the No 18 maltings in Wells with chemical treatments of the malt to shorten the cycle.[280] For a while the familiar smell of malting barley wafted over the quay as it had in times past but as production capacity increased demand fell, new production methods shortened the cycle from twelve days to two. Pauls withdrew from Wells in 1967.[281]

No 18, the last malting in operation in Wells, closed in 1967

Dewing and Kersley's mill by the railway station had seen a period of expansion when the company built the new silo behind its grand Victorian premises in 1961. Local wheat, highly suitable for cakes and biscuits, went daily by lorry to Peek Frean's factory in Bermondsey and Jacob's in Liverpool. The mill supplied retail outlets such as the

[279] F&G Smith Directors Minute Book vol.2 p.293; the arrangement was intended to finance the building of a facility for 'mechanical' malt manufacture.
[280] The cycle was reduced from two weeks to nine or ten days. Malt quality was improved, the labour force halved and production doubled: Clark p. 188. Gibberellic acid was used to improve the rate of extraction of sugars.
[281] *EDP* 25th October 1967

Co-op with bags of flour, distributed on its lorries to Norwich and further afield, both from Wells and their other mill at Fakenham. 'Sunshine Flour' it was called. The wheat came mostly from East Anglian farms and the company made little use of the railway. But the silo, conceived as a means of making the operation more efficient, proved to be its downfall. Hugely costly to build, it proved unsuitable for storing grain, which required dry conditions, and the company came to an end in 1977, also the victim of changes outside its control. The council objected but to no avail. The mill itself was taken down in 1985; the silo was finally demolished in 2022. Both Peek Frean's and Jacobs were bought out and closed by an American conglomerate in 1989.

The short, Wells had lost its employment base both from the fields, as machines replaced workers, and from the town as industries disappeared. The three farms remained but had begun to play a less significant part in the life of the town.

In town, empty buildings lay untenanted. Gradually they were sold. Grange's garage on the quay was bought by Styman brothers the grocers who transformed them into a shop with a plate glass frontage. There was a deal of waste ground apparently worthless where cottages had been. For some it was an unrivalled opportunity. Wherever there was land or property not in use or demand it could be built on. The quay was an obvious example. Charles Platten had acquired the former Vynne & Everett granary store on the quay and turned it into an amusement arcade, 'Milkobar' and restaurant.[282] He re-fronted it and eventually replaced its twin gables with a flat roof. We have already come across the story of his acquisition of the properties on either side of Sun Yard. He then bought the bait store belonging to the Wells Whelk company on Standard Road; it was to become a hardware shop. At one time he owned the entire block at the bottom of Staithe Street to the east. He picked up other parcels of land which he was to develop into housing, including a large plot at the top of Polka Road. The several maltings buildings remained, some of them empty, some having found a use. The maltings on the Glebe which Grange had converted into garages were taken over post-war by the newly formed British Road Services, the nationalised road transport concern, which had well-nigh crippled local haulage concerns. It was not a success and the Wells outlet closed, to be proposed as yet another amusement arcade.[283] Another building which outlived its usefulness was the mortuary. Built at the turn of the century it had housed the dead from out to sea who had nowhere to end their days. Even then no one particularly wanted it close by and it stood at the west end of the quay. Sensibilities and changed provision caused the harbour commissioners to ask that it be removed.

The fragility of the Wells economy was something of which local people were aware. Flint, as chairman of the council, took the trouble

---

282 *UDC Minutes* Dec. 1958 NRO DC 18/4/9
283 Application by PA Goddard *UDC Minutes* November 1960. NRO DC 18/4/9

Railway station site in 1969

to write a report to the council on the state of the town in 1950. He wrote that 'the greatest need for 1950 is a further development of its industrial life'. He noted the presence of Eastern Counties, apparently a booming concern and the Leicester lime works. Alas, he put his faith in planning, but planning was always subject to the vagaries of the market and factors quite beyond prediction.

The closure of the railway in 1964 was yet another blow. It had proved very useful for transporting material to the airfields during the Second World War but thereafter increasing competition from road transport, the chronic problem of its being a terminus and government preference for road transport made it vulnerable. Technically one could travel westwards to Heacham and King's Lynn but the line lacked the necessary capacity and was not much used. Nationalisation and the subsequent Beeching report, which recommended the radical pruning of the network, were to result in the eventual loss of the service.

The harbour branch, whose goods movements must have interrupted the lives of those living on the quay, closed in October 1952. In summer the pilgrimage excursion trains to Walsingham were stored

Diesel Multiple Unit arriving in Wells in 1964

there so as to free up the station for other traffic.[284] Pilgrimage could be described as a form of religious tourism, focussing on the revived shrines to the Virgin Mary, Catholic and Anglican, in Walsingham. Post-war both shrines became very popular and special trains, particularly from London, arrived each weekend around church festivals and in summer. While the pilgrims prayed the trains were brought to Wells to allow normal traffic to operate. The Heacham branch was closed to regular passenger traffic in May 1952; after the 1953 floods which washed the line away east of Burnham Market no attempt was made to restore it for freight traffic.

The last years of the Dereham branch saw the introduction of diesel railcars in 1955, providing the best service the town had ever seen: ten trains a day ran to Norwich. The 6.55am for Norwich arrived there at 8.34am, in good time for a 9am start to the working day. It was a good way for children to get to school in Fakenham. Freight traffic from Wells to the Ryburgh malting increased. Whelks and timber were among the freight items which left the station yard. Holiday-makers came. The bus timetables were made so as to meet arriving trains. But by 1962 closure was in the air; the council made known its opposition. The Beeching report of 1963, *The Reshaping of British Railways,* proposed the closure of the Wells to Dereham branch. Two buses a day were offered in its place; the bus company, Eastern Counties, offered eight. Closure became certain and on Saturday 3 October 1964 the last passenger train ran from Wells. Goods traffic continued for a further month. [285] Buses ran for a while from Wells to King's Lynn via Heacham, which still had a railway station, and to East Dereham. The latter was under threat within little more than a year. In truth it made more sense for there to be a service directly to Norwich but in any case the Dereham to Norwich line closed at the end of 1968. To make matters final, the parapets of the two bridges at Two Furlong Hill and at the end of Freeman Street were removed.

The station site, the station itself, the yards, sheds and turntable presented yet another eyesore, in theory an opportunity for industrial development. The council bought the station site for £9,500 intending to develop it for such a purpose.[286] Work began on clearing the yard which was to be used initially by Potters, local builders who had been responsible for many of the council houses. They were to manufacture building components. An access road from the Polka was deemed necessary, thus also providing another access from the bungalows of Northfield Crescent. The council levelled the ground with 2,000 cubic yards of crushed stone to make it more attractive to prospective users. Various firms took an interest in the land only to withdraw. Though supported by government it was never a huge success but Orchard Farm Caravans, which had a park on Burnt Street, set up shop there and greatly expanded. So for a while did

---

[284] Jenkins p. 158
[285] Ibid. p.165ff.
[286] *UDC Minutes* June 1967 NRO DC 18/4/12

North Norfolk Produce Ltd which had a lorry depot there in the 1970s; they had a processing plant in South Creake. For a long time many of the units lay empty and derelict.

For a time the vegetable processing industry experienced a boom, much of it based on carrots. In 1956 John Temple established a carrot factory on Warham Road. Carrots were washed in huge numbers in an industrial process requiring the use of quantities of water and producing the possibility of contamination. The council approved as long as the water went into the sewers. It seemed to be an effective piece of agricultural industry if only if could be made to make a

Workers at Cartwright and Butler, 1986

profit. Apparently it could not.

Carrots were much used in jam making and baby foods. Whether Cartwright and Butler's products contained carrots, the firm certainly made chutneys and similar products, initially on Mill Road. Marion Cartwright, who had been making and selling preserves from her home in Hunstanton, joined up with Charles Butler who was packing herbs from Holt in 1981. Together they set up a factory in Wells. The former council offices lying empty were rented cheaply from the new district council for the making of bottled jams and other preserves, combining Marian Cartwright's culinary skills and Charles Butler's accountancy. They bought a stove for £10 but went on to much bigger plant. Theirs was a roaring success: their products were sold in Harrods, Fortnum & Masons, even Macy's in New York and were distributed across the globe – Europe, North America, Australia and New Zealand. At the height of their success they employed 142 workers, mostly women. However, food manufacture was apt to produce aromas unwanted by local residents and after some time they moved to the new industrial estate on Maryland, taking on the offices of Dewing and Kersley, now empty close by the also defunct railway station. But just as a major contract with Marks and Spencer was being sealed in 1992, the bank withdrew financial support and the operation closed.[287]

Wells people increasingly worked out of town. Some worked on the land. Some worked at the Fakenham branch of Eastern Counties which continued after the Wells unit closed. Others worked at the huge Cox and Wyman printing plant in Fakenham whose closure in 1982 left a great hole in the very centre of the town. Ross Foods had a large facility to the east of the town for a while and food processing continued and continues there. It was and is a highly volatile industry.

GI wedding at Our Lady Star of the Sea: Sgt and Mrs Louis Nemeth (née Ryan)

Some Wells folk found jobs on the American airbase at Sculthorpe. With the coming of the Cold War, it had become important as a forward facility, with a huge support establishment, some 10,000 personnel, for its fighter and bomber force. Sculthorpe became a nuclear base but it was also engaged in the task of responding to the constant incursions of Soviet aircraft testing Western defences. There were many days when it was almost certain that a US jet fighter or bomber would be seen in the sky; sonic booms were routine. Inevitably, many of its serving staff, military and civilian, lived off the base, numbers of them in Wells. They found their homes in flats on the Buttlands, on Staithe Street, at Blenheim House where there was an informal mess, in fact, wherever there was property for rent. They played baseball and had barbecues on the Buttlands, rather exotic for those days. Likewise many Wells men and women worked on the base and were entertained there. The Americans brought money to the town and, until rationing ended in 1954, commodities unavailable to still ration-bound Norfolk. Sam Abel's garage on the A149 continued to act as a trading post. The Americans were mostly welcome but they also brought interactions which were sometimes productive of tensions. When men got girls pregnant liaison provided by the American Red Cross was essential in order to keep the peace. Local girls married them at local churches. The base did not close until 1992 but after 1962 large scale bomber deployments were severely reduced and most personnel were accommodated on the base. They had been here for nearly twenty years and their departure was keenly felt.

[287] The name was bought by a Yorkshire Bakery company, Moordale Foods, and still exists.

Abraham's Bosom on a summer's day with caravans stretching into the distance

The industry, if it can be called that, which bloomed and flourished, was tourism. The secret of the town's growth as a tourism destination was the Pinewoods camp site hard by the beach. The council had lost no time, as we have seen, in restoring the beach and the lush fields alongside the Beach Road. The then Earl's desire to preserve and enhance the Pinewoods, which he was unwilling to lease to the council, made the scene more attractive. Then in February 1950 the County Planning Committee proposed 'a coastal holiday camp' for up to 300 persons for the town. Tom Grange, quick off the mark, arranged with the Earl of Leicester for a caravan site on Beach Road and secured from the council £1,000 for toilets. The camp was an almost immediate success. Huge numbers of touring caravanners came. The site was advertised in the *Leicester Mercury* and the *Nottingham Journal.* Some came for the week; some left their caravans there for the whole summer. There were eventually some 620 caravans, all of which had to be taken off at the end of the season and stored, often within the

Sunbathing on the beach behind the lifeboat station, 1950s

town but also in nearby villages. Unprovided with mains sewerage, chemical toilets were the only provision.

The 1953 floods were a huge setback and it took until 1956 for the site to be fully restored with new roadways and the clearance of tree stumps. Charles Platten took on rental of the Beach Café. Other local providers put in their bids: concessions were granted – Pecheys the local newsagents would supply newspapers, Styman's would provide groceries and the inevitable Platten would provide milk. Also hired out by the council were the sites of the beach huts, the huts themselves being owned by the hirers. Other private contractors provided deck chairs and windbreaks.

The site included Abraham's Bosom, now restored and supplied with rowing skiffs and paddle boats for hire. Local carpenter Leslie Ellender was employed to repair and repaint them for each season, some 28 of them. An annual illustrated town guide was produced.

Success brought its own problems. As time went by and aspirations rose the management of the site became more of a strain. Winter storage was one problem, solved in part by the local people who were willing to store caravans on their land. The caravans got bigger, from eight foot wide to as much as twelve feet. This would not be the limit. Consideration was given to charging extra for the new vans which were now up to thirty feet in length. By the 1960s enquiries for pitches well exceeded capacity. In 1962 the council received a petition from 154 caravan users about the quality of the service – dust, mud, poor toilet facilities, having to queue for milk plus the need for cesspools and water closets. In 1964 it was reported that there were over 400 tents in August and upwards of 200 touring caravans. Numbers fluctuated wildly which made provision difficult. By 1967 the issue of sewage disposal had become serious. The toilet blocks emptied into a cesspit, the servicing of which occupied the emptying lorry almost full time in summer. Attempts at improving the offer were at the mercy of events, often the weather. Mains electricity was provided in1969 but in that same wet summer of 1969 flooding of the site became the problem. Tenders were sought for the putting in of mains sewerage for the site. The roadways were to be tarred.

After the 1978 floods the beach bank was raised, making the Pinewoods site seem more secure. Static caravans, not intended to be towed from place to place, became more popular. Their owners could rely on the provision of electricity, mains water and ensuite toilets. They no longer had to trek to the shower block for their ablutions. It became virtually impossible to remove the caravans for the winter period; they were too big to store and difficult in any case to move. Orchard Caravans, a local firm which supplied most of the new caravans, refused to undertake the task of removal.

After the demise of the Urban District Council in 1974, the site would be administered by the North Norfolk District Council but in 1996 Holkham decided not to renew the lease and began to impose its own regulations, including one which fixed the maximum age of a trailer, now so called, which could use the site. It was no longer a cheap holiday location. The day of the touring caravan in Wells would, before too long, pretty well come to an end. On the other hand, static caravans were rapidly becoming second homes particularly because, while the owners could not live there permanently, the caravans themselves did not have to be moved off each winter and each was connected to water and electricity supplies and mains sewerage. There were over 500 static caravans.

It is a full mile from the quay to the lifeboat station, far enough to deter people from walking except in good weather. There had long been a bus service supplied by Sam Abel and others but the idea was conceived of having a railway link. Roy Francis, an ex-naval lieutenant-commander from Forncett, south of Norwich, was a miniature railway enthusiast. The district council approached him about building a railway from the town to the beach in order to reduce congestion and to provide an additional attraction for the town. Unpropitiously as it turned out, he completed it in 1976, only 18 months before the floods of 1978 washed it away. Undeterred, he rebuilt it in time for the summer season that year. Initially powered by steam, a more powerful steam-outline diesel engine would take over hauling the carriages and Francis sold it in 1980 in order to build the much longer Wells to Walsingham light railway which took three years to build and opened on 6 April 1982.[288] The harbour railway was to pass through several owners until its closure in 2021. The lines were taken up.

Operating at regular intervals, it could take town visitors to the beach and Pinewoods visitors to the town. But there had to be something to attract people townwards. The buildings along the quay, which had been almost entirely industrial premises, had, one by one, become food outlets or amusement provision. Styman's the grocers, Platten's milk bar, Underwood's snack bar and amusement centre[289]; Gray's amusements, all opened in the 1960s. There was the inevitable rock shop. Bingo and burgers became the new offer. Buckets and spades could be bought. French's wet fish shop became a fish and chip shop. Platten opened a second chippy, a necessary rival. It was the classic combination for a seaside resort.[290]

The travelling fair, which had first brought the showmen to Wells, had visited the town for years and continued on the quay until new regulations put an end to the exhilaration of swinging out over the water on the rides. The ending of commercial shipping in 1992 would accelerate the process as the iconic Granary was abandoned to be turned into flats. Gray's arcade, next to the Granary, burnt down in 2005.

---

288 Jenkins p.191ff
289 *UDC Minutes* Jan 1966 NRO DC 18/4/11
290 Sally Festing *Showmen: The Voice of Travelling Fair People* (Shaun Tyas 2012) Ch. 5.

Reeve's grocers and wine merchants on Staithe Street 1977, by that time run by Trevor Rands and his wife Suzanne (left and right)

The change in the commercial character of the town would inevitably be reflected in its provision of services in the town itself. In the early years after the war there were seven grocers in the town. The influx of visitors, mostly day trippers and touring caravanners, meant that the shopping offer would have to change. In addition, by 1981 the number of second or holiday homes had reached nearly 14%. The town appeared to be too small for large commercial concerns to set up shop here. Larger operations such as the Co-op and the International stores came and went (and latterly came again); the latter bought the shop at the south west corner of Staithe Street in 1913 but was the victim of successive takeovers during the 1980s so that the site was bought by Leftleys who had bought Claxton's convenience store in 1971. Styman's grocers moved from Freeman Street to the quay, replacing Grange's garage; he had several outlets in the town. Nevertheless, the town was to become less and less self-sufficient in the commodities it offered. There was some stability; the chemist's shop had traded from 1925 until quite recently under the name of Kinghorn's, and was still a chemist.

Cadamy's electricians, whose founder Jack was chairman of the district council post-war, still retained its name but not the family connection; its shop front scarcely changed. Herbert Butcher, who was once a councillor too, saw his outfitting business, one of three in Staithe Street, go. Wells, drapers and outfitters on Staithe Street who once provided school uniforms, eventually pulled out in 1978. Thurgur's china and glass shop at the bottom of High Street had been there for over a hundred years. After its closure in the 1960s the building was considered as the new council offices but in 1980 it was demolished and replaced by houses.

Remarkably to the modern eye there were at one time over twenty

Claxton's self-service shop at the top of High Street in 1949 – press photo

shops in the High Street. Why they all closed or moved is a debated question. Until the closure of the railway, people routinely passed that part of town every day. Afterwards few people would pass that way. The emptying of the shops happened quite quickly once the railway closed.

Specific to the tourism industry, though not exclusively so, was the provision of food for immediate consumption. Apart from the statutory chip shops, ice cream parlours emerged, based on the local dairies. There were three dairies on Burnt Street; there was another on the quay, yet another on Staithe Street. Farmer Ernest Flint's ice cream parlour had been in business since before the war. Platten's Milkobar made money on the quay.

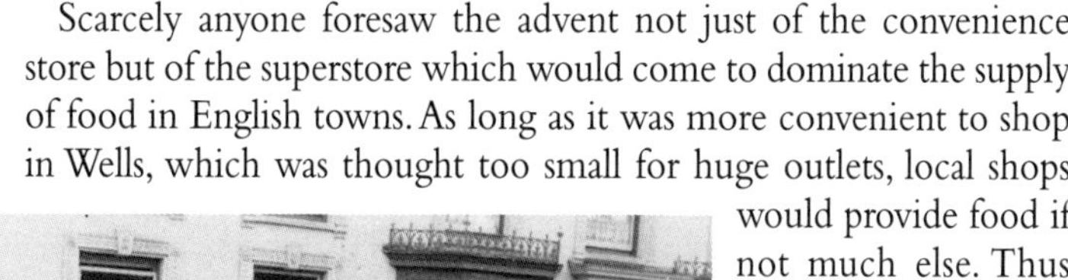

Scarcely anyone foresaw the advent not just of the convenience store but of the superstore which would come to dominate the supply of food in English towns. As long as it was more convenient to shop in Wells, which was thought too small for huge outlets, local shops would provide food if not much else. Thus when the new housing estates were planned, a parade of shops was deemed necessary. The one on Northfield Lane was to provide for all the immediate needs of residents. A similar idea for the later

Milk delivery on the Buttlands in the 1950s

Waveney Close estate was proposed but never implemented. An indication of what was to come was the opening of Claxton's self-service shop at the top of High Street in 1949.

Home deliveries, which had once accounted for the sale of bread as well as milk and, on a less regular basis, shellfish, gradually reduced. The daily delivery of milk continued longest, first from the local farms – Flint had bought a bottling plant in the 1940s and, as well as supplying nine local schools, sold over 500 pints a day in the town.[291] His Manor Farm dairy was eventually taken on by Wensum Dairies of Fakenham. Repeated take-overs and the abolition of the Milk Marketing Board in 2002 left a free-for-all market and the virtual demise of milk deliveries.

The number of shops providing for local needs inexorably reduced so that the majority sold tourist goods: books, paintings, buckets and spades and their successors; ornaments; pictures; things that no one needs but that people on holiday would buy, especially on those rainy days that retailers long for. Anything to get them off the beach. Shops which flourished during the summer often closed for the winter; the season was short.

[291] Manor Farm records 1936-2004 He also supplied the various military establishments based in the county. Cf. Correspondence with NAAFI .

6. The local community

Sharpies being brought up the slipway after a race

A local retailer in the town remarked not many years ago that 'all winter we wait for the visitors to come; and all summer we wait for them to go'. In fact, however dependent Wells is on visitors, its own social life in both summer and winter has a life of its own; one in which visitors are an ambiguous presence.

An example is the practice of leisure sailing. Sailing for fun in the harbour had been long practised mostly by locals or those who came to live in the town. The sailing club was sailing Sharpies before the war. They are boats almost unknown now on the international circuit. It may come as a surprise to know that they were a racing class in the 1956 Olympics. Described as heavy dinghies, they were gaff-rigged, built of wood and fast. Wells, together with Brancaster, had a long tradition of Sharpie sailing and was now a little closer to the centre of things. Britain gained a bronze medal in the Heavy Dinghy class though the crew, Jasper Blackall and Terence Smith, were not locals.

Another use of the harbour was for hydroplanes. In those days, the harbour was untroubled by moorings for yachts; when the tide was in it was the fishermen and the pilots who knew where the deep water was. Buoyage was irregular. The expanse of open water seemed to invite shallow drafted vessels onto the water. The Wells Motor

Boat and Hydroplane Club was formed in November 1951. Its progenitors were a group of boat enthusiasts and garage owners, men like Derek Revell, Stacey Walsingham and Sid Warren. Initially the boats had inboard engines, often marinised car engines; gradually outboards made an appearance. The 'planes' themselves were manufactured of plywood in sheds and gardens, the outboards no more than 1200cc capacity. They were to skim across the water, and so needed scarcely a foot of depth to meet their needs. On the other hand, they were less controllable than vessels having greater purchase on the water, skidding round marker buoys. Women like Evelyn Walsingham were as good a bet as drivers as men, partly it was said because they were lighter. In the years between the 1950s and the 1970s they monopolised the harbour on summer Sunday afternoons. Watched by large crowds, they were kept informed by the loudhailers announcing a forthcoming race and the results of the previous one. Vessels were handicapped according to their recorded maximum speed; some were capable of up to 30 mph. They were less admired by dinghy sailors for whom they posed a threat, liable as they were to run off course. (One ran into a fishing boat, severely damaging it.) The noise of a tannoy on a Sunday of all days did not please everyone but the social life which developed around the club and its presentation evenings was a feature of the town. Members would meet in the upstairs room of the Shipwrights, accessed via an external staircase. One of the reasons advanced for the decline and disappearance of hydroplanes was the silting up of the harbour attributed to the gravel extraction in the channel. Certainly there were some unhappy experiences of planes running onto the sand.

George Murton with Evelyn Walsingham on Zola

Gradually the channel would fill up with leisure boat moorings so that racing, whether of power boats or dinghies, would no longer be possible. The presence of moorings for sailing vessels, some of which scarcely moved during the whole summer season, would confine most boats to the buoyed channel. Beyond the lifeboat station where the channel was unsuitable for moorings, exposed to the sea as it was, the water ski club could function. Formed in 1971, at one time half a dozen boats pounded up and down the channel pulling their intrepid skiers along, raising questions about the safety of swimmers. The channel was becoming busy. Windsurfing is a hair-raising sport occasionally practised in high winds beyond the lifeboat station.

Many of the activities of the town depended on the presence of visitors. Some things were planned to attract visitors; other's drew visitors to what was practised largely by locals. Some activities were

Ted Blakey (back left) with school lifeguards

intended to supply visitors' needs but assumed a life of their own.

One of the attractions of beaches is the chance to cool off from the sun's heat just yards from a deckchair. But the sea is dangerous and the Wells channel, fast-flowing at flood and ebb, is particularly so. It may have been for that reason that in 1966 the Royal Life Saving Society proposed to the council that a body of lifeguards be recruited and trained. Teams of four to six men and women would be equipped with reels, belt and line and uniforms to work in collaboration with the RNLI. The moving spirit behind it was local policeman PC Smith; he did the initial recruitment and training and some of his colleagues from Norwich would come and help at weekends. Because the high school had a swimming pool a staff member, Ted Blakey, came to run a Lifeguards Club assisted by Mrs Terry Ashworth, a swimming instructor at the school (and wife of a Wells policeman). They would operate at weekends, on bank holidays and during the school holidays. They eventually got their own outboard-powered inflatable boat. At one time, there were over thirty members. On Blakey's retirement in 1987 Lesley Jarvis took over, followed by Emma Beck. The club only closed in 2006. It was an example of voluntary initiative providing for need but also providing enjoyment and training particularly for the young. Young people's groups flourished in those days. The Sea Scouts were another such group, which had acquired the old air-sea rescue boat *Terra Nova* whose sad fate after the 1953 floods is recorded elsewhere.

The various organisations inevitably overlapped and voluntary initiative and statutory organisations were in those days difficult to distinguish. The coastguard still had an officer in Wells which was an auxiliary station. As such it had a manned watch lookout next to the lifeboat station and was issued with an outboard powered inflatable, manned by part-time volunteers. Informal relationships established over time meant that its personnel could call upon each other and on the services of the fire brigade to provide illumination to enable a search to be conducted by night - and on the search and rescue helicopters from RAF Coltishall to share in fortnightly practice rescues, all arranged semi-informally. It was a state of affairs which was to be taken advantage of by Anglia Television which used its services in the filming of several television programmes including the Adam Dalgliesh series in the 1980s.[292] People knew each other; there were no risk assessments or other paper work to delay or prevent interaction. Lacking electronic aids and smart phones, local knowledge was essential. When the coastguard service was re-organised and the coastguard station closed in 1992, this was a loss widely mourned and only shortly afterwards the entirely voluntary Coastwatch service enabled the old coastguard station to re-open to provide daytime observation of the harbour and beach.

The same blurring of lines between tourism and locally-based activities was the Carnival. The Carnival had grown out of the Regatta and in the early days most activities took place on the quay and even on the marshes on which tents had been erected. Foot races were at one time run there. The earliest record of a Carnival Queen was Eva Claxton in 1933. Post-war revival was immediate, the first being in 1946. The Earl of Leicester agreed to be president, and the organisation was in the hands of local people from many parts of the community. In 1950 the event took place on one day with rowing races, swimming

Coronation year 1953: Ann Terrington was Wells Carnival Queen

[292] The episode *Devices and Desires* was filmed in 1991 off Wells. It was one of many films which used Wells and Holkham as a location.

and the various handicapped sailing races. The Carnival procession, which was followed by a dance, took place at 6pm. In the years that followed events on land and water took place over one weekend. In 1969 however the Carnival was extended to a week, from 26 July to 2 August and the Regatta, which was organised by the Sailing Club, took place a fortnight later in mid August. The split between land and water was not entire: swimming and rowing races all took place on the 26th. The Hydroplane races were arranged for the afternoon of the 27th to end before the Annual Lifeboat Service.

Carnival processions became more elaborate as lorries, duly decorated and loaded with members of various organisations in fancy dress, snaked their way through the town, the centre piece being the Carnival Queen who would begin her reign on a flatbed lorry surrounded by her attendants. The slightly tricky process of selecting her from a number of applicants took place a day or two earlier. Runners-up would become her attendants. There was a period when Queens might undertake a series of similar engagements at Carnivals in nearby towns such as Fakenham, Cromer and Lowestoft. It could be a busy summer for her. It would even be possible for her to be entered into a national competition. (History does not record whether any of our Queens were entered and how well they did.) Fancy dress was at the heart of it all: there were competitions for children of different ages, but also prizes for the best decorated float, for tradesmen's vehicles (duly washed down and polished), including the fire engine; for vintage cars, decorated cycles and 'perambulators', for walking adults in costume and even for the best decorated shop.[293]

Like all such events the Carnival went through its difficulties. Succession was always an issue. Also if too much money was given away to charitable causes there would be no means of carrying on the next year. It almost folded and was revived only after the 1978 floods, giving away less money but able to survive for another year. The connection between the Carnival and the Regatta became less and less

Royal British Legion, August Bank Holiday, 1994

[293] Wells Annual Regatta and Carnival Programme 1965

so that by 2000 the two had become quite separate.

Some organisations were part of national or even international umbrella bodies. Among these, as in most other larger communities, were the Women's Institute, Freemasons, Rotary, Lions, Oddfellows, and the British Legion, Much supported by incomers, these organisations were strongly represented in the town. Others like the Men's Discussion group were local.

Voluntary organisations depend upon individuals and their continuity is never assured. Thus the War Memorial Institute, the product of so much fundraising before the war had, by 1955, fallen in membership to 38 (and was to fall to 13) and was no longer self-supporting. The admission of 'ladies' to full membership in that year helped, as did an appeal to local firms for support.[294] Local grocer Derek Styman presided over a modest revival of its fortunes as chairman. League billiards and snooker were once again played. Membership continued to drift downwards so that it effectively closed. It was at that point in 1975 that Styman took the initiative and secured agreement to amalgamate with the former British Legion Billiards club whose lease on a room in a barn behind Scarborough House was about to run out. John Tuck, by now secretary and treasurer, demanded that a drinks licence be obtained and that the formerly all male Billiards Club accept women members (as the Institute already did). The interior was repainted, and membership of the Club, as it was now called, mushroomed to over a hundred members. Tuck got a band of volunteers together who enabled its resuscitation and flourishing. Thereafter it fell back for a while but then with yet another new secretary, Fred Robbins, it once again revived.[295] It was extended to provide a lounge and toilet facilities in 1985 and again shortly after. Such were the fortunes of many a voluntary organisation.

Pub outings resumed after the war; the coaches were bigger and more luxurious; pub games had never stopped. The Shipwrights Inn continued to resound to the clack of dominoes, the thud of darts and the noise of laughter. Crib was the most common card game. Tobacco smoke permeated everything, colouring walls and ceiling a dull orange. The Fleece continued as a place of refuge for the crews of the coasters. Every pub provided for leisure activities: almost all had a pool table and were part of a league. Likewise they would have a dart board and one or more teams. Not only the pubs but most men's organisations such as the coastguard, the lifeboat, the police, and the fire service had darts teams and were part of a darts league, each attached to a particular day of the week. There would be difficulties if an emergency occurred requiring the attendance of several of those organisations.

The dearth of entertainment during the war was not remedied quickly thereafter. Television did not immediately re-appear after the

---

[294] Memorial Institute Minutes October/January 1955/6

[295] John Tuck Wells Memorial Institute (and Women's Lib) WLHG Newsletter No 41 April 2009

The Scotch Disco in the Edinburgh

wartime shutdown and even when it did it closed down after an hour at 4pm and did not open up again until 8.30pm. Until 1953 very few people had a set. The two cinemas, the Regal and the Park, were the major source of provided entertainment. Sam Oliver, who ran the town gas works, was the Regal's manager; he presided over teenage couples not altogether attending to the films, a western, the adverts, none of which were local, and the main feature film. Highly rated films such as the Bond series in the 1960s and 70s would be shown a year and more after release nationally. A Saturday morning Children's Club screened films such as the *Lone Ranger*, *Lassie* and the *Three Stooges*. In time, as competition from television at home and live entertainment in the town grew, so the schedules were increasingly filled with X-rated films which excluded the young altogether.[296] The cinema closed in 1975 and was for a while a bingo hall.

'Live' entertainment in truth meant music, 'canned' or live, but also dancing – and something to drink. The primary attraction was the juke box. From the 1950s coffee bars such as Fred Raimond's on Clubbs Lane, armed with such a machine, could reckon on attracting the young to a tiny space where they would sit on bus seats when not dancing. Alcohol proved another magnet; youngsters began congregating at the back of The Fleece. Then in the late sixties the Kitsons, Michael and Mollie, son and daughter-in-law of Mary, licensees of the Edinburgh hotel, started a discotheque, the 'Scotch', on a small floor at the far end of the bar. So-called disc jockeys were employed, first by the Kitsons themselves and then by local people such as Peter and Janet Kellett and DJ Dick Platten. With two record decks the music could be virtually continuous. Ultra-violet lighting added to the fun, revealing what was underneath white blouses. By the 1970s the Scotch was operating every weekend and every night in summer. Other pubs, notably the Ark Royal and the Globe, were more occasional venues in those years.

Not all music was on disc. Local bands, formed following the arrival of rock music in the late 1950s and early '60s, played in larger venues such as the Maltings and the church rooms. The town produced its own home-grown talent. Skiffle groups, using tea chest basses and wash boards, were rapidly replaced by groups using more professional equipment. Bands like the Triffids morphed into Spencer's People, a Wells-based group that rehearsed in The Globe to save parental eardrums. They began to play at gigs all over the country, sometimes

[296] Eric Reading collection (WLHG Archive)

playing with groups that came to national attention like Marmalade. Mervyn and the Starbeats, who were to re-form thirty years later, came from Fakenham. Norfolk was well known as a place to which bands came. In the summer holidays it was possible to enjoy a long weekend: Thursdays at the Ark Royal, Fridays had live music at the church rooms; Saturday nights via the free bus heading for Cromer Royal Links or West Runton Pavilion[297] and Sunday night at the Scotch. Cromer would see such bands as T. Rex, Black Sabbath, The Who, Slade and artists like Jimi Hendrix, Chuck Berry, Lulu and the subsequently infamous Gary Glitter.

There was always the possibility of going to a dance at the Sculthorpe air base but some young GIs found their way instead to the Scotch. Discos allowed a wider range of music to be heard, including American bands. For younger teenagers, parental pick-ups at the end of the evening had to be surreptitious if embarrassment was to be avoided; most walked or staggered home. These activities were not just for locals. The adolescent daughters of visitors from the Midlands would find themselves popular in such places. The Leicester fortnight when its firms closed down was a busy time not always appreciated by locals.

Somehow it all faded away. A colossal fight in the church rooms that resulted in a hearing in the Crown Court did not help. Fist fights were one thing; the advent of knives was another altogether. Street fights were rare but they could become bloody, particularly when town loyalties were called in question. Young lads from Leicester and Nottingham, or more locally those training at Bircham Newton, came to town looking for trouble and sometimes got it. The Ark Royal and later The Globe were places from which trouble could emanate. It is a salutary thought that The Hoste in Burnham Market in those days was reputed to have a floor that your feet stuck to, not a pleasant place at all. Pubs were only beginning to sell food, albeit only basket meals, but they would improve the offering over time.

For some, there were more organised activities through membership of uniformed organisations such as Scouts and Guides, Cubs and Brownies; the Sea Scouts were popular. In 1976 scouting had acquired a new look intended to make itself more attractive: wolf cubs became cub scouts – Kipling's *Jungle Book* terminology was abandoned; Akela was gone. A Guide company was formed that year. There was the Swimming Club at the school. The young would play football; the more sedate would play bowls. As football became more serious there would be pressure to improve the quality of facilities. Hubert Spalding, president of the Wells Town football club, was indefatigable both in ensuring the future of the club and in securing finance to provide a necessary pavilion required by the league. Putting up such a building could only be justified if the club had security of tenure. The lease from Holkham Estate to the district council was due to expire in

---

[297] Julie Fielder *What Flo Said* (2013)

1996. After long negotiations a new lease was signed with the town council who were however unwilling to give exclusive use to the football club; Holkham wished to reserve the right to take back part of the land without notice. The lease for twenty-three years was finally signed in 1993. Spalding's only problem then was how to raise the money for the pavilion.

Ballroom dancing for an older generation was a serious option. Horace and Betty Kemp ran a club in the 1950s, meeting in the Church Rooms. Intended for couples, there were always more women than men so that some of the women had to take the man's part.

Members of Wells' Dancing Club in the 1950s

Tennis became increasingly popular with the formation of the Wells Tennis Club. In 1948 Rachael Chamberlain gave a piece of land opposite the council bungalows on Gales Court for a Tennis and Bowls Club in memory of her brother Ladas, after his tragic death.

Policing in the town took on a new face with the building of a new station in 1962 together with two police houses (and two more houses purchased on Northfield Waye). Sergeant Ashworth was the last sergeant for the town. On his retirement in 1972 Wells was run from Fakenham and four officers became two and then for a while one, PC Sibley. Bill Sibley was to serve out his whole time from 1970 almost until his retirement in 1994 in the town, obtaining the assistance of another officer a couple of years before doing so. He described the virtues of having a local policeman whose role was, he said, 'part tourist information officer, part social worker'; but there was still criticism about the level of cover in the town when incidents occurred. From Fakenham the operational centre moved to North Walsham, town council meetings were frequently attended by senior police officers explaining periodic shortages of police and the particular problems created by the policing of the Whitsun annual pilgrimage at

Walsingham which sucked police resources from everywhere else.

Church life, if anything, became more vigorous in the twenty years after the war. As in the secular world there was a sense that here was the opportunity for a new start. Most children in the town were christened. Whether or not you were a churchgoer you got married in one church or another. There was effectively nowhere to be buried other than in the town cemetery and most people had their funeral in church. Cremation had not yet become popular; the nearest crematorium outside Norwich had opened in 1935 but it was not until the 1970s that its use became a recognised option. Apart from anything else, it was a long way to the nearest crematorium.

Revd Alexander Stephens, extreme left, with church choir

Rector Moss had seen out the war, retiring in 1948. Donald Brown, a rector with a historical bent, had assisted Arthur Purchas in his early work on producing Purchas's history of the town. He was keen on the Sea Scouts and helped get them their boat, the *Terra Nova* (which ended up on the quay wall as we have seen). He was succeeded by the Revd Alexander Stephens who set about the repair and restoration of the church. He had the church re-roofed with slate and the side aisles in lead to which was added a new wing intended for a choir vestry, clergy vestry and toilets, a real novelty in a mediaeval church. He had the church floodlit. In his time the choir acquired a number of female choristers.

Stephens died suddenly in office in 1967 to be followed in relatively quick succession by three clergy, Howard Whyntie, Richard Page and David Chapman. Howard Whyntie came to be vicar of Wells in 1968. He attempted to put the parish on a firmer financial footing; he was thoughtful if cool. In his desire to be fair, refusing to praise some but not others, funerals that he took would not include a eulogy, something that would not go down well now. He organised a trip to the Passion Play at Oberammergau. He facilitated the re-organisation of the parishes round about so that when Cyril Lavender retired from Warham and Wighton, Whyntie worked with John Holmes, Lavender's successor, to operate the four communities of Wells, Holkham, Wighton and Warham as one unit in what was called a Group Ministry. He resigned suddenly in June 1971 and at the age of 59 went to become a school teacher; he died in 1990.

His successor, Dick Page, came from Sheffield and seems to have

Revd Dick Page and family

had a pastoral ministry particularly to non-churchgoers. During his time at Wells the children's' work and activities grew, and several younger families became regular members of the worshipping community. He was supported in his ministry by two other clergy and before too long three lay readers, ministerial forces never before or since available to the parish. However, finances were becoming straitened as the church came to rely more and more on the living membership and less on historic funds, both central and local. The printed magazine was abandoned in 1976, a symbolic loss. It would now be a duplicated publication. After a ministry in the town of seven years, Page also left for another parish in the diocese, arguably as his ministry was beginning to bear fruit. Holmes was the last vicar of Warham having retired some months earlier in 1977.

After a gap of 15 months, David Chapman from Sawley in the Derby diocese was appointed. Several clergy had turned the job down in the interim, it was thought because the new rectory was not complete. Chapman undertook yet further reorganisation as the Group Ministry was replaced by a single benefice. In this he was assisted by Geoffrey Abson, a new breed of clergyman, unpaid and locally based, whom he inherited. Chapman wrote his usual letter for the August 1983 edition of the church magazine but by September he too was gone, offered a parish in the London diocese. The parish was left in the hands of two lay readers, Roy Barrow, deputy at Alderman Peel school and Reg Winterton, who had retired to Wells. Joe Brice, a former Methodist minister who was badly disabled, held the fort during yet another interregnum.

Methodist ministers came and went on a more regular pattern organised centrally by Conference. Notable among them was Edwin Softley, who came to Wells in 1972. Highly thought of both within the church and by other denominations, he was responsible for raising funds for major repairs to the church including its reflooring. His work with young people was valued.

Revd Edwin Softley and Wells Messengers of the Cross, April 1976

He was for a while a town councillor.

Not everything was done by organised groups. The new private estates such as Mill Court and Waveney Close, built in the 1960s, were occupied by locals but also by incomers, those who would become an increasingly important group. They bought houses, bungalows for preference, as second and retirement homes. Many of them, having been involved in community life in the places from which they came, became active in local organisations. They contributed to the life of the churches, to men's and women's organisations, to such as the Wells Arts Centre, to the town twinning group, the Carnival and the hospital. Less formally the house-warming parties for new arrivals created bonds of engagement and support. Their contribution to the life of the town was to be significant. The town council would increasingly rely upon their standing for election. Their passing one by one was a serious loss to the town.

Mill Court 1970s

Some people become solitary by circumstance; some are by nature so. The keeping of an allotment – Wells had three allotment sites at one time – tends to be a solitary exercise. Required of every local authority by statute in the years after enclosure, the two large allotments at each end of the town absorbed a deal of energy and produced a lot of produce, while having given way in earlier times, to the requirement of new housing. Northfield Crescent was built on former allotments at the east end of town. The story of the west end allotments is told elsewhere.

Allotment sheds, useful to store tools, were also a place of retreat for men wishing for some solitude. Jack Cox, sometime whelk fisherman, wartime naval officer and lifeboatman, found in his shed a place to paint. The wide skies and profusion of wild life, the fishing and the coast itself had long drawn people to the town to paint. Frank Southgate's pictures had long commanded serious money. The same was true increasingly of Cox's works. Unlike the several trained painters who were drawn to Wells from elsewhere, he was untutored. He inspired others who painted and those who bought his paintings. Altogether, landscape painting became something of a feature of the town. Hazel Ashley's artists' materials shop on Staithe Street, established in 1979, found a ready trade. An arts group was started which met regularly – at one time it had fifty members. The tradition of making and catching moments in every changing land and seascape would continue using a variety of media: water colours, oils, linocuts and later photographs.

7. Two new schools

Educationally, Wells had become a hub for a number of villages in the vicinity and its new housing generated new families. By 1956 the baby boomers were of secondary school age. The secondary school was expanding. There were now eight classes in six classrooms plus a science block; additionally there were detached housecraft and handicraft rooms. A kitchen had opened in 1942. Numbers had continued to increase. It became clear that an entirely new secondary school was wanted.

There had been a programme of school building across the county since the war. The Development Plan which the County Council had produced in 1947 was supposed to give priority to the replacement of old school buildings and the building of completely new ones. The proposal was for 270 primary schools and 47 secondary schools, 39 of them new builds, thirteen new grammar schools and two new technical schools. The plan was the work of the Director of Education, Lincoln Ralphs and of Sam Peel, who had been chairman of the Education Committee of the County Council since 1941. (He had been first elected to the County Council in 1919, and had served on its Health Committee for eight years.) The two had become good friends but also allies in their attempts to improve Norfolk education. The cuts imposed by the 1951 budget put paid even to these developments in spite of proposals to put money into rural schools put forward by government in 1954 (and acted upon by Ralphs and Peel in their early submissions to government only days after the announcement). Nevertheless, according to Ralphs, progress was 'that of a cross-country goods train'. It took until 1960 for twenty-six new secondary schools to be built or nearing completion.

Donald Wadman, 1959-80

The appointment of Donald Wadman as head in 1959 had in view the building of a new school in Wells. A site on Market Lane had been identified, adjacent to the track of the old Heacham railway branch. Wadman had apparently been told that the new school could have an assembly hall equipped with a sound stage and balcony, a gymnasium or a swimming pool. A keen sailor, interested in both sport and drama, he got all three. By his second year he was able to observe the rising girders of the new school and on 20 September 1963 he attended the opening of the Alderman Peel Secondary Modern School, though it was not yet complete. Peel attended the occasion in a wheelchair; it was his last official duty. He died on 18 May 1964. (His title, that of Alderman, was granted to longstanding councillors by election by fellow council members, conferring as it did an honorific status; the system was abolished in 1974.) In the months after the official opening, as the buildings were completed, some of the furniture moving was done by staff and pupils manhandling desks and chairs along the old railway track and under the now-blocked-up bridge under Warham Road, traipsing back and forth. The school hall, still unfinished at the beginning of the new school year, provided the venue for a performance of a Christmas play, the *Song of Simeon*. The stage lighting arrived three days before and the curtains after the dress rehearsal.[298] The head was proud.

The school was important to the life of the town. Since early days teachers had come to live in the town on appointment. Many of them were to take up voluntary roles within the town: in the church, on the council, and in its social life. On retirement many of them stayed in the town. Wadman himself remained in the town, continuing to live in the old head's house. While in post he had been a keen Sharpie sailor, together with one of his staff, 'Tommy' Thomas, who lived round the corner from him. He obtained the use of six Sharpies, several owned by members of staff, so that in the summer of 1966 the National Schools Sailing Regatta was held in Wells. Over two hundred visiting competitors slept in the school hall. Less formally, pupils established friendships which were to endure over time and distance and would be revivified by the introduction, a generation or more later, of social media. Former pupils would travel across the globe and settle while keeping in touch. Education would take them further afield so that many would move out of Wells, out of Norfolk and out of the country: they went to Brisbane, Perth, Colorado, California, Texas, Kentucky, Florida, Utah, Mallorca and no doubt many other places too. It could be said that one of the prime exports from the town was its children.[299] On Wadman's watch the school began that expansion: a week's trip to Blankenburghe in Belgium was arranged. Overseas holidays were rare in those days; some pupils had never been outside the county. It was the first of many: in 1963 a party went to Switzerland and in 1965 to Austria. Trips would be organised to East Germany subsequently and skiing trips in January were to become a regular feature.

---

[298] School Magazine 1965
[299] Facebook , Down Memory Lane - various

In a strange way this was to be another tiny signal for a change in lifestyles, particularly of children. Earning money from delivering newspapers was but the beginning of it. Errand boys were needed too. At weekends and during the summer holidays girls in particular would work in shops. Some worked at Cartwright & Butler's jam factory; others at the whelk factory next to the Bowling Green; Angus's bakery, The Globe, The Crown; Holkham Pottery, Platten's café, Claxton's pop factory, Billy Neal's fish-and-chip shop on Northfield Lane.

The move to the new school left open the future of the Polka Road premises. It would become the new primary school. So after nearly a hundred and thirty years the old school would close, to become an educational Field Study Centre. Mr Metcalfe, who had taken over from Mr Clarke in 1965, supervised the move, with the ordering of substantially new equipment appropriate to the needs of small as well as larger children. He would be the first head not to live in the adjacent house. As in other areas of life the ability of the head and the managers to make decisions was becoming more and more restricted. The making of caretaking arrangements between the two schools was one example: it was decided centrally by the County on the grounds that it was 'easier to recruit head teachers than caretakers'. Metcalfe's desire to admit rising fives was met by refusal; the County was anxious to save money. The repair of the building, now over thirty-five years old, was something the authorities were less able to resist. His years would see the departure of a number of longstanding members of staff. Mrs Self, who had joined the staff in 1921 as Miss Smith, a pupil teacher, and who remained after her marriage to Fred Self, the landlord of the Ship Inn, and the birth of her children, rose to become deputy head and retired in 1966. Mrs Vera Guest, née Baker, who married a local carpenter, began her teaching career in Wells in 1923, returning in 1928 for a short time and then becoming a reception teacher in 1967; she retired in 1974. She continued as a supply teacher until shortly before her death in 1981.

A series of changes would affect both schools. The first was the remedying of the lack of any qualification obtainable by Alderman Peel children, the introduction of the Certificate of Secondary Education, a less academic qualification than GCE but which at least gave pupils something to take away with them. In the summer of 1967, the first 21 pupils took the examination, from which 28 Grade 1s were obtained, held to be equivalent to a pass at GCE. The next year some pupils took both GCE and CSE, made possible by the fact that the examination dates were different. Progress was slow, but in 1972 six pupils obtained five or more Grade 1 passes at CSE.

This seemed to cement the principle of the division at eleven but the 1970s saw two more major changes: the raising of the school leaving age to 16 and the end of selection. Depending as it did on the abolition of grammar schools, it would prove slow to implement. Wells' new school, even with a catchment of a dozen villages, seemed unlikely to obtain a sufficient school population so as to become a comprehensive school with a sixth form large enough for a wide range of subjects to be offered. Some ingenuity and persuasion would be needed.

The change to an inclusive but nevertheless examination-focussed system required new thinking and new teaching. Coincidentally therefore the turnover of staff saw the retirement of a previous generation of teachers. Among them was Mrs Haywood, who had come to the school in 1932 as Miss Wilsher, English teacher and senior mistress and after the war married the head of Maths, Tom Haywood,

Alderman Peel School, built in 1964

himself returned from active service. Another was Miss Thomson who had come to Wells in 1925 and had served under four head-teachers; she was said to have run the school under Mr Eggbeer. She taught cookery and housewifery but, in practice, she doubled as school nurse, tending cuts and abrasions and taking pupils to the doctor in her car. She had served the Wells schools for 42 years and was awarded the BEM in recognition.

Other teachers made their mark in different ways: Mr Haywood was both admired and feared; his harsh disciplinary regime included impromptu physical punishment, administered with a thrown board rubber or the flat of his hand. He was not alone in those days before corporal punishment became a sacking offence. Mr Condon was known for his ambitious musical plays and operas which in 1969 included a performance of Mozart's *The Magic Flute*. Different pupils remembered particular members of staff more or less fondly. Low expectations on the part of staff might produce resentment on the one hand or depress ambition on the other; teachers who gave encouragement seem to have been remembered with most affection. Some pupils raised money for outside charities, one of which, in 1968, was the first of a number of sponsored twenty-four-hour swims when 238 miles were swum raising £275.

With the coming of the raised school leaving age in 1973 the first statutory fifth year appeared. There were now 422 pupils in school but the process of working towards higher qualifications had been anticipated two years earlier when four pupils stayed on to take 'A' levels which two of them did, and went on to successful academic careers.

The process of creating a unified system of education began in 1977. The school was to become an 11 to 16 comprehensive, open to all within a catchment area. At the same time Fakenham Grammar school, which had new buildings, would be divided into an 11-16 high school and a sixth form college. The exercise in convincing parents that their children, who might have gone to Fakenham Grammar School, now must go to Wells included the sending of letters to prospective parents of the feeder schools and staff visits to every PTA of the feeder schools. Wells was to be a 'new school', parents were told; but the promised extra buildings never materialised. Three mobile classrooms came instead. New staff posts were created. Everyone had to be catered for: Mr Holm came as a German specialist and second deputy to Mr Barrow; Mrs Lamb was put in charge of special educational needs. In a school with a first floor those with physical disabilities were to pose problems which had to be overcome.[300]

In July 1978 the school closed as a secondary modern school and opened in the autumn term as a high school. It would, of course, take some time for it to encompass the whole ability range. In the short run with the exception of a change in colour of school uniform from maroon to blue, it looked much like the old one. The 1978 leavers, all eighty of them, included twenty-two who continued with some form of further education. Thirty-four boys went to various forms of manual work, many of them outdoors; five went to sea. Thirty-five had sat GCE of whom a quarter achieved some grades at A-C. Two years later Mr Wadman retired. He could look back on twenty-one years during which he had seen secondary education in the town transformed.

His successor, Barry Geal, faced new challenges, some of them unpredicted though some would say predictable. In 1980 there were 506 pupils; the next year the number was to rise to 551. The new head had to deal with the organisational issues that this created. He had also to deal with the fact that the buildings were already showing their defects. Acrow prop supports were needed in some classrooms and corridors. The science block had to be vacated in the August of 1983 due to roof leaks. The swimming pool was out of action for three months.

Down the road in the primary school Mr Metcalfe had his problems. The building was now over fifty years old; finances were tight: there were threats to the continuation of school dinners, numbers of pupils were falling, reductions in staffing and cleaning hours: all these pro-

[300] A pupil who had Duchenne Muscular Dystrophy posed particular mobility problems for which the school sought funding.

duced their own pressures and, to cap it all, there were issues of staff discipline. Corporal punishment was, in those days, permitted and widely practised by heads; the use of physical controls in classrooms was expected but there were limits, limits which were occasionally exceeded. Parents complained. Occasionally a member of staff would be the object of investigations. Children were said to be afraid to attend school. The head's diplomacy was put under some strain. But not all parents approved of a liberal approach. Some made their views plain that old-fashioned discipline was necessary if children were to learn that the world out there was harsh and needed to be respected if it was to be negotiated; children too had to learn to say sorry. They could be respected while maintaining high standards and children are not all the same.

Metcalfe left in 1982 with heart problems and was replaced by George Wincott from Surrey. He inherited a staff of six in the junior department and four in the infant department, together with 274 children. The ethos of the school under his leadership is indicated by a number of changes made by him. The classes were renamed after birds: Heron, Osprey, Kestrel, Owls, Puffin, Swallow, Chaffinch, Robin and Wren. He took a particular interest in children with special needs and, presaging later trends, he agreed that inter-school sports should have mixed teams from various schools so that no one school would 'win'. County advisors came in series. School numbers continued to fall, down to 220. Class names were changed to animals: Deer, Seals, Badgers and so on. Wincott retired in 1991 to be succeeded by Clive Sedgwick. Numbers dropped to 180. It fell to Sedgwick to implement the requirement of nationally organised pupil assessment, SATS as they were called. He described them as 'long and complex to administer though [they] were enjoyed by the children'. Intended to be implemented across the whole school system, they were abandoned at secondary level where there were enough examinations anyway. The National Curriculum, of which more shortly, which was introduced at the same time, applied across the board.

Perhaps the biggest headache was the occurrence of industrial action which to be fair affected the secondary school most. Teachers' salaries, which had been set in 1974 as a result of a government pay award, had eroded in value and the various unions were becoming restless. Teachers belonged to several unions, the main ones being the NUT and the NAS/UWT, resulting in differential action. Two teachers struck for a day in February 1979. By 1982 relations nationally had soured and teachers withdrew goodwill. No lunchtime duty was done; evening meetings had to be cancelled. Arbitration brought about a temporary truce but in 1984 actions resumed in earnest. Local children were sent into town at lunchtime or sent home. A NUT 'day of action' on 9 May affected the whole school other than fifth formers taking examinations. By 1985 strikes had become frequent; there were eight occasions when one of the two unions instructed teachers to strike: parents' evenings were cancelled; after-school clubs suffered. Pupils themselves made their feelings known. Several house captains and a member of the fourth form confronted the head saying that they intended to strike too! The head reported that the trouble had been 'averted so far but tensions [are] high over teachers' action and [their being] evicted from premises at lunchtime'. The production of school reports was put in jeopardy. Pupil numbers fell to as low as 80 as a result of children being sent home or making their own decisions. That there were six teachers' unions made matters worse. Because they could not agree on a common strategy, a final settlement was achieved through the Teachers' Pay and Conditions Act of 1987. The NUT, which opposed the settlement, lost a third of its members during those years; the teachers were not on the whole comfortable with refusing to exercise their professional responsibilities.

Increasingly teachers were sent on training courses following government initiatives. TVEI (Technical Vocational Educational Initiative) was a response to high youth unemployment figures and was the brainchild not of the Department of Education and Science but the Manpower Services Commission. In Wells, Miss Bannister was put in charge of coordinating it. It was said that the curriculum needed to be more vocational – members of staff were sent on courses to learn how to use computers. The long-awaited merging of GCE and CSE in 1986 required more training days. The first examinations took place in the summer of 1988. The new examination was to be seamless, allowing pupils of all abilities to take it. Rapidly it came to be assumed that grades A to C were equivalent to an old GCE pass. In-service training days during the school term, when children were not present, were introduced in 1988. They did not prevent the need for supply teachers covering for staff on courses. On many days there would be up to five supply teachers in school. Mr Geal reported on 8 January 1986, 'Normal day - for a change!' The next time he did so was in the following November. Staff pastoral responsibilities multiplied.

By 1987 the strikes had come to an end; the last was on 26 March when both major unions withdrew support for the afternoon. But by then the school had received a completely unexpected blow: three members of staff, including the head, were involved in a serious car accident. One, Mr Rumbles, was able to return within days; Mr Becket was away until half term. The head was not to return until the end of June and struggled on between operations, resigning in July 1988.

Mr Thorneycroft arrived in time for the summer term 1989 and the implementation of yet another major piece of legislation. The GCSE results which greeted him when he came to the school were pleasing. 109 fifth years were entered for public examinations, 97 of them for GCSE. The average pass rate of A-Cs was 47.9%, 97.8% of A-Fs, thus vindicating the desire of those who wanted children to leave school with some qualification, however modest.

He and his governors were to take over financial responsibility for the running of the school, setting out their own budget and taking responsibility for the hiring and firing of staff – subject to a number of safeguards. It was called Local Management of Schools (LMS). Different schools interpreted it in different ways. Alderman Peel took a moderate line, but the head reported that he had found himself negotiating the price of heating oil: 'This is a new demand on the head's time,' he wrote laconically. On 3 April 1990 he noted that, 'We are now officially devolved and responsible for our own budget of £830,000'. Sub-committees of now busier governors were formed including Lettings, Staff, Finance and Curriculum. Local professionals willing to offer their services were now much in demand. Being a governor now required flexibility in one's day job. Staff appraisal programmes were introduced to see whether they were doing their job effectively!

The Act also introduced a National Curriculum for every subject (except RE), divided into four Key Stages, two at primary and two at secondary school level, requiring yet more training courses for staff to attend. The head noted in the log book in January 1990 that a fellow head in Norfolk had resigned, 'a victim of the ERA and LMS, and probably not the last!'

The pressure on the staff continued to increase. The determination of government to assess the 'value for money' of schools resulted in the requirement that external examination results be published, thus creating 'league tables' by which schools could be compared. Inevitably the school did as every other school did, that is, to compare the syllabuses of the now privately-run examination boards to see which would suit their students best (and which seemed easiest in which to gain good grades). In order to assess the school directly, yet another piece of government legislation[301] resulted in the creation of the Office for Standards in Education (Ofsted) which could and did result in drastic action and re-organisation. The short notice given to schools, subsequently revised, caused disruption in teaching in order to meet the perceived expectations of the inspectors. Staff appraisal became the order of the day.

The 1992 examination results included four pupils who achieved nine Grade A passes from nine entries. The results for 1993 were less good, raising concerns. In 1996 results were much better, having risen to 54.1% A-Cs. Grade A passes were above the national average. One curiosity was that until 1992 boys outperformed girls by a substantial margin; thereafter the positions were reversed. It was something to which the head gave attention but without result.[302]

The school continued to suffer the effects of bad weather which delayed the arrival of buses bringing students to school. In February 1992 there were heavy snowfalls; the head recorded proudly that all the staff, bar one, got to school and 60% of the students attended. Many of course lived in town. The head's concerns a year later were different. The authorities were evidently content that seventy children

[301] Education (Schools) Act 1992
[302] Head's Report in the School magazine for those years.

were carried on one bus, with three to a seat and wished to remove the 'grace and favour' transport of children who lived within three miles of the school. The head was not prepared to have eleven-year-olds walking the narrow lanes from nearby villages. The problem was even greater in the case of primary school children; transport was provided for them up to the age of eight. Eventually bus passes were issued but parents had to pay for them. [303]

In 1994 the fall in intake resulted in a reduced number of classes in Year 7; this may have been partly due to the fall in the examination results but there was also the issue, which was to become more acute, of the fall in the number of young families in the town. Governors had always come from the town and were now of necessity recruited from the ranks of parents and professionals. Peter Scillitoe, a local businessman, saw Mr Thorneycroft in as head and presided over LMS. Sheila Griffiths Jones, a local parent, succeeded him; she followed not long after her father, Graham Cawdron, who had been chairman in the 1980s. At the end of our period that was to change; the connection with the town would weaken. Likewise, the school's early involvement in the town twinning between Wells and La Ferté St Aubin in the Sologne region of France, in which the school had played a vigorous part, did not continue. The head went on the visit, remarking on the bonds created by the process between different generations in the town. There were other matters that seemed more important. Nevertheless the school's premises were a resource in the town; plays and films would be shown there. The school played host to the Duchess of Kent when she came to name the new lifeboat, *Doris M Mann of Ampthill* in 1990. The school continued to hold its Christmas carol service in the parish church. But some of the pressures diminishing the relationship were external to Wells, one of which was that staff was less likely to live in the town, partly because of the cost of housing.

[303] Catherine Golding in *The Turn of the Tide* ed. Ian Scott (2005) p.40-1

8. The National Health Service

The health of the town continued to improve. Johnson, who had been appointed in 1948 as full-time Medical Officer of Health, produced a monthly report for the council. Unlike those of his predecessors they were short and largely uninformative. There were occasional concerns about mussels, and the odd incident of poliomyelitis. Johnson's office was in Wells in the Old Rectory, though he served quite a wide area. He also registered his concerns about the condition of housing west of The Glebe which had been identified as a redevelopment area.

On Johnson's death in harness in August 1953 he was succeeded by Dr Milne who was soon followed in 1956 by Dr WM Crichton. The latest disease to concern the medical profession was poliomyelitis followed by news of the possibility of vaccination, a huge breakthrough. By 1963 it was reported that 3,445 people in and around the town had been vaccinated against the condition. Crichton retired in 1961 at which point the office was moved from Wells to Fakenham, another example of the centralising trend. In 1966 Dr DG Poole was appointed as MOH.

Dr Hicks, local GP, sailor and town councillor

The hospital was taken over by the National Health Service in 1948, under a Regional Hospital Board. A nurses' home was proposed the following year, to be built next to the hospital building. It was completed in 1952, accommodating five nurses. The matron, Miss Jones, continued to live in the hospital itself. She retired in 1954 afflicted with arthritis. The hospital continued to rely on local practitioners such as Dr Hicks and Dr Ticehurst but also those practising in nearby villages. Dr Sturdee, who lived in Walsingham, had retired in 1945. Hicks continued to perform operations, such as hernias, appendicectomies and tonsillectomies. It was understood that one of the six beds would be kept for his purposes, a provision which the new matron, Evelyn Rowley, quietly ignored. She was to serve for thirty years.

Apart from surgery, medical care included the treatment of bronchitis and pneumonia. Fractures were dealt with. The hospital also provided what would later be called palliative care, looking after the dying. At that time the hospice movement was at an early stage and

Matron Rowley ensured that the hospital was in touch with the latest developments in understanding; she visited St Christopher's hospice in Sydenham in Kent where the most advanced palliative treatments were being tried.[304] A greater challenge, which took place in 1961, was the forced, albeit temporary, closure of the hospital due to an infection brought in by a patient. Matron Rowley herself caught it and was hospitalised in Mundesley for a couple of weeks. The incident was a reminder of the need for scrupulous attention to cleaning. Hospital visiting was restricted for similar reasons. Apart from working husbands and the mothers of small children, visiting was for two hours twice a week.

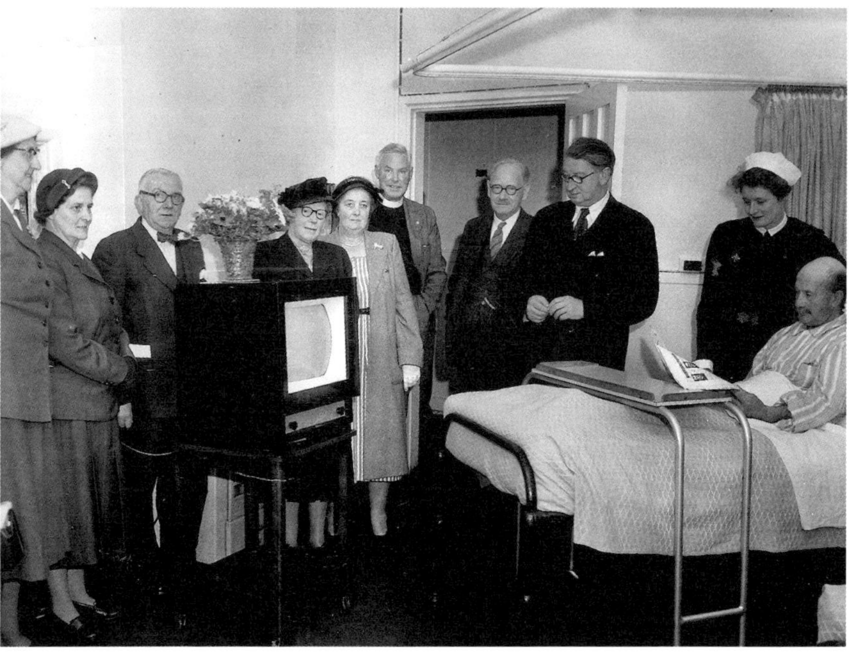

Matron Rowley (second r) and Dr. Hicks (third r) admiring the first television in 1955

Further expansion of the hospital took place in 1962 when the physiotherapy room was joined to the main building and proper waiting provision made for casualties. The new x-ray room, operated by a duty radiographer but at other times by the well-remembered Sister Faircloth, was in frequent demand. So much of what is now dealt with by specialists and dedicated departments in hospitals was done by the nursing staff, including the ordering of supplies, both medical and dietary. Further development took place in 1972 when a new ward was built, providing fourteen beds divided between men and women.

The hospital served Wells' needs and those of its visitors but it also served neighbouring villages. Recognition of that was the financial support which it received from the villages. Doctors from nearby villages, notably the Burnhams but also Walsingham, used the services

[304] Alison Christmas interview with Evelyn Rowley June 2000

of the hospital, visiting their own patients there. The demands on doctors were high. Hicks once drove a patient to Norwich Infirmary through the snow and was unable to return until the following day.

But times were changing. Rising expectations as well as litigation concerns led to the gradual cessation of operations. Dr Hicks was the last doctor to perform surgical operations, with Dr Ticehurst as his anaesthetist, assisted by nurses and auxiliaries. The most serious operations were appendicectomies and emergency abortions; the removal of tonsils and the mending of hernias were more routine. Hicks retired in 1969 – he returned to Wells to die in his own hospital in 1978. The last time that anyone was anaesthetised was in 1975. After that patients were sent to King's Lynn or Norwich. No one put up drips. What did not lessen was the number of casualties who came expecting treatment. People came off the beach with cuts and lacerations; nurses would deal with them instantly. Fractures were still dealt with. Drownings were brought in if only to the mortuary. In-patients were those suffering from medical conditions such as bronchitis and pneumonia, but also respite and convalescent patients, and the dying. The small staff of six qualified nursing staff, supported by auxiliaries, who had to cover twenty-four hours, seven days a week were very busy; there was a deal of heavy lifting to be done and the hoist, bought by the Friends in memory of Miss Rungary, was a huge help. Increasingly patients were taken directly to the general hospitals, latterly even by helicopter. It was a different world from that of Frederick Sturdee.

Vaccination and immunisation against disease remained vital to the system. As a notifiable disease, measles remained obstinately virulent but it had begun to decline. In 1949 there were 41 cases; in 1950 there were 54 cases; but by the 1960s it had all but disappeared. Protection against smallpox was given to 161 patients, against tetanus to 148, against polio to 201 and the triple immunisation against diphtheria, tetanus and whooping cough continued though in only four cases, so Dr Crichton reported to the district council. Fears were ex-

Nursing staff and assistants in 1984, Matron Rowley's retirement

pressed about the effect of immigration from commonwealth countries where tuberculosis was endemic and the town was visited by the Mass Radiography unit. In May 1962, 1,182, residents were x-rayed.

Dr Hicks' retirement left the district with only a single doctor in the town and there seemed little likelihood of a replacement. With the sale of The Normans there was no longer anywhere for a new doctor to operate from. The answer would be to build a health centre, either near to the hospital or in town if such a site could be found.[305] The council asked that there be three doctors for the town given the increasing need. The reply was negative. Worse, the Executive Committee proposed a suspension of the plans for the health centre. With a population of fewer than 2,500 and with patients taking themselves off Dr Ticehurst's list, the numbers did not add up. What persuasive arguments were used are not apparent; but the decision to suspend was rescinded and it was agreed that there should be a health centre in the town with two consultation rooms. It was built on Bolts Close in 1974 but three doctors were more than could be found. A second doctor, Dr Derek Hoddy, was recruited to start work in September 1971 to be joined shortly afterwards by Dr Charles Ebrill. Hoddy retired in 1991 to be replaced by Dr Gordon McAnsh. He in turn retired in 2022, Dr Ebrill having retired a few years earlier.

Evelyn Rowley retired in 1984, having six qualified nurses under her, Sister Faircloth, Sister Bailey, Sister Needham, Sister Clegg, Sister Wickes and Sister Sibley. Her successor, Ros Fairhead, who had been a night sister in the hospital, was to be the last matron, leaving in 1987 after which the hospital would be run by a sister-in-charge. From a staff of twenty, including cleaners and cooks, a gradual reduction would take place. Night staff had been able to rely on Matron Rowley's back-up as she had a flat in the hospital. This would no longer be the case. The main work of the hospital would be palliative care, physiotherapy and outpatients with the occasional emergency admission. There was some recognition of the work of the hospital. Helen Dunn, nursing auxiliary for forty-two years, was awarded the BEM.[306] Betty Emmerson, secretary to the hospital, active member of the Community Association and sometime chairman of the town council, was awarded the MBE in 2010 'for services to the community'.

In October 1986 the hospital received a communication from the Health Authority to the effect that discussions were taking place about the possible closure of the hospital though not 'in the foreseeable future'. This was against the background of the work of the League of Friends which had raised money for a whole range of improvements: new bed heads, a better nurse call system, various alterations and redecoration, converting the radiotherapy room for physiotherapy treatment, the surgery into a room for the treatment of casualties and making the old casualty room into a room for counselling, interviews,

305 *UDC Minutes* July 1970 NRO DC 18/4/14
306 *WTC minutes* Jan1992

nurse teaching and occasional overnight stay for relatives. The raising of the sum of £15,000 indicated a local commitment to the long-term future for the hospital.[307] Planned development by the Friends could cost in the region of £100,000. Thus in 1993 a separate men's ward was built together with a new bedded room with two toilets, an assisted bathroom and a coffee area. There was no money for extra staff but as the chairman of the Friends, Rod Travers, said, 'This will not only make it a better hospital but make it more likely to survive in the future.'[308] With changing life patterns the nurses' home was now no longer required. The Health Authority proposed to sell it. The council suggested that it could buy it. Betty Emmerson produced monthly reports on the affairs of the hospital for the council which were only matched by the work of the Friends. But larger forces were at work. Government's determination to create an internal market in the health service meant organisational change: the hospital became a trust; then it was to be run from Kelling hospital.[309]. Supported by Wells folk it was no longer run from Wells. It would be at the mercy of decisions it could not influence.

---

[307] *WTC Minutes* July 1990; letter from chairman Rod Travers
[308] *Dereham and Fakenham Times* October 29th 1993
[309] *WTC Minutes* April 1995

9. Gentrification – a small town

Caravans were stored about the town in winter

Chapters only begin and end in books. Life is more untidy. But there are moments in the life of a community which, in retrospect, divide the story into before and after. If we are searching for a date which defines the change in the character of the town it would be sometime around 1974, the year when Wells lost its status as an Urban District council and became a small town; in fact, a parish.

This was also the time when the town began to look different. It had lost most of its industry pre-war. Now the signs of that industry would begin to disappear. We know that because between 1969 and 1975 one of the staff at the town's library, Richard Shackle, took a huge number of photographs of its streets which give us pictures, literally, of what the place looked like. We can then see with our own eyes, walking around the streets, what happened to change its outlook.

It is plain that in those years, in spite of all the slum clearances, there were parts of Wells that were wretched, in some cases derelict and ruinous. Caravans, not permitted to remain on the Pinewoods over the winter, were stored around the town. There were still hay lofts, stables and coach houses, some of them with horses' harnesses still hanging up, covered in dust. Rubble from demolished buildings lay about some of the yards. There were empty houses too, their windows broken as they suffered degradation and invited vandalism.[310]

Cooking range downstairs and fireplace upstairs – no longer

A dozen former maltings, some small, some huge, had largely been left to decay. Some of them had been used for other purposes such as the bulk storage of grain, feed or fertiliser; their chimneys and cowls had been removed but little else had been done to them. Eastern Counties Farmers had put two of them to use: Pauls had only lately moved

[310] WLHG Archive

out of two more. The buildings still dominated not just the skyline but the quayside and the yards which ran down to them. A few, mostly the smaller ones, were destined to survive. Those small enough or in sufficiently good condition were converted into dwellings. The others were destined for the wrecker's jackhammers. When Richard Shackle took his pictures, they still stood, many of them having become dangerous but inviting playgrounds for adventurous children who could occasionally be seen on their roofs.

Buntings 17th century malting on Croft Yard was saved and made into homes

Those buildings which were used for grain storage remained, for the moment, busy places. Lorries owned by Borough and Strattons, later Dalgety's, would be unloaded from farms and loaded to transport elsewhere from the depot on Standard Road, just as Eastern Counties were engaged in a similar exercise from Staithe Street. There were machines, elevators and augers to move the grain about but much of the work was done by shovel. When Dalgetys moved out this was another space in the town where weeds would grow long.

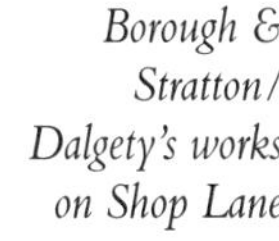

Borough & Stratton/ Dalgety's works on Shop Lane

The changes of the 1950s and 60s, already described, had been mostly on the outskirts of the town: the various estates, mostly council-built though including several privately-built closes of houses. The 1970s were to see the wholesale demolition of those industrial buildings and their replacement by houses. The Glebe marked the western limit of maltings; its modest but venerable industrial premises, which had been taken over by Tom Grange to gar-

The Glebe in 1970 with its former maltings

age his lorries, were to be replaced by a parade of seven houses built by Pottergate Properties. The owner, Walter Gould, was already building a square of town houses on the garden of The Normans, lately vacated by Dr Hicks. Now, as subsequently in several places, Gould reclaimed the bricks of the demolished sheds in order to give a more compatible appearance to the new houses. He did the same when he built six houses on Stratton's Yard on Shop Lane, called Stratton Place, and another five on the opposite side on what would become Ramms Court. A little later there would be four more cottages round the corner on Croft Yard, one of them nostalgically called Malt Cottage.[311]

The massive Pauls malting on the west end of the quay was the subject of prolonged negotiations but in 1980 all but its quayside frontage was taken down and a row of fifteen town houses was built to stretch almost the entire length of Tunns Yard, this time not by Gould but by the firm of Rileys. The district council's contribution to the building stock was to take down and replace what was probably the tallest malting in the town, clearly visible from the channel, on Jicklings Yard and to replace it with Malthouse Place, a block of flats. In 1977 it bought from the Post Office the plot of land on Staithe Street adjacent to the chemist and eventually in 1982 built Eagles Court flats.

Sid Warren's garage on Theatre Road

A number of these historic buildings remained, two in

[311] *WTC Planning Committee* minutes 1971, July 1974, July 1978, Nov. 1982

particular whose future is a story in itself, to be told a page or two hence. Confusingly both have been called the Granary; that on Staithe Street was a malting for much longer than it was Eastern Counties' grain storage; the 1904 Granary on the quay had to wait until later to be converted into flats. Others, less obviously so, were retained.

This process, sometimes called infilling, would continue. The closure of the Regal Cinema on Clubbs Lane in 1975 left the huge auditorium to be demolished and rebuilt as Oddfellows Court in 1983. Sid Warren retired from his garage on Theatre Road in 1973 which then assumed a variety of purposes – it was a boxing club for a while. It was finally demolished in 1999 to be made into a yard with eleven houses and garages, developed by a housing association, a new and increasingly important phenomenon.[312] Other garages went similarly, two on Standard Road, where more closes would be built. The huge development on Barker's garage came later. Other closes were built on former gardens, Shrublands and Beldorma Close on Polka Road. They made of Wells a residential town and, with the departure of the coasters from the quay, one which was less noisy and cleaner, a place to which people would increasingly want to move. In terms of its population, as Marilyn Smith, clerk to the council commented tartly a little later, in-filling was the only kind of development envisaged by the District. This did nothing to add to the needed provision of houses for local people.[313] In retrospect its approach was short-sighted.

During this period Wells was numerically remarkably stable. In 1951 its population was 2,491 according to the Census; in 1991 it was 2,445. What had changed was the demographic make-up of the town. In 1981 13.66% of the housing stock were second or holiday homes; in 1991 this had increased to approximately 16%.[314]

Another feature of the town, affected by wider commercial changes, was the closure of a number of public houses. The major breweries, Bullards and Steward & Pattesons, both of Norwich, jointly bought out Morgans' who had a minor presence in the town, in 1961. Two years later, in 1963, they were themselves bought out by national brewers Watneys who proceeded with a programme of pub closures: The Vine in 1965, the Prince of Wales in 1966, the Eight Ringers in 1970, the Park Tavern in 1973 and the Shipwrights in 1985. All may have been only modestly profitable but Watneys had a policy of aban-

The Vine on High Street before conversion to a private house

[312] *WTC Planning Minutes* April 1975; the development did not in fact take place until 1999.
[313] Evidence to North Norfolk District Council para 3.3 13th February 1996
[314] Ibid.

doning draught ales in favour of keg beers. These were places where men, mostly, had met, played darts, dominoes and crib, had belonged to leagues and with their families went on coach outings. Beer was never hugely profitable and even before the advent of supermarkets,

Derelict malting in 1975, replaced by Malthouse Place, 1983

the remaining houses turned more and more to the provision of food.

Going back to that same turning point, 1974, we can now look at the processes by which the town attempted to exercise its reduced authority and to exercise some control over events. Wells had run its own affairs since 1844. The Improvement Commissioners created by statute in that year had given way to the Urban District Council in 1894 whose course we have followed in preceding chapters in its exercise of wide decision-making powers, subject only to central government. It was now to pass virtually all its powers to the newly formed North Norfolk District Council. In truth a number of responsibilities had been lost since the war. Nevertheless the sudden almost total loss of control was a shock to the members of the new town council whose membership was identical to that of the old UDC. It was reduced to being an amenity body while the decision-making process which had been carried on in Wells for eighty years had moved to Cromer. For six months the old and new systems ran side by side and there was provision for shared functions, but the request that Wells should continue to manage the beach and the caravan site was denied; a similar response was received to the request to manage the Staithe Street maltings 'for recreational, social and educational purposes', the Buttlands, the public conveniences and various pieces of open land. Only the cemetery and the footway lighting were to be the responsibility of the town council, 'as it was felt that

Blackhorse Yard and Freeman Street 1970

the activities relating to the holiday industry should be planned and developed as a whole through the [district] council's area'.[315] A revised order from government provided that town greens and burial grounds should be transferred back to the parishes. A public meeting was called whose resolution was to the effect that all of the town's former property should remain with the town. A petition attracted 850 signatures. But Cromer was not in the mood for compromise; the positions of the two councils were irreconcilable. The new district council, having taken over the caravan site, proposed to reduce the number of static caravans. Subsequent town meetings were often reduced to submitting requests to the district to do or refrain from doing various things: use a piece of land as a play area; put up a No Cycling sign; repair a public seat; deal with pollution in the harbour; address residents' parking concerns; which requests were routinely ignored. It was a total change of role. Two councillors gave up the fight and failed to attend meetings, thus after six months ceasing to be members of the council. A plea to the government minister to intervene was met with a claim that he did not have the power to do so. The council was left with the cemetery, the Buttlands and responsibility for street lighting. True to form, Charles Ramm, who was now also a councillor of the new district council, opposed all attempts by the town council to retain some measure of control, as a result of which he received a motion of no confidence from the town council.

The contention, often advanced, that Wells, being at the far end of the district, was of less concern to its councillors, is difficult to resist. Certainly, the larger settlements to the east, Cromer, Sheringham and North Walsham, had many more councillors and the agenda of the

[315] *WTC Minutes* Jan. 24th 1974

district, as well as the direction of financial decisions, were bound to occupy the greater amounts of energy. Having now lost not only its legal powers but also its access to government borrowing, the cost of smartening up the town would have to come from outside the town or from local people's pockets. Its tourist season, though growing, was still very short, a mere six weeks it was said. Amenities for locals and to attract visitors were lacking. There were of course a number of hotels, Scarborough House, Clarence House, the Prince of Wales and the Crown, but they were small considering the later demand for accommodation. There were a few bed and breakfast establishments though they were not of a standard which would be acceptable in today's market.

Wells Maltings in 1970

The first major intervention by the town council in which it proposed to take on the district concerned the Staithe Street maltings. The former UDC had bought it but it was now in the ownership of Cromer. Still wanting to retain it for community purposes, the District instead proposed to demolish it in order to build flats.

The town council assembled a steering committee to look into the feasibility of converting it, consisting of representatives of a number of organisations in the town. It was suggested the building could provide a home for the youth club, the playgroup and the football club among others. It might house a museum, an indoor bowling green, and additional premises for the already existent arts group. A feasibility study was carried out, including costings for the repair and conversion of the building.[316] But the means did not exist and on the proposition of Charles Ramm the council resolved that 'in view of the high financial commitment needed to use the Maltings for a community

[316] *WTC minutes* March 22nd. 1976

centre we notify the North Norfolk District Council that we will no longer pursue the matter but request a piece of land be earmarked for a community centre as soon as possible'.[317] There were in fact two maltings adjacent to each other, both of which it was sought to save; the assistance of Sir John Betjeman, poet and lover of Victorian buildings, was solicited. One was saved; in the opinion of the chairman of the steering group, John Christmas, the lesser of the two. The other was eventually to become a block of flats. At the time it was not clear how either might be saved. The Granary (then so called because that had been its use by Eastern Counties) on Staithe Street was in a poor state.

Regal Cinema on Clubbs Lane closed in 1975

The buildings were still, in part, in use. When the old UDC bought them from Eastern Counties two years previously, an offer was received from a small group of people from the arts world to run it as the council had intended. The Sackhouse was to be an art gallery, with a coffee bar and changing facilities for a theatre which was to be set up in the Granary, originally proposed as a 700 seater. (In the event it

---

[317] Ibid. June 21st. 1976;

would accommodate fewer than a hundred.) The group's chairman was Ronald Stennett Willson, a glass designer from King's Lynn who was later to set up Langham Glass; his vice-chairman was the actor Michael Gough who had just finished filming *The Go-Between* nearby and who had come to live in Norfolk. Michael Hooton was to be its administrator, Jonathan Field its artistic director. Its focus was on high and somewhat rarefied culture; the town council's interest was more towards a community facility.

Baulked by Cromer (and by finance) the council turned its interest to the recently closed Regal cinema. However, concerned about the cost and the condition of the building, public opinion, which had been in favour, now wavered. In the event a singing and dancing licence was refused by magistrates and the sale did not proceed. The district meanwhile got planning permission (from the town council planning committee by the chairman's casting vote) to demolish the Granary and build thirty flats on the site.

The death of Charles Ramm in October of 1976 altered the balance of power. Thus when the Arts Group, having raised the necessary funds, applied for change of use so as to 'form a small theatre' in the Granary, the motion to reject the request 'as superfluous to the needs of the town' failed by five votes to four.[318] The District had changed its mind too. It appeared that because of government cuts to its 1978-79 housing programme the number of houses required in the District was reduced by a third. At its November meeting in 1977 the council received news that the District was prepared to offer the building for development as a community hall. Money still remained a problem, one that the newly formed Community Association, chaired by councillor Myrtle French but widely supported, had to solve. It was a long slog. Only in 1984 was sufficient money raised, £18,000, to enable the signing of the lease so that the work of converting the building could begin. Empty for twelve years, it was full of brick rubble, pigeon muck and all manner of refuse. Its ceilings, supported by cast iron uprights, were too low, designed as they were for malting. They had to be removed, together with the timber floors which they supported.

Voluntary effort could do so much but eventually Stuart Offord, son of the Association's chairman and an architect, was employed to design a new community space. Supported by grants from the County and District totalling another £25,000, it was opened in 1987 by Viscount Coke. After that it hosted dances, discos, banquets and wedding receptions as well as scores of fundraising efforts. The upstairs remained unused and still derelict until the Freemasons, made homeless in 1992 having been ejected from the Congregational Hall, offered to refurbish it and create two useable rooms which they did. The Arts Centre next door with its theatre continued with increasing difficulty. It closed in 1991 to be taken over by the Community Association. That

---

[318] WTC Planning Committee July 1977

the theatre was refurbished and continued to put on shows and to invite theatre groups was owed to yet another group often at odds with its neighbour, the Friends of the Granary. For them amateur dramatics and popular arts were a Wells tradition, stretching back to the early days of the Fisher theatre nearly a hundred years before, which was not to be lost. The Granary Players became both a nursery for local talent and a draw to talent from elsewhere, putting on ambitious productions on its small stage. It was a narrow stream which its members were determined not to allow to dry up. Nevertheless, the twin enterprises of arts and community use faced an even bigger question as to whether the building, including most essentially its roof, could be saved. That required the kind of money which local initiative could not raise.

The council continued to administer the three sets of allotments in the town whose deeds it held in its possession. The west end land, some nineteen acres, had been partly converted into a grazing paddock after the abortive attempt by the old council to build houses on it; the rest remained as allotments. It was now being let out by the District which asked for the deeds to the entire site. Contending that it was all allotment land, the town council refused to hand over the deeds.[319] For once it was in the stronger position. The town had formerly been responsible for the provision of housing and had been vigorous in its extension of housing supply. The council therefore felt itself justified in bringing to the notice of the District the fact that no houses had been built since 1974 and that there was a need for houses for young families. It drew attention to the fact that the District had graded Wells as 'a disadvantaged town' and wondered what it was going to do about it. The District continued to press for the handing over of the deeds of the west end allotments to which the clerk was instructed to reply that the deeds would be transferred when it became clear that the land was definitely to be used for housing, whether council or private. 'The Chief Planning officer [was] to be urged to lift the planning prohibition on the land as nearly all other housing sites in the town [were] now being developed.'[320] A further letter from the District was responded to as follows: '[the clerk] was instructed to reply that if the Planning Department would confirm in writing that the land is to be released for housing and that negotiations with Holkham for lifting the covenant are proceeding favourably, then the council would release the deeds'.

The matter was to rumble on for years. The District came up with a proposal to build 150 houses, rented, sheltered and low cost, for which reason they renewed their request for the deeds. All that was required was a positive response from Holkham.[321] Myrtle French took the initiative and contacted the Estate 'and received a favourable response'. The agreement of the Department of the Environment

---

319 *WTC minutes* October 2nd 1978
320 Ibid. October 3rd 1983
321 Ibid. Sept. 1989

had to be obtained. Allotment holders had to be consulted. After much to-ing and fro-ing, only in 1992 was a much smaller development agreed to, providing the town with an additional seven dwellings to be built at the western end of the plot. This time it was the District's chief planning officer who stopped it.[322] Frustrated, the council declared its disappointment that having negotiated and co-operated with all parties, including Cromer, the attempt to provide some additional housing had been blocked. The planning officer replied that 'a solution to problems was relocating the proposed development to the south eastern area'.

The District's Local Plan for the period 1988 - 2006, presented in draft to the town council in 1994, should have enabled the re-examination of the housing for the whole town in theory. In fact, its strategy was driven by the fact that, in its estimation, the District had already exceeded its 2006 target for housing so that it proposed minimum development, seeing itself moreover as an enabler rather than a builder of housing.[323] It thus stated its intention to retain the town's development boundary (which had not changed in thirty years) going back on the proposals not only of 1972 but also of 1987 which latter was for the development of the eastern end of the Two Furlong Hill/Mill Road triangle for residential purposes.

The matter did not rest there. Having rejected the town's proposal to build on the Mill Road triangle, the District, not three years later, made a fresh attempt to build social housing on the part of the land which had become a horse paddock, the south eastern end, in return for which the western sector on which there were allotments would become or remain the property of Wells town council. The town council was sceptical of the District's intentions and the impasse was overcome by the District's transferring the whole nineteen acres to the town council with the unspoken proviso that if the town succeeded where the District had failed and got all round agreement to build, the District would exercise an option to purchase within twenty-one years and would thus deprive the town of any benefit from its efforts. Grazing on the paddock would continue. In exchange, the Bases Lane allotments were to be transferred to the District which proceeded to build on it.

That year the now ageing sewage treatment plant was to be replaced by Anglian Water with a fully automated facility.

Housing would ever remain a political football. Having taken over the council housing stock in Wells, the District handed over the entire stock to a housing association, a so-called registered social landlord,[324] to be called Victory Housing, which had been set up for the purpose. The council would continue to administer the housing list but everything else would be in the hands of the board of the association. Decisions as to whether to sell houses, deemed uncon-

322 Ibid. Minutes Aug. 1992
323 North Norfolk Local Plan 1998 passim; see 8.11ff
324 Housing and Planning Act 1986.

omical, would rest in its hands alone.

The inability of the council to effect changes was evidenced in another area of town life, the hospital. The proposal of October 1986, already referred to, from the Health Authority indicating that the hospital might close was received by 'total and utter horror'. The monthly reports to the council by Betty Emmerson in the event did nothing to influence decisions.

A role created for the town council by legislation was to bring together all the various elements of the institutional life of the town by the holding of an annual town meeting. The same Act which abolished the Urban District required parishes to hold such a meeting. Reports were asked for from the schools, the harbour commissioners, Wells United Charities, the county council, the district council, the town football club, the Citizens' Advice Bureau and a raft of local organisations. The chairman of the town council gave a full report. But it was never well supported. People turn up to meetings when there is a live issue on which they may wish to voice their opinion, very often when there is a threat to their way of life. They did not attend to hear what had already happened and which they could in many cases discover by other means.

The church, thought of as an immoveable bastion against change, showed itself to be no less vulnerable. After another long period of vacancy in the rectory, William Sayer, previously assistant chaplain at Sandhurst, was inducted in September 1984. Bringing stability and also a forceful personality to the post, he stayed for eighteen years, retiring to a house in Holkham. During his tenure he was instrumental in making the main service every Sunday a Communion, himself wearing vestments; he attempted to improve the parish's finances by selling off the Church Rooms across the way from the church, a controversial act in the town. No less controversial was his re-ordering of the church creating a nave altar on a temporary wooden dais and removing some of the pews. He would have had more of them taken away but a Consistory Court, held at the behest of some of the congregation, ruled that he could not.

Roman Catholic priests tended to stay longer but in 1987 the Marist fathers, who were the religious order in charge of the parish, sent Fr Philip Graystone to become superior of the order from its base in Hull. He had been parish priest for some eighteen years. Wells would henceforth be served from Walsingham and for a while by Anglican clergy who had 'converted'. Until 1965 the Catholic church internationally had not officially recognised other churches as even Christian, but the Second Vatican Council convened by the Pope changed all that, recognising not only other Christians but those of other faiths and more fundamentally allowing participation, albeit tentatively, in worship and action in the town. Graystone had taken up the new possibilities with enthusiasm. Fr Michael Simison, one of his successors, even brought his congregation to worship in St Nicholas's while his church was having new heating installed. The churches worked well together, using the parish magazine as a vehicle to advertise their doings. For a time the town council's meetings were reported there.

However, nationally, the churches were becoming less influential. Most noticeable was the drop in the use of occasional offices, baptisms, weddings and funerals across the country. Wells was no different from anywhere else: in 1968 there were 29 Anglican baptisms; the following year there were 32; but thereafter numbers fell almost consistently dropping to 18 in 1974, gradually rising until 1978 but then by 1985 they had slumped to just six, around which figure the numbers remained. Funerals, which now tended more often to take place partly or wholly at a crematorium, alone held up at around 20 per annum. Sunday attendance at St Nicholas in the 1970s did not immediately diminish; what happened was that the average age of the worshippers rose inexorably. The young, acculturated by their parents into the faith and who were represented by Sunday Schools and Youth Clubs, did not stay into adulthood; soon they would be gone.[325] Many of the young in any case moved away from the town.

The evening service, once popular in the 1960s, had virtually disappeared. The replacement of Morning Prayer by a Communion service, a process started by Whyntie and made a weekly event by Sayer, did not stem the ebb tide; nor did the later introduction of modern language forms of service or of so-called Family Services which were tried on a fourth Sunday for a while. The lack of continuity between clergy had an undoubted effect. The replacement of Whit week by the secular fixed spring bank holiday in 1967 and the later legalisation of Sunday trading did not help.

The truth was that in Wells, as elsewhere, cultural Christianity had largely atrophied. People were becoming more mobile and, apparently, when people move house they often re-adjust their social relationships, of which churchgoing is one facet. Whereas most people were married in church in the 1960s, weddings were more and more secular affairs even when couples got married at all. Wells may not have swung during the '60s but national attitudes towards duty were certainly changing. An exception was the observance of funerals when the church would routinely be full and sometimes packed with people standing at the back, particularly in the case of those associated with the sea. Christmas services remained popular. Spirituality had become privatised as had social behaviour. Most public institutions were viewed critically and the shortcomings of the clergy did not help the image of the church; several left under a cloud. On the other side, those who engaged cheerfully with people and who ministered to tragedy and need found themselves forgiven by those who had been heard and helped. Clergy, after all, are human. The same was true of secular public figures whose actions were more public and so have been described in these pages. Such a person might be liked for the

---

[325] Wells Church magazine 1967-1985 (WLHG Archive)

favours he or she did for individual townspeople, even if what was done was not strictly impartial. In a small community it is difficult to be even-handed.

The latest change is partly evidenced by buildings, their re-use, their modernisation and new private housing, but also by those who live in them. As already stated, the size of the population had changed very little over seventy years. In 1991 it was 2,445, a couple of hundred fewer than in 1921. But it had become older and less 'Wells'. This can be overstated. There had always been movement in and out of the town. However, as Marilyn Smith, town clerk, noted in a letter to the District Council in 1996, the council's insistence on retaining the thirty year-old development boundary 'would appear to remove any hope that affordable housing can be provided for local people'. She pointed out that, according to the 1991 Census, those over 60 numbered 867; those between 16 and 24 numbered only 243. Current house building was on infill sites 'geared to the holiday and second home market, and is unsuitable for family housing. Demand for such housing does, in any case, inflate prices beyond the reach of local people… who are directed to find housing in other areas such as Fakenham.' She quoted a locally conducted survey in 1990 which indicated a need for housing for local people. The town council had identified, she said, the eastern part of the Mill Road/Two Furlong Hill for development for such housing, not 'vast estates', it said, 'but small scale groups of family houses'. (What she and the council did not note was the demographic bombshell of the inexorable rise in the number of elderly people.)

Meanwhile former industrial areas had now become residential, which included the quay, the most significant building of which had become a block of flats. As a result, expectations would change. The working class pub culture had begun imperceptibly to dissipate.

Lack of employment was a major issue. Industries had gone and were not replaced. Agriculture employed fewer and fewer people. Employment opportunities were mostly for unskilled jobs at lower wages, with the important exception of the building and decorating trades. The issue was no different in surrounding villages and in some cases the impact on social provision was greater.[326] South Creake had, in 1981, a church, a school, a butchers, a general store, a grocer and a fruit and vegetable stall. It had previously had another butcher, two bakers, a confectioner, a fishmonger, a hairdresser and a blacksmith. By 1991, the church and the fruit and vegetable stall remained.

---

[326] J Martin Shaw in *Social Issues in Rural Norfolk* ed. Moseley (Norwich 1976) pp.77-102

10. Afterword

The closer one gets to the present day the less easy it is to keep a sense of proportion and perspective. Judgements made about the living or even the recently dead are bound to be problematic. However, remembering how difficult it has been to recover events of quite recent date which fall out of memory, it seems worthwhile to note some of the major events of the new century.

Alderman Peel School went through a number of changes after the sudden departure of David Thorneycroft. Several head teachers have come and gone. Cheryl Crawford and John Platten were succeeded by Alastair Ogle who left in 2022, in turn to be followed by Matt Hardman. The school had become a Sports Specialist College; specialisation was a means by which a school could attempt to stand out in the competition for places. Having a flood-lit multi-use outdoor sports area as well as a swimming pool and a large games field put the school at some advantage.

Government intervention in education continued at the same rate. The Labour government of 1997-2010 introduced the idea of academies as a means of refreshing failing schools. The incoming administration decided that academy status, which put schools outside the jurisdiction of the County Council, should become available to all schools. Thus, in 2017 the school became an academy. As such it joined a trust based in Norwich, consisting of ten other schools including Wells Primary School and Burnham Market. The role of governors, which had grown considerably as a result of successive requirements that governors include local people, including parents, and that they should manage the school's budget, was now much reduced. As in so much of the world's affairs change is never consistently in one direction. Perhaps it is no more than fashion. The relationship with the town, which had long held the school in affection, was also changing. The popularity of Wells as a holiday destination created its own pressure. If young families were priced out of the market the school's population would be likely to fall, though there would be a time lag of ten years before that would happen. There would be limitations on how many pupils could be recruited from nearby and not so nearby settlements by continuously high standards.

The hospital's fate was sealed in 2002. A shortage of staff coupled with the long-term sickness of two of the nursing staff resulted in the decision to reduce the opening hours for its minor injuries unit and the number of beds from fifteen to twelve[327]. Only days later the hospital was shut for three months for 'badly needed' building work. It

[327] *Dereham and Fakenham Times* 5th December 2002

re-opened in February but the issue of staffing continued to be a problem and in December 2004 it closed for good. The initial reasoning was the temporary closure due to an outbreak of 'winter vomiting' but the chief executive of the Primary Care Trust stated that there would be a review of options about the hospital's future which would include 'a community-run health resource or healthy living centre'; in other words with no beds. The response was as dramatic as any the town had seen: in cold December winds over 200 people came to demonstrate outside the hospital; the local MP, Norman Lamb, promised his support. A public meeting packed the Maltings hall.[328] Subsequently it was admitted that the future of the hospital had been under review for two years and that staffing was not the only issue. Patient safety was the immediate problem, but the underlying issue was that the hospital cost £400,000 to run which could not be justified 'in the current restrictive climate'.[329] Local support remained strong, however, and the hospital re-opened in 2005 as a charitable trust. The League of Friends purchased an ultrasound machine, operated by a consultant radiologist twice a week. Initially it dealt with twenty local patients in a clinic, but it was not supported centrally and it lay idle for a while and was eventually given to King's Lynn hospital. Physiotherapy remained for a while but the hospital would come to depend on private facilities, the dental surgery, a

An extension to the Maltings replacing the old tourist information centre and car park

[328] *EDP* December 18th 2004, January 8th 2005
[329] *EDP* January 15th 2005

dialysis unit for visitors to the town and the desire that it could extend its usefulness to other areas.

Shops continued to come and go and, to the frustration of some shopkeepers who traded throughout the year, many closed out of season, making Staithe Street less attractive to casual shoppers. Betty Tipler, who moved to the town in 1968 and who recorded its comings and goings on film over a period of 35 years, noted that, for instance, in 1991 over half a dozen shops closed for the winter, and some of them permanently at least with the current offer.

More visible and more central to the infrastructure of the town was the initiative to seek external funding to repair and substantially extend the Staithe Street maltings; the idea was to make of it a community and arts centre on a scale only dreamt of by the Community Association of fifty years before. The state-endorsed National Lottery profits provided huge amounts of money for community causes; a successful series of bids for money made by a fundraiser employed by the trustees produced enough money to completely reroof and refurbish the building, extending it southwards onto the former car park and demolishing the old tourist information centre. A new state-of-the-art theatre would show films and live productions; there would be an art gallery and café. Inevitably there was controversy over the design of the extension with its metal cladding and the commercial decision to put the community space upstairs, placing a café and bar in the foyer.

The harbour meanwhile experienced a quantum change. The decline of the coastal trade had left the harbour commissioners with a very small income, operating out of a hut on the quay. Income was

Albatros *moored on the quay during the very high tides of March 2007*

mainly derived from harbour dues from fishing boats and leisure craft, and the parking of cars on the quay. Thus when the need came to replace one of the huge York stone blocks along the quay edge, because it had been damaged, this was likely to cost in the region of £1,000 to £1,500, crippling the spending capability for the rest of the financial year.[330]

Then came the wind farms. Climate change had resulted in government encouragement of the building of the means of obtaining energy from nature. Wind energy could be turned into electricity. Offshore wind farms were more expensive to install than those on land but they were more likely to benefit from greater and more constant wind speeds. The harbour commissioners offered Wells as a base for the construction of a wind farm on Sheringham Shoal and for its subsequent maintenance. Scira, a Norwegian state-supported wind farm company, agreed to use Wells during both the construction and the maintenance phases of the farm. It would consist of some 88 turbines. They took over the former Field Study Centre as their interim land base while building a new facility at Egmere. The support vessels needed to be able to put to sea, if not at all times of the day and night, then more regularly than the four or five hours in a day that vessels moored at the quay were able to make use of. A pontoon immediately behind the lifeboat station was proposed, a mile nearer the open sea; piling began in 2009. It became apparent that, in the face of adverse weather conditions, vessels moored on the pontoons would be vulnerable to wind and waves. The commissioners thus decided to build a full-blown outer harbour consisting of banks to the

The second of two pontoons next to the fishermen's shed

[330] Christine Abel in *The Turn of the Tide* ed. Ian Scott(2005) p. 54

east and south, thus creating a rectangular lagoon with entry to the north. A dredger, *Kari Hege,* was bought on loan for £1,000,000. This enabled the dredging of the channel out to sea and the creation of a bank or berm to its eastward side running out as far as the No. 1 buoy. The outer harbour would become a nesting site for sea birds.

The increased income has enabled improvements to the buoyage and much better shore facilities for visiting vessels. Two more pontoons were built, the first adjacent to the harbour office with shower and toilet facilities for visiting leisure craft and a second which is used by leisure fishing vessels. The departure of the wind farmers in 2021 made for another change of gear. New enterprises would have to be sought.

The dangers of overfishing were demonstrated in the years leading up to the end of the century. Scottish vessels began to come down to fish for whelks. Local whelk fishermen had left their pots only five miles out, but they were forced to go further and further out. Catches dropped dramatically so that it became uneconomic to fish at all. Local fishermen then turned to crabs which were fished some distance out from Cromer, in huge abundance; but this fishery also was unsustainable at such levels. At the same time velvet crabs, small ferocious swimming creatures with paddles for feet, appeared in quantity and were sold to the Spanish. Not really compatible with brown crabs, they seem to have been fished out within a very few years, leaving a sustainably policed and profitable lobster and crab fishery. Recovery took time but in the last ten years, up to the time of writing, the whelk have become more abundant and catches have been good in both summer and winter, with up to five tons brought home, leaving decks awash, a precarious practice only to be carried on in calm seas.

There was some interruption for the fishery with the installation of the wind farms, temporarily depriving the fishermen of parts of their grounds. The compensation agreed with the fishermen's association might encourage men to sit at home but it did not keep their erstwhile customers supplied or satisfied. In any case, the popularity of shellfish restaurants patronised by visitors mean that those who went to sea were able to bring in good rewards. A different impediment has been the weather. Bad weather can keep men ashore; storms such as the notorious 'beast from the east' in 2018 can gather up gear on the seafloor and wind it into bundles too heavy to be lifted aboard. Losses of gear can be considerable. Gear can still be made up onshore though increasingly plastic is used; the losses can mount. The closure of the crab factory in Cromer in 2012 and its removal to Grimsby demanded another rethink of suppliers. Another manufactory would soon appear. Lobster, always a delicacy, could command good prices in local restaurants; crabs could be dressed in the town and taken to Billingsgate fish market in London. The development of a lobster hatchery was intended to secure the future of the fishery.

The town itself has grown, if not in the size of its resident population, then in the number of dwellings. In 2014, Holkham Estate

Mainsail Yard replaced Barker's filling station and the bakery

proposed that one of the fields of the old Manor Farm, Home Piece, lying to the south of the track of the old Heacham railway line off Market Lane, should be developed as a housing estate providing 123 houses. Called Staithe Place it is, in fact, the furthest block of housing from the 'staithe'; a tribute to marketing methods if not accuracy. It has been the largest but not the only development in recent years. Manor Farm Drive was built on the other side of the old railway track; the bakery and garage site to the west of the town had been developed into Mainsail Yard, a three-storey block of houses with garages on the ground floor in case of flood. Many of the garages have been changed to residential use subsequently in spite of the flood risk. A close of houses on Polka Road replaced a large garden. More infilling. The Home Piece estate came under the rules regarding the need to have a percentage of affordable houses and as a result Victory Housing acquired forty units for rent. More housing is being proposed by North Norfolk District Council as part of the Local Plan process; the current proposal is for 70 houses.

Meanwhile the existing housing stock was in demand and house prices rose sharply along the north Norfolk coast. As a result, whereas in the ten years to 2006 the percentage of second or holiday homes had risen from 20% to 21%, in the succeeding ten years the figure had risen to 31% and would rise to 37% by 2022. A small attempt to reverse this, or at least to slow it down, was the creation in 2010 of a local housing association, Homes for Wells, intended to provide houses for rent to local people. Some people left or lent houses to be rented out. Its largest venture was to convert the old primary school, which had recently ceased its later role as a Field Study Centre, into eleven flats.

Wells beach, 2021

One result of the increase in the number of second homes has been the extension of the tourism season. Half terms, Easter and the Spring Bank holiday fill the streets with parked cars, but any sunny weekend, even in the depths of winter, has brought visitors. Parked cars were to become a major problem as environmental bodies opposed any increase in off-street parking which was so necessary to keep the traffic flowing and the streets clear for buses and emergency vehicles. Day visitors and their children would crowd the quay to catch gillies, shore crabs, with baited nets. The Carnival, now expanded to ten days, was supplemented by Christmastide, a weekend for the early arrival of Father Christmas, the switching on of Christmas lights and the attempt by shopkeepers and pop-up stallholders to get people to spend. Dependence on tourism increased, spurred by the 2020 pandemic.

The shopping offer in the town has changed over time, as supermarkets in nearby Fakenham have taken away the once thriving grocery trade. The last butcher's shop in High Street closed before the end of our period. Of the two butchers in Staithe Street, one remains, the other having been converted into a delicatessen. A fishmonger has returned; there has been ebb and flow. There is still a greengrocer. On the other hand, art shops, selling not only pictures but artists' materials, are now no longer a feature. Photography shops have taken their place. There are many more gift shops. Eating places have proliferated and all the public houses now sell food. Gray's amusement arcade, adjacent to the granary, which had caught fire in 2005, stood gaunt and ugly for some time but finally in 2014 a daringly high block of flats was built, with shops on the ground floor; the refurbishment of the Platten's parade of shops next to the Fleece has

After some years without a petrol station a self-service facility was installed in 2019 very near to the site of Cain's garage of the 1920s

almost completed the refreshing if not the replacement of the quay buildings.

As for the provision of services there was ebb and flow, though mostly ebb. The rebuilding of the police station (and the sale of part of the land on which it stood for housing) represented the retention of a symbol of local control. Fakenham magistrates' court, however, closed in 2001. On the plus side, after some years without a petrol station, a self-serve station opened in 2019 replete with an air pump. The loss of the bank in the same year had been foreseen with the previous reduction of hours. The departure of the sole firm of solicitors after more than 140 years of local legal assistance was another sign of the changing realities of commercial life in the town.

High tides continued to overtop the quay wall, summer and winter – even one year on August bank holiday – and measures were put in place to evacuate vulnerable properties by the appointment of flood wardens. These proved necessary in December 2013 when the proverbial tidal surge raised the water level above that of 1953 and tested the flood barrier. It held, so protecting the west end of the town. The glass panels which had been installed on top of the wall made an eery sight as the water level rose up. It was like some nightmarish aquarium. No vessels ended up on the quay, unlike in previous floods. The fishing vessels had removed themselves to safe anchorages and by a feat of good seamanship, Ton Brouwer, the skipper of the *Albatros* which was moored on the quayside, managed to turn the vessel into the wind and prevent her from being carried over the quay wall. Nevertheless the water rose to chest high in some shops and those who had placed flood boards across their front doors found that the water came around the back. The harbour office was flooded but its

High Street, once a busy shopping thoroughfare, is now bereft of shops. Many properties are now holiday lets and second homes

records were safe upstairs. It was a warning.

The pressure for change has continued and is unlikely to abate. Estate agents' trade fluctuates because of all sorts of factors, but there is no sign of their disappearing from the streets of the town. The desire to have some say in the nature of development has resulted in the town council proposing to produce a Neighbourhood Plan, through which the town might regain some local control over its housing development.

This story has been about a town. But a town is lots of things: its buildings, its industry, its merchants, its workers, its men, women and children; increasingly its retired people and its visitors. These are in a constant state of change. Even if buildings, always in need of repair, remain much the same externally, their inhabitants die, sell up or move, and newcomers come and put their mark on them. Even where people remain in the same house they improve, alter and decorate it. Few distemper walls remain. An ancient yard, once full of shouting children and working women, whose husbands are out at sea or digging or shovelling or lifting or carrying, and old men in doorways quietly smoking can, in a matter of decades, become empty of people, only inhabited at weekends by folk from elsewhere hefting suitcases from their cars into what have become weekend cottages. The yard may look the same but it is quite changed. It is not the same place. In trying to preserve the past it has nevertheless quite gone. And for those who regret its passing, what such a yard once was included water from an outdoor pump, the smells of farmyard animals, outside toilets, stone floors, candlelight. People once lived in damp and cold cottages, sometimes going short, suffering arthritic pains,

Staithe Street – the word means harbour – now pedestrianised, is the major shopping street

poverty, and a shorter life span. It may have made up for that by close neighbourly ties and bonds of kinship.

This description is itself a crude comparison. There was no 'way back when'. The town has always changed. Incomers are as old as the Vikings and as recent as the coming of the Shannocks and the Kentish trawlermen. They included the Dutch, the Danes and the Americans. A welcome was sometimes lacking, sometimes reluctant, sometimes warm. Some of the incomers came to possess, some to compete, some to participate; some came and went. And some left: they went to Australia, to New Zealand, to America, to Spain; some with new husbands, some for a better life, and some for the sunshine. The rate of change varied and when it was speedy it posed a threat that might overwhelm the populace and even drive them out. A small place is always subject to larger movements of change.

Appendices

Chairmen of UDC

George F Smith	1894
Herbert Dewing	1901
F Walter Kersley	1902
George S Andrews	1903
Herbert Dewing	1904
Arthur Ramm	1907
Frederick Raven	1918
Sam Peel	1922
Herbert Butcher	1928
George Turner Cain	1930
Frederick Raven	1931
Herbert Jary	1934
George Kitson	1935
William Dalliston	1936
George Turner Cain	1937
Henry Aldridge	1938
James Blades	1940
George Turner Cain	1946
Ernest Flint	1947
TW Grange	1951
Henry Aldridge	1954
EW 'Willie' Hicks	1955
Jack Cadamy	1964
Charles Ramm	1965
Jack Cadamy	1966
Mary Kitson	1970-74

Chairmen of Wells Town Council

Mary Kitson	1974
Frank Sawbridge	1974
Myrtle French	1976
Douglas Jagger	1983
Betty Emmerson	1991
David Perryman	1993
David Jagger	1996
Andrew Benstead	1997 – town mayor
David Jagger	1999 – town mayor
Andrew Benstead	2001 – town mayor
Joyce Trett	2003

(rotating chairmanship)	2005 -7
Allen Frary	2007
Michael Gates	2018

Harbourmasters

John Parker	1845
Richard Smith	N/K
John Smith	1853
William Temple	1883
Frederick Waterson	1912
Frank 'Tender' Smith	1913
Frank Taylor	1956
Chick Smith	1974
George Smithers	1985
Graham Walker	1989
Robert Smith	2001

Lifeboat coxswains

Richard Smith	1869
Horace Hinson	1875
Capt. Robert Elsdon	1879
Horace Hinson	1880
William Crawford	1985
Thomas Stacey	1905
William Edward Grimes	1917
Theodore Nielson	1933
William Rushmore Cox	1947
David James Cox	1960
Anthony Jordan	1986
Graham Walker	1989
Allen Frary	1997
Nicky King	2018

Lifeboats

Eliza Adams	1869
Charlotte Nichols	1880
Baltic	1888
Baltic No 2	1895
James Stephens No 8	1913
Baltic No 3	1919
Royal Silver Jubilee	1936
Cecil Paine	1945
Ernest Tom Nethercoat	1965
Doris M Mann of Ampthill	1990
Duke of Edinburgh	2022

Bibliography

Books and official records
(Short articles referred to in the text have been omitted)

Abel, Christine, in *The Turn of the Tide*, ed. Ian Scott, 2005

Adcock, Steve, *Early Policing in Wells*, WLHG Newsletter No 69, 2019

Arguile, Roger, *Wells-next-the-Sea, a small port and a wide world*, Poppylands, 2014

Arguile, Roger, *History of Wells Church*, 2021

Barker, Brian, *Norfolk Carrier*, 2003

Barney, John, *The Trials of Wells Harbour*, Mintaka Books, 2000

Bartram, Len, *RAF North Creake Egmere 1940-1947 a brief history*

Beale, Chris, *The History of the Wells Discussion Group*, WLHG Newsletter 44, 2010

Clark, Christine, *The British malting industry since 1830*, Hambleton, 1998

Cornish, CJ, *Nights with an Old Gunner*, 1898

Cringle, Mike, *The Gamekeeper's Boy*, Larks Press, 2001

Cringle, Pat, *Saltmarsh and Sandunes,* Wells & District Wildfowlers Club, undated

Dalton, Nell and Ebdon Paul eds., *A Wall of Water*, Masque Community Theatre 1985

Edwards, George, *From Crow Scaring to Westminster,* Unwin, 1922

Edwards, Noel, *Ploughboy's Progress*, Centre of East Anglian Studies, 1997

Evans, George, *Ask the Fellows who Cut the Hay,* Faber, 1955

Evans, George, *Where Beards Wag All*, Faber, 1977

Festing, Sally, *Fishermen*, Shaun Tyas, 1999

Festing, Sally, *Showmen: The Voice of Travelling Fair People,* Shaun Tyas, 2012

Fielder, Julie, *What Flo Said,* 2013

Gillard, Derek, *Education in England* 2018, http://www.education-england.org.uk/ history

Golding, Catherine, in *The Turn of the Tide*, ed. Ian Scott, 2005

Green, Geraldine, in *Stiffkey with Cockthorpe – a story of Norfolk people*, Poppylands, 2013

Jenkins, Stanley, *The Wells-next-the-Sea Branch*, Oakwood Press, 2011

Hastings, Adrian, *A History of English Christianity 1920-1990*, SCM, 1991

Hiskey, Christine, *Holkham*, Unicorn, 2016

Holland, Julian, *Dr Beeching's Axe 50 years on*, David & Charles, 2013
Howkins, Alun, *Poor Labouring Men*, Routledge, 1985
Howkins, Alun, *The Death of Rural England*, Routledge, 2003
Malster, Robert, *Saved by the Sea*, Terence Dalton, 1974
Mansfield, Nicholas, *English Farmworkers and Local Patriotism, 1900-1930*, Ashgate Press, 2001
The Norfolk Crab Fishery, MAFF, 1966
Perkins, Geoff, *Wells-on-Sea: A town and its people as it once was,* 1996
Perkins, Geoff, *Some more Wells people*, 2009
Perkins, Geoff, *Heroes and Fighting men and women of Wells-on-Sea*, undated
Perkins, Geoff, *When I was a Young Lad*
Perryman, David, *How They Lived*, WLHG Newsletter No. 16, 2000
Purchas, AW, *Some History of Wells and District*, 1965
Shaw, J Martin, in *Social Issues in Rural Norfolk,* ed. Moseley, Norwich, 1976
Smith, F&G, Directors' Minute Books, 1878-1962
Seeley, Richard, *Coaster: Photographs at the Port of Wells-next-the Sea,* Wells, undated
Smith, Robert, *Crossing the Bar*, Wells Harbour, 2018
Stammers, Michael, *Shipbuilding in Wells in the 18th and 19th Centuries*, WLHG, 2011
Stone, Jean, *Recollections of Wells* 1992
Stone, Jean, *Further Recollections of Wells*, 1994
Tuck, John, *Conversations with Alderman Sam Peel OBE*, WLHG Newsletter No 46, 2010
Walker, Graham, *The Memoirs of William John Harman 1854-1944,* Walker, 1995
Weatherhead, Fran, *North Norfolk Fishermen,* The History Press, 2011
Welland, Mike, *The History of the Inns and Public Houses of Wells*, WLHG, 2012
Welland, Mike, *The Cornish family of Iron Founders,* WLHG Archive, 2016
Welland, Mike, *Wells Regattas*, WLHG archives
Welland, Mike, *The Nursery, Theatre Road*, WLHG archives
Wells Church magazine, 1967-1985, WLHG archives
Wells Cottage Hospital, Annual Reports, 1934, 1936
Wells Cottage Hospital, Management Committee minutes 1911-1944, NRO ACC 2008/268; 2009/3
Wells-next-the-Sea Lifeboat – a history, 2001
Wells School Log Books 1860-1996
Wells Town Council Minutes 1974-2001
Wells UDC Minutes 1894 – 1974, NRO DC 18/4/3-15
Wharton, Betty, *The Smiths of Ryburgh*, Crisp Malting 1990, p. 10
Wild, Susan, *The Man Who Did Different*, WLHG, 2013
Woods, Sheila, *Out with the Tide*, Poppylands, 1989
Young, Francis, ed., *Catholic East Anglia,* Gracewing, 2016

Index

(Pictured subjects are in bold)

A

B

C

D

E

F

G

H

I

L

M

N

O

P

Q

R

S

T

U

V

W

Z

Other books by Roger Arguile

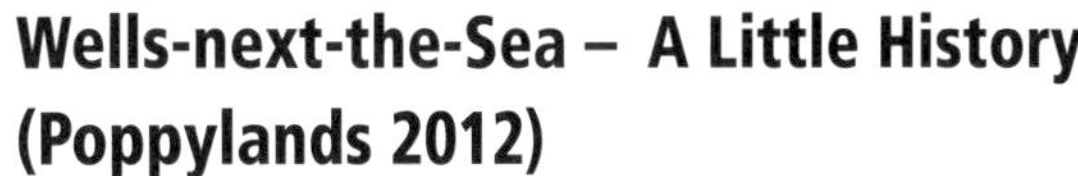

Wells-next-the-Sea – A Little History (Poppylands 2012)

Wells-next-the-Sea, whilst no longer the malting centre and busy trading port that it once was, remains a popular home and favourite holiday destination for many. This title provides a concise history of the development of the town from its earliest recorded history as the town of Guella, through to the calling of the last of the seagoing traders at the end of the 20th century and its new life as both holiday destination, marina and harbour for the North Sea wind farm industry.

Wells-next-the-Sea – A Small Port in a Wider World (Poppyland 2014)

Wells-next-the-Sea receives thousands of visitors every year. On a summer weekend the streets are packed with people who come to enjoy the beaches, the cafés and the pubs which line the quay, but it was one of the later Norfolk coastal towns to become a tourist haven. Author Roger Arguile details its busy role as a fishing centre, as a trading port and as a centre for malting, from the 11th to the 20th centuries, in this fascinating history.

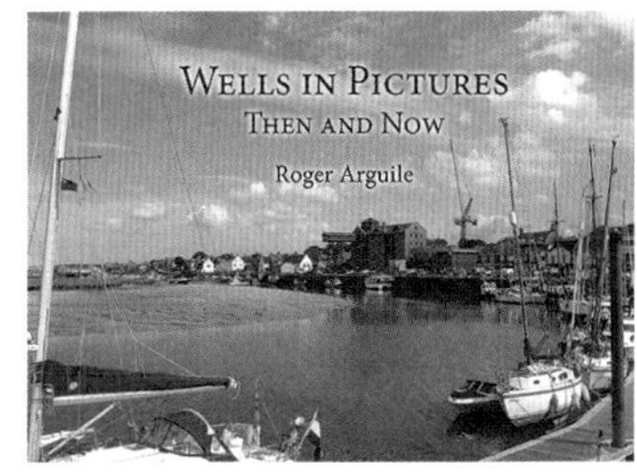

Wells In Pictures – Then and Now (Poppyland 2021)

Wells-next-the-Sea has become a much admired holiday resort. Its character is, in good part, due to its having been a port, fishery and industrial base. Now known for its shelfish, fishing has been a regular and important trade throughout its history. In the 19th century malting became a huge industrial and commercial enterprise until its collapse in 1929. Agricultural related industries continued until the 1990s when the coastal shipping ceased. In this book the author has gathered together a collection of photographs from the past and present that puts the town into its historical perspective.